Becoming Divine

Becoming Divine

Jonathan Edwards's Incarnational Spirituality within the Christian Tradition

Brandon G. Withrow

The Lutterworth Press

To Mindy, my companion in everything.

The Lutterworth Press
P.O. Box 60
Cambridge
CB1 2NT
United Kingdom

www.lutterworth.com
publishing@lutterworth.com

ISBN: 978 0 7188 9525 9

British Library Cataloguing in Publication Data
A record is available from the British Library

First published by The Lutterworth Press, 2017

Copyright © Brandon G. Withrow, 2011

Published by arrangement
with Cascade Books

All rights reserved. No part of this edition may be reproduced, stored electronically or in any retrieval system, or transmitted in any form or by any means, electronic, mechanical, photocopying, recording, or otherwise, without prior written permission from the Publisher (permissions@lutterworth.com).

Contents

Acknowledgments • ix
Abbreviations • xi

Introduction • 1

PART ONE: The Judeo-Christian Tradition of Jonathan Edwards

1 The Illuminating Word and Spirituality from Antiquity to the Early Reformation • 13

2 Scripture and Spirituality in Early-Modern Biblical Interpretation • 45

PART TWO: Jonathan Edwards's Spirituality in His New England World

3 The Seeds of Spirituality in the Young Edwards, 1703–1723 • 75

4 The Pursuit of Divine Excellencies, 1723–1730 • 108

5 The Incarnational Spirituality of the Mature Edwards • 136

PART THREE: Jonathan Edwards's Spiritual Reading of the Sacred Text

6 Unlocking the Divine Treasure Chest • 171

7 The Lasting Voice of Edwards • 197

Bibliography • 207
Index • 227

Acknowledgments

While the cover of this work bears my name, many persons willingly and graciously helped me shoulder the burden of seeing this project to completion. This book is the product of over a decade of reading, PhD research, conference papers, and conversations. What contributions it offers to the field are not the work of one mind alone.

I am deeply thankful to Dr. Douglas A. Sweeney of Trinity Evangelical Divinity School for his early encouragement, insight into the study of Jonathan Edwards, consistent feedback, and mentoring. I am honored to pass on to my students the invaluable lessons I first learned from you; thank you for setting me on this particular path. I am similarly grateful to Dr. Samuel T. Logan Jr. of Westminster Theological Seminary and of Biblical Seminary for his guidance and contagious enthusiasm. You made the many challenges of research a pleasure.

I am thankful also to Dr. George M. Marsden of the University of Notre Dame for his kind and helpful comments early in my research, and to Drs. Carl R. Trueman and Jeffrey K. Jue of Westminster Theological Seminary for their insight into the post-Reformation world. I am grateful to Dr. Stephen Nichols of Lancaster Bible College and Graduate School for generously donating the Claghorn Collection to the Montgomery Library at Westminster Theological Seminary during my research years there. Special thanks also belong to the staff (past and present) of the Montgomery Library of Westminster Theological Seminary, especially Emily Sirinides and Grace Mullen, for fielding my incessant requests for interlibrary loans and archived materials; and to the staff of Albion College for opening your rare books library, even at the last minute.

To my research assistants, Brian Cosby (Beeson Divinity School, Samford University), Joshua Arthur (Winebrenner Theological Seminary), and Kevin Vile (Winebrenner Theological Seminary): each of you is a thoughtful and diligent scholar. I look forward to reading your future contributions to your fields.

A scholar may research in solitude, but vision-broadening dialogue requires community. I extend sincere appreciation to the faculty of Beeson Divinity School (Samford University) for welcoming me during my brief time with you, and to the staff at Samford University Library for making my research efficient; your library is a beautiful place to study. I am similarly thankful for the community at Winebrenner Theological Seminary and the University of Findlay—especially Professors Jeannine Grimm and Kathryn Helleman, and Drs. John Nissley, Gary Staats, and George Fry—for the frequent and spontaneous conversations about the world of biblical interpretation and the history of Christianity. I am also grateful for the excellent assistance provided by Pam Carles and Margaret Hirschy at Schafer Library (University of Findlay).

Drs. Peter Enns and John H. Armstrong encouraged me to see this to publication, and I am indebted to them for their professionalism and insight. Many friends, among them Michael Vendsel, Jeffrey Waddington, and Craig Biehl, graciously indulged my fixation on Edwards (and only occasionally required the bribery of a drink or two).

Finally, I gratefully acknowledge my wife, Mindy, my perpetual conversationalist, best friend, and live-in editor. Your patience with me, particularly as my first reader—learning more than you ever wanted to know about Edwards—is immeasurable. Thank you for consistently standing by my writing projects and challenging every word I write.

Abbreviations

AmLit	*American Literature*
ANF	*Ante-Nicene Fathers*
AThR	*Anglican Theological Review*
BS	*Bibliotheca Sacra*
EvQ	*Evangelical Quarterly*
CH	*Church History*
Essay	*An Essay Concerning Human Understanding*
HTR	*Harvard Theological Review*
ICR	*Institutes of the Christian Religion*
IET	*Institutes of Elenctic Theology*
IJST	*International Journal of Systematic Theology*
Int	*Interpretation*
JCS	*Journal of Church and State*
JETS	*Journal of the Evangelical Theological Society*
JHI	*Journal of the History of Ideas*
JPH	*Journal of Presbyterian History*
JR	*Journal of Religion*
JTS	*Journal of Theological Studies*
MT	*Modern Theology*
NEQ	*New England Quarterly*
NPNF	*Nicene and Post-Nicene Fathers*
PG	*Patrologiae Graecae, Cursus Completus*
PhRev	*Philosophical Review*
PRRD	*Post-Reformation Reformed Dogmatics*
RefR	*Reformed Review*
RefRJ	*Reformation and Revival Journal*
Relig Am Cult	*Religion and American Culture*
SC	*Saybrook Confession*
SJT	*Scottish Journal of Theology*
Summa	*Summa Theologica*

TI	*Theological Investigations*
TJ	*Trinity Journal*
TPT	*Theoretico-Practica Theologia*
TynBul	*Tyndale Bulletin*
VC	*Vigiliae Christianae*
WJE	*The Works of Jonathan Edwards* (Yale Series)
WJO	*The Works of John Owen*
WTJ	*Westminster Theological Journal*
WSA	*The Works of Saint Augustine*
WW	*Whichcote Works*
ZAW	*Zeitschrift für die Alttestamentliche Wissenschaft*

Introduction

> The term "Calvinist" is, in these days, among most, a term of greater reproach than the term "Arminian"; yet I should not take it all amiss, to be called a Calvinist, for distinction's sake: though I utterly disclaim a dependence on Calvin . . . and cannot justly be charged with believing in everything just as he taught.
>
> —Jonathan Edwards, *Freedom of the Will*[1]

> Every believer is ingrafted into Christ, and Christ is ingrafted into every believer. . . Christ is born in the soul of the believer . . . and every believer is a mother of Christ.
>
> —Jonathan Edwards, *Images of Divine Things*[2]

A Man Out of Time

In Mark Twain's *A Connecticut Yankee in King Arthur's Court*, the legendary King Arthur and Hank Morgan, the time-traveling Yankee who transforms the Medieval simpletons with modern technology, find themselves on the business end of a gallows. Their rescue comes in a moment of stark contrast, the clash of two disparate worlds, and in a manner worthy of Monty Python, Morgan escapes, finds a telephone, and rings Lancelot for help. At the last possible moment, with the noose tightening around Arthur's neck, an "endless procession" of five-hundred "mailed and belted knights" ride in fearlessly on bicycles, with Lancelot leading the charge and shouting: "On your knees, every rascal of you, and salute the king! Who fails shall sup in hell to-night!"[3]

---

1. Jonathan Edwards, *Freedom of the Will*, vol. 1 of *The Works of Jonathan Edwards*, 131. Hereafter, all references to volumes in this series will follow the abbreviated citation, *WJE*, with volume number and page number for subsequent citations.

2. *WJE* 11:112.

3. Twain, *A Connecticut Yankee in King Arthur's Court*, 381.

Like Hank Morgan (though less humorously), Jonathan Edwards (1703–1758) is often seen as out of his place and time. Many early modern thinkers have failed to meet the test of time, but this colonial New England minister, his Northampton, Massachusetts church, and short-lived Princeton presidency have continued to catch the interests of scholars and pastors alike for three centuries. Uneasy historians attempt to return him to his natural habitat, but disagree when pressed to identify it; and many have tagged and released him only to discover him again wandering in some other world and time. Puritan, closet Catholic, Medievalist, revivalist, pastor, missionary, philosopher, scientist, Ramist, Lockean, Calvinist, Cambridge Platonist, Newtonian, anachronism, evangelical: these are but a sampling of the labels applied to him, but he remains relatively elusive. To rely too much on categorization can obfuscate context. Historical study, as Quentin Skinner writes, is "contaminated by the unconscious application of paradigms the familiarity of which, to the historian, disguises an essential inapplicability to the past."[4] Yet we persist, for without classification, he remains unknown.

Edwards is as complex as he is simple, and many have missed the proverbial tree for the forest. He was a gatherer, collecting the best of knowledge wherever it could be found. For that reason, generations of Christians, especially evangelicals, rarely fail to sing his praises. To Samuel Hopkins and others of the New Divinity (his second-generation followers), Edwards is "one of the greatest of divines" and "of remarkable strength of mind, clearness of thought, and depth of penetration . . . able, above most others, to vindicate the great doctrines of Christianity."[5] His work portrays a seeker and a significant figure of a new Christian spirituality, later to be known as evangelicalism, which owed its ideas to the past but also looked forward to a fresh and energetic future.

Edwards was not always the stalwart theologian that he is portrayed as today. His younger years were those of a tortured soul seeking redemption; but out of that turmoil was birthed a vibrant spirituality

---

4. Stout, "Puritans and Jonathan Edwards," in *Jonathan Edwards and the American Experience*, 142–59. Morimoto, *Jonathan Edwards and the Catholic Vision of Salvation*; Eversley, "Pastor as Revivalist," in *Edwards in Our Time*, 113–30; Westra, "Divinity's Design," in *Edwards in Our Time*, 131–57; Tracy, *Jonathan Edwards, Pastor*; Daniel, *Philosophy of Jonathan Edwards*; Lee, *Philosophical Theology of Jonathan Edwards*; *WJE* 6; Morris, *Young Jonathan Edwards*, 67–70; Miller, *Jonathan Edwards*, 53–62; *WJE* 11:21; *WJE* 23:15–16; Johnson, *H. Richard Niebuhr*, 123–33; Skinner, *Regarding Method*, 59.

5. Hopkins, *Life and Character*, preface.

that dominated his adult years. This book investigates this complex story of Edwards and the theological conclusions that resulted. According to Edwards, there is a strong, necessary connection between the converted soul and the spiritual reading of sacred Scripture, and this connection is found in the idea of deification modeled after the incarnation. In the incarnation, Christ became human, and in salvation, human beings are connected to the divine—participating in that divine nature and becoming part of it—the process of deification or theosis. In this, humans are both fully human, but progressively taking on the divine nature in a union reminiscent of the incarnation, according to Edwards.

Ancient Jews and Christians argued for a strong connection between union with the divine and the multilayered reading of the sacred text. For Christians in the East and West, this was informed by a belief in deification that resulted in a spiritual reading of the Bible. The world of Edwards is informed by this history. As a young man, Edwards struggled to experience conversion, which he understood to be accompanied by fears of the divine, but when that day finally arrived, he discovered instead a "surprising, amazing joy" and a new perspective on God and Scripture that he had never seen before. The Christian, according to Edwards, has access to the divine mind and even possesses the Trinity itself, and therefore can find in the sacred text a pleasure that is only available to those united to God. As Christ is both divine and human, the Christian experiences a second-sort of incarnation, that is, he or she is human but participating in God. Even Scripture itself is both divine and human, and therefore follows an incarnational analogy.

Becoming Divine provides a detailed account of this complex theological construction by honing in on two key theological elements of his Christian spirituality, often dryly labeled *biblicism* and *conversionism* today, and placing that thought at the intersection of the broader traditions of Christianity and his narrower New England and Calvinist context. What emerges from this exploration of his life and thought is a figure whose mind was keenly aware of the issues of his day while simultaneously finding solace in a spirituality that belongs to the past.

Out of his personal struggles he weaves together—with the help of a belief in divine participation modeled after the incarnation—a complex perspective on conversion and Scripture on which his spirituality hinges. Certain theological themes from the Christian tradition, such as union with Christ and justification by faith, show themselves to dominate his ruminations as hinging doctrines. In short: Jonathan Edwards's reading of Scripture is inseparable from his understanding of conversion, and while his perspective on both finds particular meaning in his early-modern and pre-critical context, he is, nevertheless, very much indebted—though he is not always aware of it—to the long-standing and colorful traditions of his theological ancestors.

Edwards remains a complicated figure, and like Hank Morgan, his life offers plentiful moments of stark contrast in the clashes of disparate worlds. He is both a theological throwback and an ingenious inventor with an eye for the future.

Edwards and Evangelicalism

That someone is indebted to long-standing traditions is not a groundbreaking statement, but in the case of Edwards and the continued confusion over who he is as a thinker, it remains an open and necessary discussion. Over a decade and a half ago, David Bebbington wrote his *Evangelicalism in Modern Britain: A History from the 1730s to the 1980s*, in which he called for an understanding of evangelicalism as a movement that began out of Enlightenment ideas in the 1730s. Jonathan Edwards, as Bebbington sees it, was one of the movement's pioneers. The evangelical movement of Edwards's day was very different from the current media stereotype fueled by the outrageous sound bites of Pat Robertson. Amidst the long reign of a more clinical approach to theology, Puritan leaders with pietistic influences drew attention to a need for personal holiness. The language of transformation in this era incurred serious criticism from Reformed leaders in New England due to its highly mystical tones. The evangelical movement was unexpected and therefore potentially dangerous to established Reformed theological traditions.

Attempting to define such a movement is difficult, but Bebbington identified at least four important characteristics: *conversionism, activism, biblicism,* and *crucicentrism*. For Bebbington, the origins of evangelicalism have less to do with mysticism and more to do with an Enlightenment epistemology. While his thesis is still being challenged or even revised, these terms are generally accepted for the purpose of the argument found here. However, the Enlightenment premise is only a part of the picture. Two elements of Bebbington's quadrilateral, conversionism and biblicism, represent central themes for early evangelical development, especially for Jonathan Edwards's vibrant spirituality and theological imagination.[6]

Conversion is "the belief that lives need to be changed," as Bebbington defines it. It is a transformation of the soul. For centuries, Christians of both Eastern and Western persuasions understood the light of Scripture to be inseparable from the light in the transformed soul. The light in the soul is the result of the union of the converted individual with the incarnated Christ. This union effectually connects the human to all that is divine, shedding the light of the divine mind that wrote Scripture upon the mind of the newly changed Christian reading it. Saint Athanasius once asserted that God became human so that humans might become God. That powerful notion of incarnation and deification long has been entrenched in the imaginations of Christians and has been the basis for seeing Scripture as containing deeper layers of spiritual meaning. Ancient Christians like Origen of Alexandria and Augustine understood the literal and plain message of the Bible to be a form of divine baby talk, but the soul that participates in the divine is able to transcend the lower message to a higher message, one that is found in the mind of God and made possible by the Holy Spirit.

Edwards also sees this important connection between the illumination of the soul (and therefore the mind) and the Word illuminated by the Spirit. The spirituality of eighteenth-century colonial evangelicalism is infused with the view that one's conversion involves a transformation. For Edwards, this is made possible by the work of the Spirit in uniting the converted soul to Christ, the God-Human, thereby giving each Christian everything that belongs to the Trinity itself. The Christian "doth really possess all things," writes Edwards in his notes, and by "all things," he does mean *all*:

> God three in one, all that he is, and all that he has, and all that he does, all that he has made or done—the whole universe, bodies and spirits, earth and heaven, angels, men and devil, sun moon [and] stars, land and sea, fish and fowls, all the silver and gold, kings and potentates as well as mean men—are as much the Christian's as the money in his pocket, the clothes he wears, or

---

6. For a critique of Bebbington's work, see Williams, "Was Evangelicalism Created by the Enlightenment?," 283–312. Sweeney and Withrow, "Jonathan Edwards," in Haykin and Stewart, *Emergence of Evangelicalism*, 278–301.

> the house he dwells in, or the victuals he eats; yea more properly his, more advantageously, more *his*, than if he [could] command all those things mentioned to be just in all respects as he pleased at any time, by virtue of his union with Christ . . .[7]

With words just as bold and powerful as many of his mystical Christian ancestors, Edwards plunges into the depths of his spiritual tradition. As the Trinity consists of three persons but one nature, and as the incarnated Christ consists of two natures but one person, for Edwards, conversion is about becoming one body with Christ, with Christ as the head of that body. From this, the newly converted soul enters a vibrant spiritual life that participates in the divine being and is full of holiness and joy. In conversion, the human mind is spiritually united to the divine, and through spiritual sight, the Christian can see the divine being everywhere.

His interest is not simply academic, nor mere curiosity—though he possesses plenty of both—but the work of a tormented soul. His own spiritual journey, which began nearly from day one in the Puritan world of his youth, was fraught with disappointment and failures. He constantly sought what he considered true conversion, only to become dissatisfied with the results. In his resolution of May 26, 1723, he wrote himself this reminder: "Resolved, constantly, with the utmost niceness and diligence, and the strictest scrutiny, to be looking into the state of my soul, that I may know whether I have truly an interest in Christ or no; that when I come to die, I may not have any negligence respecting this to repent of."[8] As a child, Edwards thought he had experienced true conversion; later, when he came to mature faith, he dismissed his early belief as the notion of an illuminated but deceived mind. The day of what he comes to see as his actual conversion delivers a surprise both supernatural and disconcerting. For all its realness, Edwards's transforming experience does not fit the form of conversion that his father and grandfather had told him to expect. Rather than experiencing fear and trembling, he discovers "surprising, amazing joy," and his theology—and the theology of the new movement that will become known as evangelicalism—is transformed.

Via conversion, the biblical text becomes more than black letters on a white page; it is now the unlocked lid of the treasure chest of God. It becomes a thing of beauty and excellency that is impossible to know

---

7. Bebbington, *Evangelicalism in Modern Britain*, 3; *WJE* 13:183, 184 ("Misc." ff.).
8. *WJE* 16:757 (Resolution 48).

outside of the transformation of conversion and divine participation. Ancient Jewish and Christian thinkers followed Plato in seeing this world as merely a shadow of the heavenly reality. Christians understood Christ's incarnation as bridging the gap between heaven and earth, providing a reading of the earthly words in the Bible with a deeper, spiritual, and often allegorical message. Edwards too understood his new connection to the divine being through the incarnation of Christ as providing a window into a deeper, spiritual message, one bathed in divine beauty. The Bible is more than human words; for Edwards, it is access to a heavenly treasure chest.

Like many in his day, he is concerned with defending Scripture's veracity from the attacks of early-modern deists. One may note his use of the term "infallible"—a popular evangelical term today nearly equaling its cousin, "inerrancy"—in his *The Distinguishing Marks of a Work of the Spirit of God* (1741). In this he writes: "we are to take Scriptures as our guide . . . this is the great and standing rule which God has given to his church, to guide them in all things relating to the great concerns of their souls; and 'tis an infallible and sufficient rule."[9] Edwards harbors a strong trust in the words of Scripture, and this trust goes beyond the text, because, as he sees it, it is God thinking aloud. It is here that *biblicism*, defined by Bebbington as "a particular regard for the Bible," is important.[10] However, what is striking is how Edwards's incarnational spirituality brings his reading of the Bible to new heights and inevitably connects him to the existing tradition.

That Edwards is a biblicist has become an "embarrassing family secret," as Douglas A. Sweeney writes, and for some, a disappointment. "Three hundred years after Edwards' birth, and half a century into what some have called the Edwards renaissance," he adds, "few have bothered to study Edwards' extensive exegetical writings." Current scholarship takes a great interest in Edwards the philosopher or Edwards the scientist, but "modern scholars have yet to come close to understanding the ways in which Edwards' life was animated by what he deemed God's Word."[11] Unless one reconsiders or revises Bebbington's Enlightenment premise, one may forget that Edwards's understanding of the Bible is no

---

9. *WJE* 4:227.

10. Bebbington, *Evangelicalism in Modern Britain*, 3.

11. Sweeney, "'Longing for More and More of It,'" in Stout et al., *Jonathan Edwards at 300*, 25–26.

stranger than that of his spiritual ancestors. While it does carry with it early-modern concerns, his handling of the text bathes the concerns of the early-modern commentary in the mystical waters of ancient hermeneutics. Through direct and indirect contact, Edwards's intellectual commitments span the ancient, Medieval, Reformation, and contemporary generations. He is both a leader of a colonial sea change within Western American Christianity, and a chimera, benefiting from the diverse contributions of his theological ancestors. In other words, there is good reason scholars wrestle over how to label him.

Edwards's writings paint the picture of one who embraces the Protestant doctrines of the past (especially the Reformation), while harboring a conviction that he is a leader of a new generation, called to improve these ideas using the newest discoveries available—both scientific and philosophical. With this in mind, Bebbington's thesis finds some reevaluation in this book. A fresh look at Edwards from this perspective offers new light on America's early religious consciousness. In his unparalleled biography of Edwards, George Marsden writes that Edwards "has many ardent admirers, many detractors, and many who attempt to rehabilitate him by making him over in their own images." Among Marsden's goals is to "depict [Edwards] in his own time and in his own terms."[12] This is my goal here as well, and I hope Edwards's voice comes through loud and clear.

To that end, Part 1 of this book looks at the precedence for Edwards's thought within the tradition, from the time of antiquity to the time of his birth. In this section (chapters 1 and 2), I examine the various intersecting trajectories that set up the body of Christian work available to Edwards in his day. Precedence is not established by mere transmission of information, but, as will be seen, Edwards's thought evolves as the result of a web of beliefs that inform his world. From East to the West, and from Origen to Calvin, the connection between union with the God-Human and biblical interpretation is explored. Ending in the Enlightenment, we see that the world of Edwards's intellectual development challenges standard scholarly presuppositions.

Part 2 looks more closely at the world of Edwards from the time of his youth, including the many historical, cultural, and intellectual troubles that informed his own personal story and reading choices. In this section we find a young man driven to understand himself and his

---

12. Marsden, *Jonathan Edwards: A Life*, 2.

religion, struggling with the prospect of challenging his tradition (and by default, his parents), and suffering from depression. Not many persons whose religious experience they describe as a "surprising, amazing joy" might sink into depression, but for Edwards it required a retro-engineering of his conversion to make sense of that experience. The outcome was a hybridization of sorts, benefiting from a mind desperate to meet the expectations of his religion and keenly aware of the philosophical and scientific claims of his day. What he discovers is an understanding of union with Christ that is vibrant, incarnational, and reminiscent of many theologians before him. It is a theological perspective that restructures his understanding of salvation, and even incorporates Medieval categories into the science of Newton.

Part 3 demonstrates how this new spirituality influences Edwards's biblical interpretation. Centuries-old methods of interpretation—based on a mystical spirituality—that engage in multilayered hermeneutics (see Part 1) are reflected in Edwards's own approach to the biblical text. But a child of the Protestant Reformation he is, and the literal reading of the text serves as the foundation for his typological lens. Moreover, he is keenly aware of the questions raised by those skeptical of Christianity and anything spiritual. What is seen in this section, then, is an incarnational view of Scripture capable of engaging the questions of his day with the answers given to the questions of the past.

This volume will provide a detailed look at this chimera with a healthy respect for his complexity. It will show that his reading of Scripture must be understood as inseparable from his understanding of conversion; and that grasping this context requires a better reading of the web of beliefs—early modern and ancient—that inform the intellectual world of Jonathan Edwards.

PART ONE

The Judeo-Christian Tradition of Jonathan Edwards

1

The Illuminating Word and Spirituality from Antiquity to the Early Reformation

> There is nothing that tells us of such glorious things as the word of God. These things are above all that could be found out by human reason, more excellent than man can obtain the knowledge of, or communicate by, human learning, more excellent things than either men or angels could reveal to us.
>
> —Jonathan Edwards, "Heeding the Word"[1]

> It is probable that when Paul ascended into heaven, that he there received his gospel . . . heavenly things themselves should be communicated in heaven itself.
>
> —Jonathan Edwards, "The Blank Bible"[2]

"THERE CAN BE NO doubt," declares David Bebbington, "that Edwards was the chief architect of the theological structures erected by Evangelicals in the Reformed tradition. That was sufficient to ensure that they were built on Enlightenment foundations."[3] Though it is apparent from his notes that Edwards never fails to notice the latest tomes and buzzwords of the eighteenth century, Bebbington's conclusion is an overstatement. Edwards belongs (only partly self-consciously) to a long tradition that an eighteenth-century aristocrat from a theological

---

1. *WJE* 19:46.
2. *WJE* 24.2:1077.
3. Bebbington, *Evangelicalism in Modern Britain*, 65.

dynasty could not avoid. He engages that tradition only selectively in his notes but understands its value nonetheless. This present chapter looks broadly at that tradition, from ancient beginnings to its transformation in the early Reformation.

Much like the mystics of earlier centuries, Edwards understands union with God as allowing the soul to see the divine being in all things, including both the book of nature and the book of Scripture. Christians of all generations have understood the light of the Bible as inseparable from the light of salvation; the illumined word and the illumined soul always have some connection for the Christian faith; and this is no less true for Edwards. Human beings transformed by the Spirit think God's thoughts after him because they are united to him through their union with the incarnate Christ by the bond of the Spirit. In this union, everything appears much grander; i.e., ancient Christians found in this an opportunity for allegorizing the biblical text, and Reformed Christians who discarded allegorism in favor of stronger literalism still embraced its cousin, typology.

Edwards is a man between worlds. He is neither a conservative literalist nor a liberal allegorist, and he does not see a need to build tension between the two. "There is a medium," he writes, "between those that cry down all types, and those that are for turning all into nothing but allegory and not having it to be true history; and also the way of the rabbis that find so many mysteries in letters."[4] To understand Edwards, then, is to first understand the changing themes in the world of biblical interpretation and its connection to the theology of a transformed soul, particularly as themes of divine participation (deification) and incarnation were explored from the ancient world to Reformation Christianity. Many ancient thinkers understood the reading of Scripture as a participation in something beyond this world, an ascent of the soul into paradise, and this has important implications for the spirituality of Edwards centuries later. In the midst of the Enlightenment's rejection of this form of thinking, these ancient themes not only connect Edwards to the broader Christian tradition in significant ways, but also help transform his understanding of his own conversion and his reading of the sacred text.

---

4. *WJE* 11:151.

The Spirituality of Ancient Jewish Interpretation

The Bible, while not the oldest human document, has a long history of interpretation that transcends languages and cultures. That might seem to be stating the obvious, but it can be easy to forget that modernist or postmodernist approaches to Scripture are mere newborns in the history of biblical interpretation. In reality, biblical interpretation began long before the Bible itself was finished, especially in its Christian-specific form. The Hebrew Bible, or the *Tanak*, namely the *Torah* (Law), *Neviim* (prophets), and *Ketuvim* (writings) were not created in a vacuum. Thus scholars are not surprised to find the writer of the biblical book of Daniel (9:24–27) offering a prophetic inner-biblical commentary on the prophecy of seventy years of captivity to Babylon found in the biblical book of Jeremiah (25:11; 29:10). And as a larger Christian book, the Apostle Paul, in his Epistle to the Galatians (4:24), interprets the Genesis narrative with the fresh paint of allegory.

Between the time of the Tanak and the Christian New Testament, an entirely new interpretive tradition arose. The Apocryphal (meaning "hidden things") and Pseudepigraphal (meaning "falsely attributed") books offer their own perspectives on the Tanak. Circulating during what is called the Second Temple period (516 BCE—70 CE), some of the apocryphal texts make it into certain canon lists during the earliest Christian periods, only to be removed by subsequent generations, the most famous removals being those by Protestants during the Reformation who treat them as useful for reading but not for dogma. Some of these Second Temple texts, like First Enoch (1:9), for example, were considered acceptable enough to be quoted with some authority by the author of the New Testament book of Jude (14–15), but not acceptable enough to be considered canon by subsequent generations of Christians. A history of biblical interpretation was already in place before a finished Bible existed, and such an interpretative history sets precedents for new approaches to follow.

Mirroring their neighboring cultures, ancient Jewish and Christian interpreters engaged in creative methods of biblical interpretation that became well entrenched by the Middle Ages. The ancient Jewish fourfold sense of interpretation (or *PaRDeS*, known as *peshat, remez, derash,* and *sod*) best represents this creativity. The acronym became short for "paradise" and was understood by Jews in late antiquity to consist of multiple heavenly layers, traditionally seven layers (based on ancient descriptions), though scholars are not in agreement on that number as a standard. For the Apostle Paul in his own mystical experience, the number of levels is said to be three in Second Corinthians (12:2). To find the deeper layers of interpretation in a text is to be taken into paradise.[5]

Peshat is the plain or literal sense, which includes elements of grammar, history, etc. It is the philological, linguistic method of interpreting the text that is, as Philip S. Alexander writes in his *The Targum of Lamentations*, "less guided by scientific principles and accumulated scientific knowledge."[6]

Remez is the allegorical reading of the text. In this sense, the text symbolically points to some abstraction or eternal truth, but never states it explicitly; the erotic Song of Songs, from this perspective, is not about frolicking lovers, but should instead be understood on an ethereal plane, and therefore is about the spiritual love life of Israel and God.

Derash (meaning "to seek") is often paired with *peshat* as the second most important interpretative layer. This is *Midrashic*, and it has two essential elements: the locating and engaging of textual elements of interpretation, and their moral or tropological interpretative results. As to the first:

> ... *Derash* senses that a word in one verse is alluding to an occurrence of the same word in another verse and draws a homiletic meaning from this. *Derash* is a way of reading into any part of Scripture an overarching theological system that is seen as the primary context of meaning.[7]

When read, words mean far more than they appear, and this layer of interpretive reading is the process of deciphering revelation hidden within its words and structure.

While *peshat* is a plain and literal reading, or God speaking in human words, *derash* is looking for deeper, theological intention in those words. When encountering the text from this perspective, the reader needs to pay close attention to word forms and shared roots. Repetition of words or their roots across sections or even across different books of

---

5. For further discussion, see Harlow, *Greek Apocalypse of Baruch*, 46–50; Wright, *Early History of Heaven*; Fonrobert and Jaffee, *Cambridge Companion to the Talmud*, 203–4.

6. Alexander, *Targum of Lamentations*, 39; see also, Halivini, *Peshat and Derash* (1991).

7. Alexander, *Targum of Lamentations*, 39.

the Tanak may draw the reader to this fresh method and deeper insight. For example, Lam 1:1 reads, "How lonely sits the city that once was full of people! How like a widow she has become, she that was great among the nations! She that was a princess among the provinces has become a vassal" (NRSV). One might be surprised at how much depth a Midrashic interpretation can find in this passage due to one word. In *The Targum of Lamentations* the word "how," or *'eikhah*, points the interpreter to a deeper connection with another passage:

> 1. *Jeremiah the prophet and high priest said:*
>
> How *has it been decreed against Jerusalem and her people that they should be condemned to banishment, and that "'Eikhah" should be pronounced over them in mourning, just as Adam and Eve were condemned, when they were banished from the Garden of Eden, and the Lord of the World pronounced "'Eikhah" over them in mourning?*[8]

The appearance of a word in one biblical passage draws the reader's mind to a similar parallel in another text, in this case, Genesis and the expulsion of Adam and Eve from Paradise. To the casual modern reader, there may be no apparent connection, but a single word and a sleight of hand can bring mysterious connections to light.[9]

For modern readers, to take a word and invest it with such an unlikely connection may sound like an exegetical song and dance, but for the ancient scholar this methodology is gold, assisting the seeker to find something more divine in the text—something beyond the pure literal reading. It is a search for God's hidden, but not silent, voice. As to the second use of this layer, the moral or tropological meaning, Michael Fishbane notes that "the words of the text help to illumine personal experience, and life-experience helps one to penetrate the human issues of the text."[10]

This ancient method of interpretation laid the foundation for midrashing, or filling in the gaps. Certain words or phrases left unexplained were often followed, like a loose thread, to their hidden but intended spiritual meaning. Out of this the ancients spun their own undying folklore. For example, in Gen 4:1 Eve says of the newborn

---

8. Ibid., 109.
9. See Alexander's discusson in ibid., 109 n. 2.
10. Fishbane, *Garments of Torah*, 119.

Cain, "I have produced a man [*Ish*] with the help of the Lord." *Ish*, or "man," drew the attention of Jewish interpreters. Why a man? Why not a baby? *Ish*, after all, is never used of a baby or a boy. This question led to an historical tradition that said that Cain was born a grown man, a gruesome half-breed, the result of a sexual relationship between Eve and Satan himself. This child was marked for life, interpreters argued, and this view of the text made it into the Christian tradition as well. "Having been made pregnant by the seed of the devil . . . she brought forth a son," wrote Tertullian in his *On Patience* (5:15). For Medieval writers, this lore provides the background for the fictional tale of Beowulf, whose famous enemy, Grendel, is the spawn of Cain. In antebellum America, this interpretation became a popular biblical justification for slavery, as black slaves were considered the offspring of Cain and cursed by God.[11] Because of this approach, the text took on a remarkable life of its own.

The fourth and last sphere of interpretation is *sod* (meaning "mystery" or "secret"), the mystical reading. To interpret the Bible in this way is to look at the biblical words esoterically, offering a creative interpretation, where the literary and mystical meanings are one. As a method, it is most often associated with Medieval Kabbalah.

Jonathan Edwards demonstrates his awareness of these approaches beyond the reference quoted above. His notes show that he is intrigued by the ancient *prisca theologia*, and that he looks for books to improve his understanding of other religions and their practices, including Kabbalah. Far from being a pluralist—he concludes in these notes that all non-Christian religions would be overthrown in the coming apocalypse—he nevertheless is interested in the connections between other religions and Christianity. What ray of truth appears in their teachings? How much did God reveal to them? These are his concerns.

His first experiences with Judaism came in 1722, when he moved to New York to serve as an interim pastor of a small Presbyterian congregation. The big city gave him experiences he could not find in his small New England hometown. His Jewish neighbor in New York, whose window was directly across from his, was the "devoutest" person he had ever met.[12] Books on religion, which included discussion of Kabbalah, made their way into the young pastor's notes (where he copied long passages

---

11. Kugel, *Bible as It Was*, 85–96.
12. *WJE* 2:165.

from his reading) and into his Catalogue of Reading. It remains difficult, however, to know the extent to which he was influenced by them.[13]

Nevertheless, an ancient tradition of seeking the mind of the divine—and therefore greater layers in the text—long preexisted the common era. Why seek these other layers? To seek the hidden mind of God in a sacred text is not something limited to the Jewish belief system. The Greek world engaged in such pursuits since the fifth century BCE, and it is Greek philosophy that informs later Jewish approaches to the text. Ancient writers reasoned, as William Yarchin writes, that "due to the inherent limitations of human understanding, there will always be something in the sacred text that remains undisclosed to the unglossed reading. *Mystery, then, was characteristic of sacred texts*." Each generation had to appropriate the ancient text or myth so as to bring it into relevance to their traditions or cultural circumstances, and this crossed cultural borders. (The Jewish sect known as the Essenes, for example, interpreted scriptural references to the messiah and the prophetic pictures of the "remnant" [e.g., Jer 23:3] as referring to their community and founder.)[14] Allegorical interpretation eventually became the emphasis and the tool to make this repurposing of the biblical text possible.

The Collision Between Jewish and Greek Worlds

Among the Greeks, ancient stories of flawed and no longer relevant gods and goddesses were made acceptable to the philosophical elite when interpreted as abstract metaphors and allegory. "For the ancients," writes Yarchin, "it was not a matter of exposing what is hidden in the text but rather a hope to be guided through figurative reading into a sharing of the divine mind."[15] Making sense of the gap between this world and the eternal has classically been the task of philosophers. The things of this world represent the reality in shadow, a concept exemplified by the history of the *Logos*. The Greek term, defined as "word" or "reason," finds its origins around the sixth century BCE with Heraclitus (ca. 535–475), and early Greeks understood it to refer to the organizing principle of the world. Heraclitus uses the term to refer to the stability or balance

---

13. As Wallace E. Andersons warns: "it is important to not over-emphasize the explicit influence of Cabala." For more on the connection, see *WJE* 11:25.

14. Yarchin, *History of Biblical Interpretation*, xii.

15. Ibid.

between the elements of the world, or that which ties together all things (humans, the divine, the world); "all things are . . . one," says Heraclitus.[16] As the Jewish and Greek worlds collided, the development of the *Logos* idea was not lost on Jewish interpreters. Jewish spirituality and views of their own sacred text developed significantly.

Following Heraclitus, Plato (ca. 429–ca. 348 BCE) also refers to the *Logos*. For him, the *Logos* is the word, speech, or organizing intelligence or rationality between the reality and this concrete world. He illustrates this connection between the real world and the shadow world in his well-known cave allegory.[17] Behind this world is the unchanging World of Forms—a world of eternal ideas that provide the archetype for all things in this earthly, concrete world. The created world is modeled after those perfect universals. In the World of Forms, the universal and immaterial model has all the necessary attributes that allow humans to identify all things material, no matter their diverse characteristics. Forms communicated by the Logos make sense of the world, according to this system, and give it an intelligence. This works in tandem, that is, as long as it is remembered that they are derivative in nature, the concrete elements of this world are also necessary for humans to discover the World of Forms. More importantly, the preexistent soul, before its bondage to matter, was part of the World of Forms and therefore should long to return. As Andrew Louth explains:

> . . . the search of the soul for knowledge of the Forms is, in a sense, its homecoming. The soul is naturally divine and seeks to return to the divine realm. And it does this in the act of contemplation—*theoria*—of Being, Truth, Beauty, Goodness. This act of *theoria* is not simply consideration or understanding; it is union with, participation in, the true objects of true knowledge.[18]

For Plato, the soul's ascent begins in this world, but there are limitations. And unlike the body, because the soul is immaterial, it must be immortal. The cyclical act of reincarnation is part of the process of learning to separate the immaterial from the material, a process of improvement and engaging the other world.[19]

---

16. Kittel *et al.*, *Theological Dictionary of the New Testament*, 506; Heraclitus, *Fragments*, 51; see also Hippolytus, *Refutation of All Heresies* 9.9.1.

17. Plato, *Republic* 7.514–20.

18. Louth, *Origins of the Christian Mystical Tradition*, 3.

19. Segal, "Incarnation," 122.

Others after Plato continued to build on his cosmology. For example, the Athenian Stoics (from *Stoa* or "porch," named for the school with a painted porch where Zeno of Citium taught philosophy in Athens around 300 BCE), looked to the *logos spermatikos* to make sense of the universe; they conflated nature, rationality, and God. The universe is one and the same with God, and its order is evidence of his existence. The Logos is the "creative force," like a seed, and responsible for holding all things together, filling everything.[20] This interpretation does not escape the notice of the ancient Jewish philosopher-theologian Philo of Alexandria (20 BCE—50 CE), and it is to him that innumerable scholars have gravitated as representing the world of New Testament biblical interpretation.

Philo

"The history of Christian philosophy begins not with a Christian but with a Jew, Philo of Alexandria, elder contemporary of St. Paul," writes Henry Chadwick.[21] Ancient Alexandria was the intellectual center of the Greek world, the home of the allegorical interpretation of Scripture, and teaming with Platonists. Like a good Alexandrian, Philo understands God as beyond human reach, transcendent, and beyond the eternal Forms themselves. The connection between the divine being and this world is generally understood by the Greeks to be the job of subservient beings. For Philo this poses a serious problem, particularly in that it is not compatible with his Jewish monotheism. His solution is to brand these as *powers*, which, as J. N. D. Kelly notes, are "not so much distinct beings as God's operations considered in abstraction from Himself."[22] The gap itself is closed, according to Philo, by the Logos. Philo's combination of Jewish thought with Platonism gives the Logos a deeper dimension. He is more concerned (than earlier Greeks) with reinforcing the connection of God to the world itself, and the Logos serves his purposes—a perspective that, as Chadwick notes, "anticipates not only Plotinus, but also the Christology of St. Paul in Colossians."[23] Thus Philo writes in *On the Confusion of Tongues*, using terms familiar to Christians, that:

20. Peter, *Monotheists*, 39.
21. Chadwick, "Philo," 137.
22. Kelly, *Early Christian Doctrines*, 10.
23. Chadwick, "Philo," 143.

> . . . if there be any as yet unfit to be called a Son of God let him press to take his place under God's First-born, the Word [logos], who holds the eldership among the angels, their ruler as it were. And many names are his, for he is called "the beginning," and the Name of God, and His Word, and the Man after His image . . .[24]

In contemplating the Logos (the Forms), human beings can learn about God. "As intermediary between God and the universe," explains Kelly, "the Logos has a double role: it is God's agent in creation, and it is also the means by which the mind apprehends God."[25] In Exod 31:2–3, for example, God calls out Bezalel, a man filled with "divine spirit," to do work in gold, silver, and bronze. Philo's comments go to the heart of this double role:

> Bezalel means, then, "in the shadow of God"; but God's shadow is His Word, which he made use of like an instrument, and so made the world. But this shadow, and what we may describe as the representation, is the archetype for further creations. For just as God is the Pattern of the Image, to which the title of Shadow has just been given, even so the Image becomes the pattern of other beings, as the prophet made clear at the outset of the Law-giving by saying, "And God made the man after the Image of God" (Gen. 1.27), implying that the Image had been made such as representing God, but that the man was made after the Image when it had acquired the force of a pattern.[26]

The act of creation may move from Logos to world—from the spiritual to the material—but in the hope of knowing God or The Good, the flow is the opposite. Interpretation is a spiritual exercise, a connection of the immaterial part of humanity to the immaterial God. For Philo, it is just as important to be observant of ritual as it is to understand that higher principle behind it. One requires the other and between the two is the spiritual entity known as the Logos. "The highest level occurs when a person not only *understands* that the Logos is identified with the One reality," writes S. Daniel Breslauer, "but actually experiences that unity together with the Logos itself."[27] In the spiritual journeys, according to

---

24. Philo, *On the Confusion of Tongues*, 146.
25. Kelly, *Early Christian Doctrines*, 10; Philo, *Migration of Abraham*, 174.
26. Philo, *Allegorical Interpretation*, 3:96.
27. Breslauer, "Philosophy in Judaism," 165; see also Kugel, *How to Read the Bible*, 17–18, and Louth, *Origins of the Christian Mystical Tradition*, 17–34.

Philo, human beings should reach beyond this literal world to the Word (*Logos*). Philosophical contemplation takes the soul to the Logos; interpreting the biblical text is no different. The written Word points to the immaterial Word.

When it comes to the Torah, the allegorical, as Yarchin puts it, "brings the reader into immediate apprehension of the divine truth Moses seeks to communicate . . . allegory is necessary because of the unspeakable difference between Creator and creatures."[28] Speaking of Abraham's call to leave his homeland and to sojourn, Philo calls it an emigration "of soul rather than body, for the heavenly love overpowered his desire for mortal things." Much the same, when the person interprets the biblical text, "migrations as set forth by the literal text of the scriptures are made by a man of wisdom, but according to the laws of allegory by a virtue-loving soul in its search for the true God."[29] Speaking on this passage, James Kugel writes:

> Here, Philo admits that the biblical story in Genesis is literally talking about an event from the past, the time when "a certain wise man," Abraham, left his home in Ur. But taken allegorically, the text is really not talking about Abraham at all, but about the human soul. Any soul in search of God, Philo goes on to say, must like Abraham, leave its "home," the world of trusting only in the senses of sight, hearing, and so forth; such a soul must migrate to another "city," that is, to another way of perceiving.[30]

The soul is lifted up so it can see more and be "emancipated," in Philo's words, from the bonds of this world, from its own "travail." In so doing, humans ascertain a higher meaning. Philo records his own experience in this way, where "under the influence of Divine possession," he went into a "corybantic frenzy" and obtained "an enjoyment of light" and "keenest vision." It is a calling to leave one's self behind, to "approach . . . work empty," as Philo describes his experience.[31] Looking for the allegorical interpretation in the text is dutifully submitting to a higher calling.

When it comes to Scripture, the reading experience remains inseparable from the spiritual experience; the one assists the other. The

---

28. Yarchin, *History of Biblical Interpretation*, 18.

29. Philo, *On Abraham*, 15:66, 68.

30. Kugel, *How to Read the Bible*, 18–19.

31. Philo, *Migration of Abraham,* 32–35; Chadwick, "Philo," 153; Yarchin, *History of Biblical Interpretation*, 19.

spiritual sense of Scripture requires the spiritual or mystical side of humanity. To know the text, the soul has to have a spiritual connection to the Logos; to make sense of that connection in this imperfect world, individuals need the text.

The first few generations of Christian interpreters, having Jewish and Greek origins and living in the same quarters of the intellectual world as Jewish interpreters, reflect these same multilayered, even heavily allegorical approaches. The significant difference for these ancient Christians, however, is the doctrine of the incarnation of Christ; and because of this, even when the language of Greek philosophy enters into their biblical interpretation, they engage not merely in old-fashioned allegory but also in typology. Allegory is an extended metaphor, the taking of a narrative—where the words mean one thing literally—and giving it a more abstract or figurative meaning. Typology is similar to allegory, but, in the words of James Kugel, where allegory points to the vertical, typology is "horizontal."[32] The New Testament writers use allegory sparingly, giving typology more of a leading role, whereas post-apostolic interpreters consider both to be useful tools that fall under the general label known as the *spiritual sense*. It is, however, a mistake to believe that ancient writers made strong distinctions between typology and allegory.

Look, for example, at Gal 4:21–31. Here Paul introduces the biblical story of Sarah and Hagar, which he interprets as a story of two Jerusalems, with, "Now this is an allegory: these women are two covenants." It is not, however, Paul's normal method of interpretation to appeal to direct allegory. When he ventures away from strictly literal-letter writing in which he gives advice or lays out a command, he is more prone to typology. For example, in Gal 3:16, the promises to Abraham's "seed" are understood to foreshadow Christ. While allegory, in Greek terms, looks at the narrative of this world as representing the heavenly, or the Forms, typology takes into consideration authorial intent and looks forward in time, that is, to things to come. In the case of Christianity, a New Testament typology understands the Old Testament to foreshadow Christ and his work of redemption.

Scholars are not in full agreement on the connection between New Testament books like Hebrews and the writings of Philo. Both Philo and the writer of Hebrews appeal to a similar Platonic language of shadow. In the book of Hebrews, for example, Platonism appears to inform the

---

32. Kugel, *How to Read the Bible*, 21.

cosmology of the writer, as evidenced by the vocabulary used in statements like 8:5: "They offer worship in a sanctuary that is a sketch and shadow of the heavenly one; for Moses, when he was about to erect the tent, was warned, 'See that you make everything according to the pattern that was shown you on the mountain.'" Both Philo and the author of Hebrews bring in the language of the Logos (Word), with the most notable comparison being:

> Hebrews:
>
> Indeed, the word of God is living and active, sharper than any two-edged sword, piercing until it divides soul from spirit, joints from marrow; it is able to judge the thoughts and intentions of the heart (Heb 4:12).
>
> Philo:
>
> God severs by his own all-cutting word all those natures one by one that seem joined together and united—both of bodies and actions.
>   God sharpened the blade of his all-cutting word and divided the substance of everything, formless and without quality as it was.[33]

Their similarities can be overdrawn, and as Kenneth Schenck sees it, the two have probably spent time in "closely related circles," that is, both writers seem to have Alexandrian backgrounds. This may account for the similarities more than anything else does.[34]

The Platonist vocabulary of Hebrews is fused with a typology that provides the primary hermeneutical methodology but with a significant difference. Thus, while things on earth are shadows of the things in heaven, they also are shadows of things to come (10:1): "Since the law has only a shadow of the good things to come and not the true form of these realities, it can never, by the same sacrifices that are continually offered year after year, make perfect those who approach." This forward shadowing is possible for one very good reason: while for Philo the things of earth are shadows of the Forms or the Logos, for early Christian interpreters the Logos is not confined to the heavenly. The Logos became human in

---

33. Philo, *Who is the Heir of Divine Things?*, 130, 140.

34. For differing approaches to the Philo-Hebrews discussion, see Spicq, *L'épitre aux Hébreux*; Williamson, *Philo and the Epistle to the Hebrews*; Hanson, *Allegory & Event*, 83–93; and Schenck, *Brief Guide to Philo*, 81–86.

the incarnation, and in becoming human added not only the vertical reflection of the heavenlies, but also a horizontal reflection; that is, the Logos is the God-Human and the Logos is both earthly and heavenly.

By understanding the Logos as the incarnate God-Human, Christianity changes everything; the earthly and heavenly divide is no longer a problem. The Logos is no longer untouchable. As the Gospel of John (1:14) sees it, "the Word [*Logos*] became flesh and lived among us, and we have seen his glory, the glory as of a father's only son, full of grace and truth." For Philo, the Logos (the pattern for all creation) is the form of God, but not personally connected to that creation. For the Apostle John, however, Christ is the "form of God," but willingly took on another form, that of humanity.

Prior to the incarnation, there was a supposed disconnect between this world and the ultimate world. The spirit of the person hoped to transcend the shadows to get a look at the Logos, and a layered interpretation of the sacred text opened a door into that world, with the words as the connectors. In Christianity, Scripture is the Word of God, pointing the reader to the ultimate Word or Logos, namely Christ, and furthermore, there can be a real connection because this same Word became flesh and in so doing bridges the gap between two worlds. More importantly, the Logos makes it possible for humans to experience the divine. For this reason, Christian spirituality will always be connected to its sacred text in an intimate and vital way.

The Christian *Quadriga* and Deification

From the perspective of early Christian interpreters, while Philo brought heaven and earth a little closer, the incarnation of Christ clothed the Logos in a fleshly garment. No longer was there an unbridgeable gap between God and humans because Christ, the God-Human, became the bridge. A Christian's union with the God-Human supplies him or her with the logic of the "spiritual sense"; it connects the divine mind with the human's. Edwards would agree with Athanasius's maxim that "God became man so that man might become God."[35]

Following Philo, early Christian theology is very much connected to the world of Middle Platonism. Christian thinkers like Augustine (354–430) utilized the work of Plotinus (204/5–270), the founder of

---

35. Athanasius, *De Incarnatione*, 54 (NPNF 4:65).

Neoplatonism. It would be incorrect, however, to see Christians of these early centuries as merely repeating Platonic ideas. The role of the incarnation changes the basis for Christian theology, and Christian philosophy takes on a confirming role, rather than one of a primary authority. Origen, for example, who shared the same teacher as Plotinus, engages Platonism in his theological meanderings yet considers himself a Christian first.[36]

Origen of Alexandria

The primary authority for Origen is the biblical text (though the modern reader may not immediately recognize this commitment). For this reason he writes significant commentary on the Bible, in which he explores in depth the allegorical meaning that occurs to him during his reading. Platonism provides the epistemological basis for his hermeneutic, as well as his general view of the world. Origen engages in a highly mystical theology, one that provides the backdrop for future discussions of participation in the divine, and is centered on reading the Bible. The Platonist side of Origen emphasizes the need for contemplation in order for the soul to ascend, but he distinctly rejects the World of Forms and places them in the Logos; it is in the Logos that they derive meaning and receive intelligence. Through contemplation, human beings find access to them, an access made possible by the incarnation.[37]

For Origen, as with many of the Greek Fathers, a proportionate relationship exists between divine knowledge and the condition of the soul. To know the mind of God means becoming more like God by participation in the Logos. Though the world of the Logos is obscured, the incarnation provides a way beyond that roadblock. Scholars disagree, however, on how much emphasis Origen puts on the incarnate and fleshly Christ: Gordon Rudy, for example, argues that Origen has less interest in the human nature of Christ in terms of the material body and more in the soul of Jesus, while J. A. McGuckin sees Origen as finding significant "hopes for the *theosis* of the human race" in the reality of the flesh.[38] Whichever it is (and Origen appears inconsistent in his terminol-

---

36. Louth, *Origins of the Christian Mystical Tradition*, 52–53.

37. Ibid., 59.

38. Rudy, *Mystical Language of Sensation*, 33; McGuckin, "Strategic Adaptation of Deification," 111 n. 11.

ogy and emphases), one cannot underestimate the importance of the incarnation for him. He writes:

> For Christians see that with Jesus human and divine nature began to be woven together, so that by fellowship with divinity human nature might become divine, not only in Jesus, but also in all those who believe and go on to undertake the life which Jesus taught, the life which leads everyone who lives according to Jesus' commandments to friendship with God and fellowship with Jesus.[39]

The incarnation breaks down the barrier sin creates between human beings and God. The incarnate Logos connects the world of the divine with the world of the human. So "all beyond the Very God is made God by participation in His divinity," Origen writes; by the Logos "they became gods" or "images."[40]

Not only is a friendship and fellowship gained by the incarnation, but a new level of understanding as well.[41] The human being, who is spiritual, longs to return to the spiritual; humans have not only five physical senses for the acquisition of knowledge, but also five spiritual senses. The attribution of spiritual senses goes back to Parmenides but is explicated in greater detail by Plato and Philo, particularly as it relates to the sense of spiritual sight.[42] These five spiritual senses, according to Origen, are tools for taking the soul further into spiritual knowledge as it relates to contemplating the divine in general and as humans look for greater meaning in Scripture specifically. "For the names of the organs of sense are often applied to the soul," writes Origen, "so that we speak of seeing with the eyes of the heart . . . so too we speak of hearing with the ears when we discern the deeper meaning of some statement."[43] The soul's spiritual sense organs and the door opened by the work of Christ give humans access. "Origen thinks the physical humanity of Christ is absolutely necessary as a medium that allows human beings to attain the

---

39. Origen, *Contra Celsum*, 3:28.
40. Origen, *Commentary on John*, 1.2 (ANF 9:323).
41. Christensen and Wittung, *Partakers of the Divine Nature*, 25–26.
42. The discussion of the five spiritual senses has a long history, but one should look at Rahner, "'The Spiritual Senses' according to Origen," 81–103. See also Balthasar, *Origen: Spirit and Fire*, 218–57; Hauck, "'Like a Gleaming Flash," 557–73; Louth, *Origins of the Christian Mystical Tradition*, 66–67; McGinn, *Foundations of Mysticism*.
43. Origen, *On First Principles*, 1.1.9.

spiritual realm," writes Rudy. The God-Human "draws our attention to the Logos," from whom divine knowledge can be obtained.[44]

As Jesus Christ in human form points other human beings to the Logos, so does Scripture in written form. C. W. Macleod points to this connection, writing that for Origen the "Scriptures themselves are the vehicle of divine inspiration . . . indeed, since both they and Christ are the Logos, Christ can be said to be incarnate in them."[45] Moreover, Scripture is, as Gordon Rudy explains, "the teaching of the logos," thus Scripture must also contain human (bodily, or literal) readings and divine (spiritual, or allegorical) readings, or as Origen explains in his *On First Principles*, Scripture has a threefold sense: body (literal), soul (moral), and Spirit (spiritual) senses.[46] Most often, Origen engages the literal and spiritual, mixing allegory and typology, though the distinction is neither clear nor consistent. Human spiritual sensation, enhanced by the grace of God, can engage the *sensus divinus* or spiritual message and discover the allegorical meaning of Scripture. In the Gospels, says Origen, there is "an inner meaning," one "which is the Lord's meaning, and which is only revealed through the grace that was given to him who said, 'We have the mind of Christ . . .'"[47] Louth helpfully draws out Origen's emphasis:

> Understanding Scripture is not for Origen simply an academic exercise but a religious experience. The meaning found in Scripture is received from the Word, and the experience of *discovering* the meaning of Scripture is often expressed in "mystical" language; he speaks of a "sudden awakening," of inspiration, and of illumination . . . a large part of the content of *enoptike* is the discovery of "spiritual," "theological" meanings in Scripture through allegory. In this . . . Origen enters more and more deeply into communion with God—and leads others into this communion . . .[48]

The Spirit of God, according to Origen, intentionally puts markers or "stumbling-blocks" in the biblical text that are intended to leave human

---

44. Rudy, *Mystical Language of Sensation*, 34.

45. Macleod, "Allegory and Mysticism in Origen and Gregory of Nyssa," 371.

46. Rudy, *Mystical Language of Sensation*, 20; Origen, *On First Principles*, 4.2.4–5. For a helpful discussion see Hanson, *Allegory & Event*, 235–58.

47. Origen, *On First Principles*, 4.2.3. Origen is referencing 1 Cor 2:16, where Paul is talking about spiritual knowledge.

48. Louth, *Origins of the Christian Mystical Tradition*, 63.

beings asking questions.[49] Like Jewish interpreters, when Origen sees something unusual or unexpected in the text, he believes there must be more to the text than the grammatical meaning. The Spirit inserts things "less probable" into the biblical narrative, even that "which could not have happened at all" so that "we should be led on to search for a truth deeper down and needing more careful examination . . ."[50] "What man of intelligence," asks Origen regarding Genesis 1, ". . . will consider it a reasonable statement that the first and second and third day, in which there are said to be both morning and evening, existed without sun and moon and stars, while the first day was even without a heaven?"[51] When he finds markers like these, he looks for allegorical or typological or spiritual meaning (he does not always distinguish between these) and therefore a deeper message that takes him beyond this world into the world of the Logos.

For Origen there is an intimate connection between Christ the Word and the Word of God, between contemplation and knowing or discovering the message of the Logos. Finding light means going beyond the mere letter, as finding light here means going beyond the shadow world to the Logos. Later Greek exegetes will continue this tradition and will also build intensely on the connection between allegory and asceticism.

Later Greek Fathers

The Greek Fathers emphasize participation in the divine and its connection to the divine Logos—though not all engaged in allegory, notably Basil.[52] As Gregory Nazianzus writes, Christ's "inferior Nature, the Humanity, became God, because it was united to God, and became One Person because the Higher Nature prevailed," and this happened, again in Gregory's words, that "I too might be made God so far as He is made Man."[53] The effects on Christ's humanity as a result of being incarnationally united with the divine are paralleled in the Christian's union with Christ. Only through the person's union with Christ can the soul experi-

---

49. Origen, *On First Principles*, 4.2.9.
50. Ibid.
51. Ibid., 4.3.1.
52. Sheldon-Williams, "The Cappadocians," 132.
53. Gregory Nazianzus, *Oration* 29:19 (*NPNF* 7:308).

The Illuminating Word and Spirituality from Antiquity to the Early Reformation 31

ence the divine light (or darkness as it may be at times), grow in it, and have the spiritual sense.

The model of spiritual sensation envisioned by Gregory of Nyssa, as he explains in his allegorical *Life of Moses*, is the person drawn "from the beauty which is seen to what is beyond" and given a longing "to be filled with the very stamp of the archetype."[54] The "eye," says Gregory, continuing the metaphor of spiritual senses in his *Catechical Orations*, "by virtue of the bright ray which is by nature wrapped up in it is in fellowship with the light."[55] A large portion of the scholarship on Gregory of Nyssa has focused on his apophatic theology, that is, his belief that the Christian finds the impenetrable darkness of God in his or her union with his being. Gregory's focus on darkness is often said to be the difference between he and Origen, but this is an overstatement, as both understand divine light is as much a part of the theological program for the soul united to God in Christ.

Current scholarship has given more attention to the role divine light plays in Gregory's theology. Martin Laird's work *Gregory of Nyssa and the Grasp of Faith* is a good example of clarity on the issue.[56] Laird points out that while Plotinus does not place the emphasis on faith in his work, the late Neoplatonic world of Gregory as found in Porphyry (c.233–309) and more specifically Proclus (412–485) does have a concept of faith as important for being united with the Good.[57] Gregory, however, places a greater emphasis on faith as effective for union with God. Faith, because it unites humanity to the divine, is transformative. "But most of all Gregory presumes in faith a real relationship with the Incarnate Word," explains Laird, "immanent in creation, in sacred scripture and in the person of Jesus of Nazareth."[58] The incarnation, in Gregory's view, remains central for human faith and knowledge. God unites "himself with our nature," writes Gregory, "in order that by its union with the Divine it might become divine. . . ."[59] In this union the soul finds illumination.

---

54. Gregory of Nyssa, *Life of Moses*, 114.
55. Gregory of Nyssa, *Great Catechism*, 5 (*NPNF* 5:478).
56. Laird, *Gregory of Nyssa and the Grasp of Faith*, 15–33.
57. Ibid., 12–13.
58. Ibid., 14.
59. Hardy, *Library of Christian Classics*, 302.

Human beings are not to be forever separated from God as longing lovers but are to be united with the divine.[60] Why? Gregory explains: "For needful it was that neither His light should be unseen, nor His glory without witness, nor His goodness unenjoyed, nor that any other quality observed in the Divine nature should in any case lie idle, with none to share it or enjoy it. . . ."[61] In other words, if human beings are created to be partakers "of the good things in God," says Gregory, then it stands to reason that they could be "adapted to the participation of such good" as well.[62]

What makes such participation eternally possible is Christ's incarnation and the union of human beings to the incarnate God-Human. Lewis Ayres puts Gregory's position this way: "the union of all with Christ brings all to share what Christ has from the Father. . . ." In his commentary on 1 Cor 15:28, Gregory explains:

> Unity then means to be one body with him. When the good pervades everything, then the entirety of Christ's body will be subjected to God's vivifying power . . . Christ unites all mankind to himself, and to the Father through him . . . he who is in the Father effects our union with this very same Father.[63]

Through the incarnation humans share in the divine, but they continue to long for the beauty of his light that is beyond.[64] For this reason, Nyssa also connects the contemplative life with the soul's ability to see deeper into the biblical text. He sees a significant connection between allegory and asceticism in interpreting Scripture—particularly in terms of Song of Songs—because in turning away from the literal reading of the biblical text toward the spiritual parallels, the ascetic turns away from "material to intelligible realities," as Verna Harrison puts it.[65] The allegorical is

---

60. McGuckin, "Strategic Adaptation of Deification," 104.

61. *Great Catechism*, 5.

62. Ibid.

63. Ayres, *Nicaea and Its Legacy*, 305.

64. Writing in his treatise on 1 Cor 15:28, Gregory argues that in the final end of this world, when Christ is victorious and subjects all things to the Father, "evil will pass over into non-existence." "When we all are free of evil in imitation of the first-fruits, then the whole mass of our nature will be comingled with the first-fruits and we shall become completely one body . . ." (Gregory of Nyssa, "Sermon on 1 Corinthians 15:28, [32–44]," 257–58).

65. Harrison, "Allegory and Asceticism in Gregory of Nyssa," 113–20. For a discussion of some of the differences between Origen and Nyssa see Ludlow, "Theology

part of that light that is found in the soul's union with the divine and is made possible through the incarnation.[66]

The kind of methodology employed by Origen and Nyssa was not the only system being employed by their contemporaries, however, and it did receive some criticism. In their day, the Antiochene school—particularly Diodore of Tarsus (ca. 330–390) and John Chrysostom (ca. 347–407)—took a more literal interpretation, that is, literal for its day but not in a modern parlance. In reaction to the heavy allegorical methodology, the Antiochene school employed the idea of *theoria*, meaning "insight." Scholars often overstate the differences between the Alexandrian and Antiochene approaches. For the Antiochenes, a deeper spiritual insight remained, but never at the expense of the literal and historical meaning. The deeper spiritual message was something literally intended by Spirit, a typological message that was connected strongly to the details of the historical record and New Testament verification.[67]

Chrysostom read with more flexibility on the spiritual insight than did Diodore, though he did attempt to connect his typological reading to the literal. For example, when Jesus feeds the five thousand with five loaves and two fishes in John 6:1–14, Chrysostom connects it to the feeding of the Israelites in the wilderness by Moses's bread, manna. He is justified in making this connection because Christ himself does so in John 6. In verse 32, Jesus tells the crowd, "Very truly, I tell you, it was not Moses who gave you the bread from heaven, but it is my Father who gives you the true bread from heaven." Chrysostom finds a strong contrast here in connecting Jesus's words to the historical Exodus. "He calls that bread 'true,' not because the miracle in the case of the manna was false," says Chrysostom, "but because it was figure, not the reality." Both the manna and Moses are types of Christ.[68]

Chrysostom's restrained *theoria* does not come with a rejection of deification. "Seest thou how by degrees He leads us up into the very arches of Heaven," he tells the congregation in his homily on the Gospel

---

and Allegory," 45–66. On spiritual reading and the fathers, see Ward, "Allegoria: Readings as a Spiritual Exercise," 272–95.

66. For a comparative discussion on Origen's and Nyssa's apologies for allegory see Heine, "Gregory of Nyssa's Apology for Allegory," 360–70.

67. Kelly, *Early Christian Doctrines*, 75–78.

68. John Chrysostom, *Homily 45*. For an extended treatment of Chrysostom on John 6, see Hylen, *Allusion and Meaning in John 6*, 3ff.

of Matthew (5:46).[69] Theosis language is restrained, however, and is primarily connected with the community, especially in the sharing in the Eucharist.[70] When writing on 1 Cor 10:17 ("Because there is one bread, we who are many are one body, for we all partake of the one bread"), he finds in it a deeper significance. Paul "intended to express something more," says Chrysostom, "and to point out how close was the union: in that we communicate not only by participating and partaking, but also by being united. For as that body is united to Christ, so also are we united to Him by this bread."[71]

The multilayered and multifaceted spiritual sense guided by the spiritual senses was significantly more popular in the East than in the West despite the existence of these two groups, which picked up the methodology through imported works of Eastern Christians.

Western Christianity

Western theologians also engaged in allegorical interpretation founded on an understanding of the soul's spiritual status. Philo's methodology, as carried on by figures like Origen and Nyssa, made its way into the Western hermeneutics of Ambrose and Augustine—the latter learning it from the former, and the former benefiting significantly from Origen. In his work on the Song of Songs, Origen ties the deeper meaning of the text to the ascent of the soul. As F. B. A. Asiedu shows, "For Origen, the allegorical reading of the Song is reserved for those who have advanced through the first two stages [natural and moral levels]," requiring "deeper contemplation that yields the mystical meaning of the Song."[72] Ambrose carries on this perspective and teaches it to the skeptical Augustine, who struggles with the essential veracity of the literal reading.[73]

As a Neoplatonist, Augustine (354–430) identifies the World of Ideas with the mind of God,[74] with Scripture as the gateway from the spiritual senses to God's mind. And much like his Platonist predecessors and Eastern counterparts, Augustine, too, finds something of value

---

69. John Chrysostom, *Gospel of Matthew: Part 1. Hom. I–XXV*, 281.

70. Christensen and Wittung, *Partakers of the Divine Nature*, 111 n. 12.

71. John Chrysostom, *Library of Fathers of the Holy Catholic Church*, 327 ("Homiley 24").

72. Asiedu, "Song of Songs and the Ascent of the Soul," 312.

73. Augustine, *Confessions*, 5.

74. Augustine, "Miscellany of Eighty-Three Questions," XLVI.

in deification. While it is recognized that Augustine does not speak of deification with exactly the same enthusiasm as some of the Greek Christians, neither does it escape his notice or approval.[75] In his well-known Christmas Sermon, he writes: "Designing to make gods of those who were men, He, who was God, was made man."[76] In this sermon he clearly reflects the words of Athanasius, but he seems to connect this more thoroughly to the Pauline doctrine of adoption, whereby all Christians are made "sons of God" through the incarnate Christ. In his homily on John 1:11 ("He came to what was his own, and his own people did not accept him"), he says that God sent his son so that he might adopt sons, and then proceeds to peel away the depth of this relationship: "Let us possess Him, and let Him possess us: let Him possess us as Lord; let us possess Him as salvation, let us possess Him as light."[77]

Augustine acknowledges a relationship between the person's spiritual status and having access to divine light. According to his *Confessions* (7.10), God's light comes from spiritual sight and spiritual hearing, which human beings find internally in the heart moved by God's grace. These senses of the heart allow the person to spiritually see God's light and hear God's voice. Given his views of deification and his understanding of the spiritual senses, it is no surprise, then, to find Augustine appealing to a fourfold sense in the biblical text. In his *Unfinished Literal Commentary on Genesis* he explores the fourfold method of interpretation, which for him includes the historical (literal), allegorical, analogical, and aetiological, though he appears to find the first two most helpful.[78] Likewise, in his *On the Profit of Believing* (section 5) he spells out the same four levels, defending the use of allegory or typology for reading the Old Testament Law with a deeper meaning, a meaning that he finds available to the pious.

Shortly after Augustine, Gregory the Great (540–604) offers a threefold method including the historical (literal), allegorical, and moral or tropological. "First we lay the foundations of historical fact," writes Gregory, "then we lift up the mind to the citadel of faith through al-

---

75. Bonner, "Augustine's Conception of Deification," 369–86. Also see the follow-up essay by Robert Puchniak, "Augustine's Conception of Deification, Revisited," 122–33. The latter essay is based on Augustine's newly discovered manuscripts.

76. Augustine, *Sermons for Christmas and Epiphany*, 112 (Sermon 192).

77. Augustine, "Tractate 2" (NPNF 7:17).

78. Augustine, *Unfinished Literal Commentary on Genesis*, 1.5.

legory; finally through the exposition of the moral sense we dress the edifice in its colored raiment."[79]

By the thirteenth century, Augustine of Dacia (d. 1285) provided the well-known and pedagogically apt mnemonic that has withstood the test of time: *Littera gesta docet; quid credas allegoria; moralitas quid agas; quid speres anagogia* ("the letter teaches us facts; the allegorical what to believe; the moral how to live; the anogogical what to hope for").[80] This fourfold sense, or *quadriga*—*sensus literalis* or *sensus historicus* (the literal or historical sense)*; sensus tropologicus* (moral sense); *sensus allegoricus* (allegorical sense); and *sensus anagogicus* (eschatological)—is a trip into the deeper reality behind the text.[81] The literal interpretation remains the foundation of the allegorical, but it is hardly the stopping point of a good theologian. For the *via antiqua* this world is a mere shadow of the ultimate reality; so also, in Scripture, the literal meaning is a mere shadow of the spiritual.[82]

Many medieval exegetes recognized problems with unfettered allegorism and tried to bring some balance. Albert the Great (ca. 1206–1280) and Thomas Aquinas (1225–1274), notes Richard Muller, "were largely responsible for a major shift in the emphasis of medieval exegesis away from the Gregorian allegorism toward a great emphasis on the letter."[83] Thomas admits as much in his *Summa*, writing, "These three, history, etiology, and analogy, are groups under the one general heading of the literal sense."[84] But neither fully escaped the confines of realism.

For interpreters of the Reformation era, the added dimensions are connected to elements of the Spirit and union with Christ (and therefore the entire Trinity). The incarnate Logos or Word connects heaven and earth; the Bible, God's Word, fills in the details for both. During the Protestant Reformation, union and incarnation remains central for the Reformed, but the *quadriga*, though it does not disappear, receives a serious blow.

---

79. Gregory the Great, *Moralia*, 1.3.

80. Attributed to Augustine of Dacia in his *Rotulus Pugillaris* and quoted in Pokorný and Roskovec, *Philosophical Hermeneutics and Biblical Exegesis*, 301.

81. Spivey, "Hermeneutics of the Medieval and Reformation Era," 101–15.

82. Oberman, *Luther*, 117.

83. Muller, *PRRD* 2:35–36.

84. Aquinatis, *Summa Theologica*, 1a.1.a.10.

The Reformation Challenge to the Ancient World

Descriptions of Edwards's exegesis are generally concerned with typology. The typological interpretation of Scripture is bound up in Edwards's understanding of the "spiritual sense" and the participation in the divine by union with Christ. Leading this discussion, Stephen J. Stein argues that Edwards's employment of typology or a spiritual meaning in the text is markedly different from his Reformation heritage:

> Edwards shared certain assumptions with the Reformation tradition, but in other ways he departed from prevailing patterns of Protestant exegesis. In contrast to the Reformation accent upon the sufficiency of the singular literal sense of the Bible, he underscored the multiplicity of levels of meaning in the text and the primacy of the spiritual.[85]

Stein recognizes that Edwards is committed to the Reformation's literal sense of Scripture but adds, "the literal meaning Edwards pursued was not singular in appearance."[86] Edwards does emphasize the typological reading of Scripture, but Stein may be overstating the apparent contrast. During the Reformation the fourfold sense was treated with varying degrees, and even Calvin, try as he may, does not adhere to a purely literal reading of the biblical text.

Nevertheless, changes did occur in the Reformation. In contrast to the *via antiqua*, the *via moderna* followed a different route, paying homage to the leader of nominalism, William of Ockham. For Ockham, words do not have a reality outside of the mind; words and the concepts based on them are "constructs of reason and based on experience," explains Heiko Oberman, and "they possess no independent reality."[87] Only the person is real, and when it comes to ideas, words are not shadows of the forms. Martin Luther's understanding of Scripture as the only authority derives from this nominalist perspective.[88] (Though he does not borrow wholesale from nominalism, it does play a significant role in his early theological development.)[89] Due to the rejection of realism, nominalism contributes to both the Protestant Reformation doctrine

---

85. Stein, "Quest for the Spiritual Sense," 100–101.
86. Ibid., 107.
87. Oberman, *Luther*, 117.
88. Ibid., 117.
89. Trueman, *Luther's Legacy*, 57–71.

of *sola scriptura* and the Copernican revolution.[90] Reformation exegesis shifts away from the spiritual to what the words literally represent, where true meaning can be found and measured. Allegorism, as the Reformers see it, left declarations of truth unchecked and uncertain; furthermore, the Magisterial Reformers find no comfort in the church as the arbiter of truth. Thus, declaring "Scripture alone" best fits their nominalist epistemology and challenges to church authority.

John Calvin and the Reformed Faith

The Reformers, for all their zeal to overthrow authority, never fully abandon church tradition. Calvin, for example, though he does not quote the church fathers as "authorities," does quote them as "partners in conversation," as David Steinmetz puts it.[91] Church tradition, subject as it is to change, muddies the clarity of Scripture and undermines its authority, as Luther and Calvin see it. Thus the Reformers usher in something new, which Bernard Lohse describes:

> What is decisively new in Luther over against medieval tradition is that though till the onset of the indulgence controversy he ranked authorities such as the church fathers, the councils, and the *ratio* alongside Scripture, in the course of his dispute with Rome he was forced more and more to give Scripture critical value against specific traditions and doctrinal opinions in tension with or actually opposed to Scripture.[92]

The literal sense, driven by the historical and grammatical, provides the Reformers a sober, clearer approach to truth, one that avoids the digressions of unfettered allegorism and unquestionable authority.

As a result of the new emphasis on the literal reading of the biblical text, the Reformers emphasize the clarity of Scripture by engaging more thoroughly in the art of the *commentarius*.[93] The design of the commentary is to bring the reader a clear, perhaps even raw, understanding of the biblical passage. While there was no single concept of a *commentarius*, the kind of commentary that Calvin engages in is, according

---

90. Oberman, *Dawn of the Reformation*, 179–203; see also Oberman's, *Impact of the Reformation*; Lohse, *Martin Luther's Theology*, 18ff.; Ozment, *Reformation in Medieval Perspective*, 107ff.

91. Steinmetz, *Calvin in Context*, 136.

92. Lohse, *Martin Luther's Theology*, 187.

93. McKim, *Historical Handbook of Major Biblical Interpreters*, 123–24.

to Richard Muller, "a running analysis of an entire text consisting in brief annotations and explanations, unencumbered by digressions or expansions."⁹⁴ Calvin clearly indicates in his preface to Romans that he is familiar with various commentary models, such as those of Melancthon and Bucer, but is deliberately doing something "different."⁹⁵ He wants to avoid Bucer's bloated model (that tended toward wordiness) in favor of *"perspicua brevitae,"* or lucid brevity.⁹⁶ And he also wants to avoid Melancthon's tendency to selectively comment on *loci*, often in order to digress into *disputationes*.⁹⁷ If Scripture is perspicuous, Calvin reasons that the commentary form should reflect the brevity and literal meaning of that scripture. To digress from the Scriptural text at hand in a commentary is to detract from the meaning of Scripture and to risk committing the reader to "boredom."⁹⁸ Therefore, *brevitas* not only respects

94. Muller, *Unaccomodated Calvin*, 29. On the term *commentarius*, in connection with tradition, Kenneth Hagen offers some helpful background. Hagen argues that the term *commentarius* was not understood "uniformly" in the sixteenth century (Hagen, "What did the term *Commentarius* mean to sixteenth-century theologians?" in Backus and Higman, *Théorie et Pratique de l' Exégèse*, 13). The word *commentarius* meant many things in classical Latin; Hagen notes particularly that it could be a notebook, memorandum, brief explanation, or even notes on a lecture (ibid., 17). In secondary literature, Hagen found that the word was understood broadly in terms of biblical exegesis. It could include the philological, theological, philosophical, and historical (ibid., 19). For others, such as Erasmus, Hagen says that a commentary involves the "discussion of the interpretation of others," and "the clarification of difficult texts" (ibid.). At times this resulted in a form of commentary called a "paraphrase." Ultimately, Hagen says, the "common denominator" for the commentary traditions of the sixteenth century is that *commentarius* was a note and "referred generically to a work on Scripture" (ibid., 37).

95. Calvin, *Epistle of Paul the Apostle to the Romans and to the Thessalonians*, 3.

96. Calvin, *Commentarius in Epistolam Pauli ad Romanos*, 3:3 (402.9).

97. There is a continuing discussion over Calvin's intended use of *brevitas*. Richard C. Gamble argues that Calvin's emphasis on *brevitas et facilitas* is tied to the clarity of Scripture (Gamble, "*Brevitas et Facilitas*," 15). According to Gamble, Calvin understands Scripture to have a "rhetorical beauty," a "simplicity" and "style" that Calvin wants as "his own" (ibid.); see also Gamble, "Exposition and Method in Calvin," 153–65. According to Gamble, it is a "hermeneutical method," one that includes concision and clarity. Calvin, as Gamble argues, understood this method to best reflect Scripture's own method (Gamble, "*Brevitas et Facilitas*," 15). Richard Muller disagrees, saying that "these often cited forms, *brevitas* and *facilitas*, must be understood, *contra* the view of Battles and Gamble, as stylistic or rhetorical and methodological rather than as hermeneutical principles. They cannot, in other words, be seen as Calvin's grounds for ruling out the 'allegorical' exegesis of Origin or Augustine" (Muller, *Unaccomodated Calvin*, 236 n. 94).

98. *ICR* 1:5.

Scripture's clarity but is also better pedagogy. (Diversions could be left to his other books, namely, the *Institutes*.)[99]

Despite this emphasis on clarity, literalness, and brevity, it is a mistake to see Reformed literalism as "singular," as Stein calls it. Edwards's primary tradition, Calvinism, has more depth than strict literalism. "For all its deep interest in literal meaning and historical context," writes Muller, "Calvin's exegetical method stands in an intellectual and theological continuity with earlier Reformation models and, through them, with some of the basic interests of medieval exegesis."[100] Calvin does not reject the deeper, spiritual meaning of Scripture. For example, commenting on Gal 4:22, Paul's great allegory of Sarah and Hagar, Calvin warns heavily against allegory, saying, "Let us know, then, that the true meaning of Scripture is the natural and simple one"; but he also proceeds to acknowledge the use of the anagogical and allegorical senses, so long as there is no "departure from the literal meaning."[101] The anagogical and allegorical senses are prefigurative and therefore more typological, founded on and supported by the literal sense.[102] This is more than a singular literalism—it is a literalism with many theological branches. The typological is kept in check, as Calvin understands it, by measuring it against the literal.

The literal, however, is not simply the reading given by the human author. The message understood by the human author may not be the same meaning intended by the divine author. Calvin, allowing the New Testament to serve as commentary on the Old, looks for the authorial intent of the Holy Spirit. He believes that though most readers of Scripture can ascertain the literal message of a passage, the spiritual, typological, or christotelic meanings can be identified or understood only by those who are in relationship with Christ and therefore have minds enlightened by the Holy Spirit. As will be true for Evangelicals coming after him, conversion and biblical interpretation are inseparable at this point for Calvin: "God works in his elect in two ways: within, through his Spirit; without, through his Word. By his Spirit, illuminating their minds and forming their hearts to the love and cultivation of righteous-

---

99. Ibid.
100. Muller, "Hermeneutic of Promise and Fulfillment," 81.
101. Calvin, *Epistles of Paul the Apostle to the Galatians*, 84.
102. *PRRD* 2:472.

ness, he makes them a new creation. By his Word, he arouses them to desire, to seek after, and to attain that same renewal."[103]

To understand the divine, and therefore spiritual, mind behind the biblical text, the interpreter must have that same mind residing in the soul. Calvin sees the Bible, writes John L. Thompson, as a "unified book with a unified plot, inspired in its wording by the same Spirit that was needed to guide its reading, its interpretation, and its application."[104] An inseparable link exists, therefore, between Spirit and Word, that is, between the work of the Spirit in the soul and the ability to apprehend the message of God or between conversion and biblical interpretation.

Reading the biblical text, however, is not simply a matter of the Spirit of God working within the interpreter. The work of the Spirit is far more intimate than that, and that intimacy is reflected in how Calvin understands the incarnation of Christ and the union of the human being with the God-Human. The Greek Fathers emphasized deification and divine participation as giving the Christian a privileged or unique position. For Athanasius, "God became man so that man might become God."[105] The parallel for Calvin, as it is for Augustine, is found in his understanding of adoption and union with Christ.[106] Christ took on human flesh as a first step toward becoming the brother of humanity: "according to our teaching," writes Calvin, "Christ made us sons of God with him by virtue of a bond of brotherhood. For in the flesh that he received from us he is the only begotten Son of God."[107] Salvation requires more than the mere flesh of the incarnation, says Calvin; it requires "the Spirit through faith."[108]

The Greek Fathers saw a parallel between Christ's incarnation and the kind of union the Christian has with Christ. Calvin thinks along similar lines. The incarnation of Christ, the fact that the divine and the human natures are united in one person, is the direct result of, or is made possible by, the work of the Spirit. This understanding has been labeled Calvin's Spirit-Christology. The "Spirit has chosen Christ as his

103. *ICR* 2.5.5.

104. Thompson, "Calvin as a Biblical Interpreter," 67, 68, 71.

105. Athanasius, *De Incarnatione*, 54.

106. Trumper, "Historical Study of the Doctrine of Adoption in the Calvinist Tradition," 119.

107. *ICR* 2.14.7.

108. *ICR* 2.13.2.

seat," writes Calvin, "that from him might abundantly flow the heavenly riches of which we are in such need."[109] E. David Willis argues in *Calvin's Catholic Christology* that he "never loses sight of the role of the Holy Spirit in the Incarnation." The Spirit does not so much serve as a material cause (to use the language of Aristotle) as he becomes something more like an efficient or instrumental cause of the incarnational Christ, allowing for both divine and human natures (including the human mind) to be fully at work in the hypostatic union. "Christ's existence and ordering reality beyond the flesh are in large measure to be accounted for Pneumatologically," writes Willis; "the Son is never effectively active in creation or redemption without the Spirit. What the incarnate Lord accomplished was never without the transforming presence of his Spirit."[110]

The Spirit's role, for Calvin, is also essential to the mystical union of the Christian with Christ incarnate. The Spirit unites the believer to Christ and "Christ stands in our midst, to lead us little by little to a firm union with God."[111]

> Therefore, that joining together of Head and members, that indwelling of Christ in our hearts—in short, that mystical union—are accorded by us the highest degree of importance, so that Christ, having been made ours, makes us sharers with him in the gifts with which he has been endowed. We do not, therefore, contemplate him outside ourselves from afar in order that his righteousness may be imputed to us but because we put on Christ and are engrafted into his body—in short, because he deigns to make us one with him. For this reason, we glory that we have fellowship of righteousness with him.[112]

The *unio mystica* is such that "we ought not to separate Christ from ourselves and ourselves from him"; Christ "has been so imparted to you with all his benefits that all his things are made yours, that you are made a member of him, indeed one with him. . . ."[113] The intimacy of this relationship cannot be underestimated: "Everything that belongs to Him is ours," Calvin declares.[114] The Spirit is that by which human

109. *ICR* 2.15.5.

110. Willis, *Calvin's Catholic Christology*, 82–83; see also Tamburello, *Union with Christ*, 84–101.

111. *ICR* 2.15.5.

112. *ICR* 3.11.10.

113. *ICR* 3.2.24.

114. Wallace, *Calvin's Doctrine of the Christian Life*, 17 (translation of Sermon on Acts 2:1–4 [*Calvin Opera* 48:633]). Wallace writes that "it is at the same time essentially

beings are united to him, and "by the grace and power of the same Spirit we are made his members, to keep us under himself and in turn to possess him."[115]

Any mind with this kind of connection to Christ must be able to see more of Christ in the text, Calvin argues. The typological, then, is the message of the text that Christians see through their union with Christ and his Spirit. Christ is apparent in the biblical text to those that have eyes to see, so the call for literalism is tempered by the belief in the meta-author, namely, the Holy Spirit. The biblical text can have a deeper meaning because the Spirit of God intends the text to foreshadow the future work of Christ. For example, in commenting on Paul's spiritual interpretation of the rock Moses struck as Christ, Calvin says of these typologies, "That Christ may be seen by us today through the Gospel, Moses and the Prophets must take their place as forerunners." Calvin sees these pictures of Christ as anagogical, in that they, from the perspective of an Old Testament writer, are images of things to come. "Assuming the principle that the visible rites of the Law are shadows of spiritual things," he continues, "he shows that Christ must be sought in all the legal priesthood, in sacrifices, in the order of the sanctuary."[116] Calvin does hesitate to see Christ in the Old Testament, and he also sharply criticizes Origen's extreme allegorical interpretations, but he also recognizes that faith in Christ "is the centre and sum of Scripture."[117]

Transition to the Seventeenth-Century Post-Reformation World

In the century following the Reformation, the subject of the next chapter, biblical interpretation took another radical turn. Calvin's ideas were developed by the Puritans, who fought intensely for the Reformation ideals of biblical authority. It is Calvin's understanding of types that, in the words of Mason I. Lowance, "released to Puritanism a view of

---

a spiritual union effected by the power of the Holy Ghost in such a way that there is no 'gross mixture' of Christ and ourselves" (ibid.).

115. *ICR* 3.1.3.

116. Calvin, *Matthew, Mark, and Luke*, 235, 236.

117. Calvin, *Second Epistle of Paul the Apostle to the Corinthians*, 329, 41, 330; see also Forstman, *Word and Spirit*; and Neuser, *Calvinus Sacrae Scripturae Professor*.

the Bible filled with prophetic and eschatological symbols."[118] However, Puritanism was not the only movement to interpret Scripture in this era. Baruch Spinoza and other like interpreters began to question biblical authority and called for the elimination of any idea of a spiritual sense. The Bible is to be interpreted as any other book, according to Spinoza, and he helped lay the foundation for future generations of deists. While this way of reading the Bible caused a Puritan uproar, it also moved other Christians, like the Cambridge Platonists, to incorporate Neoplatonism into their reading of the Bible, and Latitudinarian ministers to employ an interpretative method that focuses on the morals of the Bible, arguing that the Bible does not have to be perfectly accurate or empirically verified to be trusted. And thus the further evolution of biblical interpretation in the seventeenth century will supply Jonathan Edwards with an even wider range of ideas to explore.

---

118. Lowance, *Language of Canaan*, 26.

2

Scripture and Spirituality in Early-Modern Biblical Interpretation

> The church of Christ sets the crown upon Christ's head in the day of his espousals to his bride, i.e., in the conversion of the soul. Christ is crowned as king by God the Father, and not only so, but also by the church, his mother.
>
> —Jonathan Edwards, *Blank Bible*, on Song of Solomon 3:11[1]

> Marriage signifies the spiritual union and communion of Christ and the church, and especially the glorification of the church in the perfection of this union and communion forever.
>
> —Jonathan Edwards, "Images of Divine Things"[2]

IN THE BUSY JEWISH quarter of Amsterdam in 1632—just a few steps from the Houtgracht channel, on the Burgwal thoroughfare—Baruch Spinoza was born to the Portuguese businessman Michael de Espinoza. Primarily speaking Portuguese but praying in Hebrew, they were one family among many Jewish-Portuguese immigrants enticed to this republic known for its religious toleration and economic promise. Perhaps it is not surprising that Spinoza, growing up in such relatively diverse circumstances, dared to think differently from his Jewish and Christian counterparts on the nature of Scripture. As free as Amsterdam was, Spinoza's views on the nature of the biblical text and his rejection of key points of orthodoxy, including biblical authority and Mosaic authorship,

---

1. *WJE* 24:617.
2. *WJE* 11:52.

were met initially with fear and communal shunning, but ultimately transformed the world of biblical interpretation.

Spinoza and others like him were willing to ask forbidden questions. Must we believe that the Bible is God's revelation to humanity simply because it or the church says it is? Who is the privileged interpreter of Scripture? Who is to say that one person's reading of the biblical text is more enlightened by the Spirit than another's? Spinoza and the thinkers encouraged by him were troubled by what they saw as a sacred text that did not stand the test of scientific investigation.

As seen in the previous chapter, ancient and medieval Christians explored the depths of the biblical text with little fear, finding no need to question its authority since any number of possible readings, including the allegorical, were available when a literal reading posed a problem. But the Reformers had challenged these tactics; and in one sense, the Reformation's questioning of the church's authority and allegorical readings of the Bible set the stage for the willful opposition and pre-critical thinking of Spinoza. Scholars of the seventeenth century now had to deal with a serious challenge to the Bible and to their own respective theologies. Among these scholars, Spinoza represents a minority, one that often delayed publication of books for the sake of avoiding persecution, but the majority were visible members of movements like Puritanism and Cambridge Platonism or their progeny, the Latitudinarians.[3] These latter groups resisted each other as much as they resisted Spinoza. The Puritans resisted the Church of England because their theology was too "Romanized," the Cambridge Platonists and Latitudinarians because they were too "liberal," and Spinoza and Descartes because they purportedly placed authority in the individual. The Cambridge Platonists and the Latitudinarians resisted Spinoza for throwing out the baby with the bathwater, and the Church of England and the Puritans for being too dogmatic and, consequently, brutal. There was no united front.

Edwards's New England world was far from untouched by these controversies. The changing historical and intellectual climate of

---

3. Many of these interests can be found in his citations, quotations without citations, but particularly in his "Catalogue of Reading" and "Account Book." Writing on the sources listed in "Account Book," Thuesen notes that, "Of the approximately seventy-seven strictly theological works mentioned in the document [the 'Account Book'], two in seven are 'polite' (Anglican, Latitudinarian, or Enlightenment) volumes, while the rest ["impolite"] may be classified broadly as Nonconformist or Reformed" (Thuesen, "Edwards' Intellectual Background," 26).

seventeenth-century European cultures of the Bible made possible the theological controversies of the eighteenth century, represented by a flurry of books and pamphlets that made their way into European and American universities and colleges, culminating in the first major controversy to hit Yale and coinciding with Edwards's first personal theological crisis. A contextualized perspective on Edwards's theological crisis in the early 1720s, requires some examination of the preceding intellectual issues and historical movements that inform his immediate world.

Post-Reformation Puritanism

Between the 1530s and 1640s, England experienced tumultuous religious and political uncertainty. The Puritans, carrying on the Reformed doctrine of Scripture and conversion, sought (among many priorities) to shed the imposition of ritual from the Church of Rome as it was found in the Church of England and dictated by the monarch. The battle was pursued on economic, political, and ecclesiastical fronts. At the beginning of the seventeenth century, when James VI of Scotland became James I of England (1566–1625), many Presbyterians expected an ally, but he quickly sided with Episcopalianism. With the Millenary Petition in 1603, Puritans of all stripes raised questions regarding ritual, subscription, and discipline. In response, James called the Hampton Court Conference in 1604 to discuss the issues, but at the mention of Presbyterianism—which would end his power to discipline from the throne and his "divine right" to rule the church—James called off the meeting. He was keenly aware that a loss of power over the church would result in the loss of control over church money and property.

Pressure continued to build in subsequent years as Charles I (1600–1649), considered a crypto-Catholic by the Puritans, upheld the positions of Archbishop William Laud (1573–1645). Laud served on the King's Privy Council, whose vision of the church primarily concerned a uniformity of worship. As a result of his attempts to enforce this uniformity, Puritan lecturers were censored and liturgical practices were instituted that were considered by Puritans to be "Roman." For many Puritan millenarians who eagerly took on the role of watchdogs, looking for indications of the end of the world often focused on any sign of possible "papists" in the Church of England. Laud's efforts to instill liturgical practices further widened the divide between the Puritans and the Church of England. "In an effort to deter further anti-papal polemics," writes Jeffrey K. Jue, "from 1633–1640, Archbishop Laud forebade the publication of any material identifying the pope as Antichrist. The Laudians were already suspected of being crypto-papists, and this intolerance therefore unleashed a flood of anti-papal fear." Parliament had even sanctioned the publication of Joseph Mede's *Clavis Apocalyptica* as a "timely propaganda piece in attacking the ecclesiastical establishment endorsed by Charles I."[4]

Continued instability forced some English Puritans to immigrate to the Netherlands, bringing with them their theological contributions.[5] Evidence of this international dialogue is not hard to find. English books found their way into Dutch Reformed libraries and vice versa; both Richard Baxter and Owen had significant numbers of Dutch books on their shelves.[6] "The cluster of Puritanical intellectuals in exile had a lively dialogue on polemical and learned topics," writes Keith Sprunger. "Unorthodox notions flourished alongside scholarly orthodoxy. Freedom of ideas produced 'Amsterdam Babylon' and 'Amsterdam Babel.'"[7]

During these exiles, significant work was done on Protestant biblical interpretation. William Ames (1576–1633), a contributor to the Synod of Dordrecht in 1618 as an unofficial English representative of Calvinism and an advisor to Johannes Bogerman, the presiding officer, was at the front of the discussion.[8] It is his *Medulla Theologiae* and *English Puritanisme* that helped define Puritan Calvinism. For Ames, the doctrine of Scripture is the heart of all things Puritan. In 1610 Ames republished William Bradshaw's (ca. 1572–1618) *English Puritanism* (1641) in his own name, editing it and adding an introduction.[9] According to this volume, Puritans understood the pope to be the "Antichrist," one who saw his authority as higher than Scripture. But it is Scripture that has the highest authority, according to Ames, a doctrine that unites all Puritans:

---

4. Jue, "HEAVEN UPON EARTH," 40, 43.

5. Sprunger, *Dutch Puritanism*, 355, 356.

6. Trueman, "Puritan Theology as Historical Event," 259; Trueman, *Claims of Truth*, 15.

7. Sprunger, *Trumpets from the Tower*, 47. On this trafficking of ideas, see Schoneveld, *Intertraffic of the Mind*.

8. Sprunger, *Learned Doctor William Ames*, 54.

9. Ibid., 32.

> *They hold and maintaine,* that the word of God contained in the writings of the Prophets and Apostles, is of absolute perfection, given by Christ the head of the Church, to be unto the same the sole Canon and rule of all matters of *Religion,* and the worship and service of God whatsoever. And that whatsoever done in the same service and worship cannot be justified by the said Word, is unlawfull. And therefore that it is a sin, to force any Christian to doe any act of Religion, or Divine Service, that cannot evidently be warranted by the same.[10]

For the Puritan, all one needs for life and religious duty are to be found in Scripture, not in the decrees of the monarch or the bishop.[11] Scripture is the foundation of the Puritan approach to science, education, capitalism, and charity.[12] Nevertheless, while Scripture is plain enough to be applied to all areas of life, it is not plain to all, and there is a deeper meaning. "It is one thing to say that *all necessary truth* is plainly and clearly revealed in Scripture, which we do say," argues John Owen, "and another, that *every text and passage* in the Scripture is plain and easy to be understood, which we do not say, nor ever thought . . ."[13] There is a supernatural layer to Scripture that is sometimes hard to discern. While Scripture is plain, it contains something "mysterious" and "surpassing the comprehension of any man in this world."[14]

This mysteriousness is, however, never a subjective message. Puritan biblical interpretation, in keeping with earlier Reformation interpreters, retains as a fundamental element the clarity of Scripture found in the literal meaning.[15] Like Calvin (and Luther), the literal interpretation—the interpretation proper (as understood by the human authors)—is not the only literal interpretation; a "work-around" exists, made possible by the main author of the Bible, the Holy Spirit. His intended meaning, the typological, is the second literal interpretation.[16] "In interpreting the Scriptures," writes William Ames, one should be "waying [sic] the propriety of the tongue, wherein they are written" and

---

10. Ames, *English Puritanisme,* 20, 1.
11. Sprunger, *Dutch Puritanism,* 458.
12. Morgan, *Godly Learning,* 14, 18.
13. *WJO* 14:276.
14. *WJO* 14.276.
15. Packer, "Puritans as Interpreters of Scripture," 191–201.
16. Lewalski, "Typological Symbolism," 81.

"waying [sic] the Circumstance of the place, by comparing one place with another, and by considering what is properly spoken, and what tropically or figuratively."[17] In another place he explains, "Some things were known by a natural knowledge and some by a supernatural."[18]

As with Calvin, the Puritans also demand a spiritual sense to understand the spiritual message of the Holy Spirit. For example, James Durham (1622–1652) notes in his *Exposition on the Song of Solomon* that Scripture contains a literal meaning, equivalent to the historical sense, but it also contains another literal sense: the sense literally intended by God. Solomon's book "carrieth the authority of the Holy Ghost engraven upon it," writes Durham. The text thus has two authors:

> This Song must either be attributed to the Spirit, as the chief author of it, (though Solomon was the penman) or we must say, it was not only penned, but indited [sic] merely by some man, (Solomon, or whoever he be) led by his own spirit, or some other spirit, without the Spirit of God: but none of these last can be said.

This is what he calls a "two-fold literal sense of Scripture." Given that he is discussing the book of Solomon, one of the more controversial books in the history of interpretation, Durham cannot resolve himself to see the sexual and romantic overtones as offering any "edification." "Running in the night through the streets, and slighting him at the door . . . by no means can admit a proper, literal, and immediate sense," he insists, "but must needs aim at something figurative."[19] Herein is the logic: Scripture cannot include a book that focuses on such themes, therefore, biblical books like the Song of Solomon must be read differently (overlooking, of course, that such a book's presence in the Bible might, in fact, support the rejected premise that the Bible can indeed include books with sexual themes.)

Durham is not alone in his conclusions. Other Reformed commentators of his day approach the biblical text with similar attention to literal meanings, applying the spiritual sense when perceived as required by the text. A look at Matthew Poole's *Annotations Upon the Holy Bible*, for example, reveals this Puritan exegetical ethic in play. The subtitle of

---

17. Ames, *English Puritanisme*, 10–11; see also Richard Baxter's statements affirming the same thought in *The Practical Works of Richard Baxter*, 478.

18. Ames, *Marrow of Theology*, 186.

19. Durham, *Exposition of the Song of Solomon*, 26, 28, 30.

Scripture and Spirituality in Early-Modern Biblical Interpretation 51

the volume, "The Sacred *Text* is Inserted, and *various* Readings Annex'd, together with Parallel *Scriptures*, the more difficult *Terms* in each Verse are Explained, seeming *Contradictions* Reconciled, *Questions* and Doubts Resolved, and the whole Text opened," promises too much hermeneutically. Poole begins his commentaries on books of the Bible with a brief introduction, describing the content and message of the book using redemptive language. Then, verse by verse, he examines the biblical text, pulling from the historical context as well as the grammatical and contextual framework. The verse appears first with the explanation underneath; the literal interpretation gets the priority. Citing numerous cross-references, Poole guides Scripture in commenting upon Scripture, harmonizing it doctrinally. There is little wonder as to why this was a favorite commentary for many of the Reformed, including Edwards.

Notwithstanding what may be perceived as a tedious handling of the Greek and Hebrew, various translations of texts, and less-than-colorful commentary, Poole rarely fails to indicate the spiritual meaning of the text as well. When Moses and Aaron, in Num 20:10–11, gather the congregation together, Moses lifts up his hand and strikes the rock, causing water to flow out; according to verse 11, "water came out abundantly, and the congregation drank and their beasts."[20] Poole does not shrug off that this was a literal, historical event; but he does immediately focus on a deeper meaning: "To the men it was a sacrament, 1 Cor. 10.3, 4. but to the beasts it was no holy but a common thing."[21] As promised in his encompassing subtitle, Poole is harmonizing the Old and New Testaments, explaining that the water pouring out of the rock was more than just flowing water but also a "sacrament," something spiritual, a foreshadowing of the work of Christ. He inserts 1 Cor 10:3–4 as a cross-reference because this is the New Testament commentary on the Numbers passage, which according to Poole, provides the greater and intended meaning of the Holy Spirit: "And did all drink the same spiritual drink for they drank of that spiritual Rock that followed them, and that Rock was Christ" (1 Cor 10: 4). *The Annotations* then follows through with an explanation of the spiritual meaning of the text:

---

20. When referencing Scripture passages in discussing these English interpreters, I will cite the King James Version to remain faithful to their historical contexts.

21. Poole, *Annotations*, no page numbers (Num 20:10–11). Hereafter all citations for both volumes of this commentary will reference the biblical passage.

> And all the Jews, as well those that perished in the Wilderness, as those that were preserved to go into *Canaan*, they drank of the water which came out of the *Rock* . . . which water was *spiritual drink* in the same respects that the *Manna* was spiritual meat, being miraculously produced, and being a figure of Christ. For, [saith] the Apostle, *That Rock was Christ*, that is, the Rock did signifie or prefigure Christ, the Rock was Christ in the same sense that the *Bread in the Lords Supper* is the *Body* of *Christ*.[22]

Like Durham, when Poole approaches the Song of Solomon he resorts not only to a prefigurative or typological interpretation, but also to one that is prejudiced by the allegorical. Noting the outlandish figures of speech and the supposed indecency between the groom and his bride, Poole concludes that *"this Book is to be understood mystically or Allegorically concerning that spiritual Love and Marriage which is between God or Christ, and his Church, or every believing Soul."*[23] Another popular commentator of the day, Matthew Henry (1662–1714), comes to the same conclusion, arguing that the book is "an allegory, the letter of which kills those who rest in that and look no further, but the spirit of which gives life . . . It is a parable which makes divine things more difficult to those who do not love them, but more plain and pleasant to those who do."[24]

Though the Puritans approach Scripture with more freedom than their predecessors to find figures or allegories in the text, their approach remains in the spirit of Calvin, controlled by the text and the belief that the Holy Spirit and their regeneration gives them access to the hidden,

---

22. Poole, *Annotations*, 1 Cor 10:4.

23. Poole, *Annotations*, "Introduction" to "Canticles." Poole offers a general description of an allegory in his commentary on Gal 4:24 in *Annotations*. Here Paul describes Sarah and Hagar as representing allegorically both heavenly and earthly Jerusalems. "That is called an *Allegory*," writes Poole, "when one thing is learned out of another, or something is mystically signified and to be understood further then is expressed. Scripture hath a peculiar kind of *Allegories*, wherein one thing is signified by and under another thing." Poole notes that Moses did not intend an allegorical meaning when he wrote about Sarah and Hagar. Rather, the Apostle Paul judged that there was not only a literal meaning to the text, but also a mystical sense that could be applied to the historical context. Similarly, Matthew Henry writes, "*These things*, says he, *are an allegory*, wherein, besides the literal and historical sense of the words, the Spirit of God might design to signify something further to us, and that was, That these two, Hagar and Sarah, *are the two covenants*, or were intended to typify and prefigure the two different dispensations of the covenant" (Henry, *Matthew Henry's Commentary*, 6:699).

24. Henry, *Matthew Henry's Commentary*, 3:1053.

mysterious, redemptive-historical message that is, in some sense, the metanarrative of the entire Bible. As Matthew Poole writes, commenting on 1 Cor 2:11-12: "but there are deep things of God, Mysteries in Scripture, which till the Spirit of God hath revealed to me, they know not nor understand; for none knoweth them originally, but the Spirit of God, who is himself God, and *searcheth the deep things of God.*" Likewise, Edwards will also later write of 1 Cor 2:11-12 that "in these two verses is contained an invincible argument for the insufficiency of human reason without a divine revelation in things of that nature which the gospel reveals..."[25] It should be no surprise, then, that the typological interpretation of Scripture popular with Edwards and given so much attention by scholars is founded primarily on an existing Reformed methodology. The Bible is—for Calvin, the Puritans, and Edwards (assimilating and building on his forebears)—the source of all things mysterious in the divine mind. It is, therefore, a divine treasure chest containing hidden gems for those who dig deeper into it. More than simple reading is required, however; one must be guided in this by the Holy Spirit—and therefore be in relationship with God—in order to access the treasures locked in the chest.

The question of who has the Spirit of God, or who can perceive the true voice of the Spirit in interpreting the Bible, then, is a crucial question for seventeenth-century biblicists. Among those quick to challenge, Spinoza is a prime example.

Seventeenth-Century Challenges and Responses

Spinoza

Spinoza's Amsterdam teemed with business and intellectual pursuits, such as those of Spinoza's famous neighbor, the artist Rembrandt Harmenszoon van Rijn. As a young man, Spinoza divided his time between his schooling—under teachers like Rabbi Menasseh ben Israel (1604–57), a progressive who promoted Jewish-Christian dialogue by instructing his students in the New Testament—and working in his

---

25. Poole, *Annotations*, 1 Cor 2:11-12. First Corinthians 2:11-12 reads in Edwards's KJV, "For what man knoweth the things of a man, save the spirit of a man that is in him? Even so the things of God knoweth no man, but the Spirit of God. Now we have received, not the spirit of the world, but the Spirit which is of God, that we might know the things that are freely given to us of God" (*WJE* 24.2.1038).

father's vegetable import business. His early educational experience and contact with others in his father's business exposed Spinoza to a broad world of ideas. At age fourteen, he left his Jewish schooling altogether and ventured into business fulltime, pursuing training in Latin and exploring the many intellectual and philosophical trends of his day through a secular education.[26]

By 1656, when Spinoza left his father's business, his beliefs were in a state of rapid flux. Because of his evolving views on the Mosaic authorship of the Pentateuch, his growing acceptance of pantheism, and his rejection of the immortality of the soul, he was eventually excommunicated from his congregation and community. Now earning his living as a lens polisher, his intellectual transformation led him to publish several books on his new theological outlook, one of the most important being the *Tractatus Theologico-Politicus,* a strong critique of the Bible and politics.

The *Tractatus*, a landmark in the history of biblical interpretation, heralds a change in the treatment of Scripture and the role of the biblical commentator. Spinoza's radical thinking was a significant factor in setting the tone of seventeenth-century European biblical interpretation (especially early Deism) and eighteenth-century American reactions. "While certainly only part of a diverse and very broad culture of critique," writes Robert Brown, "Spinoza's treatise represented one of the most thoroughgoing applications of a demonstrative method to the epistemological estimation of the biblical narratives. In this sense, its appearance was something of a precipitating moment." Or as Leo Strauss says, "from our time, scholars generally study the Bible in the manner in which they study any other book . . . Spinoza more than any other man laid the foundation for this kind of Biblical study."[27]

From his excommunication until his death in 1677, Spinoza argued that the Jews were arrogant in insisting that they were the only chosen people, and his writing continued to push for social reform leading to freedom from binding religious thought and to a promotion of a pluralistic democracy.[28] The Bible was a major obstacle for his agenda and needed to be understood and interpreted outside of the walls of dogma.

26. Nadler, *Spinoza*, 176–79.

27. Brown, *Jonathan Edwards and the Bible*, 34; Strauss, *Spinoza's Critique of Religion*, 35.

28. Harrisville and Sundeberg, *Bible in Modern Culture*, 44.

Western thought, he argued, needed to break away from the presuppositions that held the mind back from using reason to ascertain the nature of being. According to Spinoza, whether Jewish, Catholic, or Protestant, these presuppositions were fortified in their respective institutions. For the Protestant, especially the Reformed, this meant letting go of the doctrine of scriptural authority.

While the Reformers did reject radical allegory and church tradition as merely human authorities, it is clear from Spinoza's work that he sees their doctrine of *sola scriptura* as irrational, placing a human and therefore flawed book above the mind and critical examination. The added notion of being illuminated by the Spirit appears to Spinoza as an elitist and unaccountable form of interpretation, a convenient replacement for the church tradition the Reformers had rejected. In its place Spinoza advocates a scientific approach guided by the light of reason.

Like Descartes, Spinoza's search for certainty requires him to attempt to dismiss his presuppositions. Inspired by the Cartesian *ordine geometrico*, Spinoza seeks to recognize, as obligatory for all as is mathematics, only those self-evident ideas which have necessary corollaries and which may lead to ultimate philosophical truth.[29] Known as *infallibilism*, this epistemology judges so-called claims to truth or knowledge as if they are mathematical conclusions, certain and binding.[30] Guided by the light of reason, human beings are able to escape the superstitious fears of religion that only lead to engulfing humanity in violence and hatred. Through reason, according to Spinoza, one will be able to analyze the Bible using the same tools used to interpret the text of the Babylonians or any other people group.

> If we would separate ourselves from the crowd and escape from theological prejudices, instead of rashly accepting human commentaries for Divine documents, we must consider the true method of interpreting Scripture and dwell upon it at some length; for if we remain in ignorance of this we cannot know, certainly, what the Bible and the Holy Spirit wish to teach.[31]

---

29. Brown, *Jonathan Edwards and the Bible*, 31–34; Kenny, *Oxford History of Western Philosophy*, 146–51.

30. Brown, "Edwards, Locke and the Bible," 363, 364.

31. Spinoza, *Theologico-Political Treatise*, 1:99. "I may sum up the matter by saying that the method of interpreting Scripture does not widely differ from the method of interpreting nature—in fact, it is almost the same" (ibid.).

With this belief in mind, Spinoza demands that the Bible be treated like any other book, subjected to the reason of human beings and proven through testing and logic.[32]

Undermining the idea of the Bible as revelation, Spinoza goes right to the heart of its treatment as the infallible word of God. Spinoza does not want the interpreter to take the claim that it is God's literal word too seriously, since he believes it is the result of a misunderstood idiom. According to him, the Jews do not discern between first and second causes. Rather, he asserts, they "refer all things directly to Deity . . . if they make money by a transaction, they say God gave it to them; if they desire anything, they say God has disposed their hearts toward it; if they think anything, they say God told them."[33] Essentially, Robert Grant explains, "it could be claimed that Hebrew idiom was responsible for [the Bible's] attribution to God."[34]

Spinoza sees no special need for such supernatural transformation. Ironically, the divine and supernatural light, a source for certitude and clarity in Reformed theology, offers too many individual and unchecked interpretations, according to Spinoza. It provides too much room for any person or institution to justify any dogma or action of intolerance. The truth, he claims, is that when the Bible is understood in its plain language, neither the redeemed nor the reprobate has an advantage over the other.

> For as the highest power of Scriptural interpretation belongs to every man, the rule for such interpretation should be nothing but the natural light of reason which is common to all—not any supernatural light nor any external authority; moreover, such a rule ought not to be so difficult that it can only be applied by very skilful philosophers, but should be adapted to the natural and ordinary faculties and capacity of mankind.[35]

Whether it was his Jewish community or the institutionalized Christian church (Protestant or Catholic), truth in these systems, according to Spinoza, was deemed as the sole property of that institution. The advantage of being the chosen ones made the Scripture a handy tool to beat down anyone with whom they were at odds. But human equity,

---

32. Strauss, *Spinoza's Critique of Religion*, 35.
33. Spinoza, *Theologico-Political Treatise*, 15.
34. Grant, *Short History of the Interpretation of the Bible*, 106.
35. Spinoza, *Theologico-Political Treatise*, 119.

tolerance, and true democracy occur when everyone realizes they are on an equal playing field.

Spinoza argues that when interpreters claim that "the light of nature has no power to interpret Scripture, but that a supernatural faculty is required for the task," they give themselves too much credit. "If we look at their interpretations," he insists, "they contain nothing supernatural, at least nothing but the merest conjectures . . . Let them be placed side by side with the interpretations of those who frankly confess that they have no faculty beyond their natural ones; we shall see that the two are just alike—both human, both long pondered over, both laboriously invented."[36] His point, to paraphrase, is that everyone puts on their pants one leg at a time. Each interpreter may not have the same level of natural faculty, but none of them has a supernatural faculty. Ultimately, no props are needed; only the light of natural reason, possessed by all, is necessary to understand Scripture.

For Reformed Protestant Christianity, Descartes and Spinoza represented the start of a new threat to biblical authority and interpretation. Both Descartes and Spinoza were met with intense opposition from post-Reformation exegetes, especially Dutch and English Puritans who intended to continue the Reformation understanding of Scripture's sole authority.[37] Dutch theologian and professor at Utrecht, Gisbertus Voetius, accused the new philosophy of indirect atheism. Voetius charged his students with the task of taking on Descartes; one student, Dutch theologian Peter van Mastricht, would become Voetius's successor.[38] Van Mastricht's disagreement with Descartes is focused on Scripture as the source of unequivocal authority.[39] He argues that Scripture has eight characteristics, all stemming from its divine authority. Scripture, according to van Mastricht's explanation of 1 Tim 3:16–17, is God's word and as such carries his authority. Being divine, it must be

---

36. Ibid., 114. "The difficulty of interpreting Scripture arises from no defect in human reason, but simply from the carelessness (not to say malice) of men who neglected the history of the Bible" (ibid.).

37. On reactions to Descartes and Spinoza, see Pünjer, *History of the Christian Philosophy of Religion*, 407–45; Preus, *Spinoza and the Irrelevance of Biblical Authority*; see also my "Introduction" in van Mastricht, *A Treatise on Regeneration*, vii–xxxii.

38. For an overview of the Cartesian debate among the orthodox Reformed, see Bizer, "Reformed Orthodoxy and Cartesianism," 20ff.; and van Mastricht's *Novitatum Cartesianarum Gangraena*.

39. Bizer, "Reformed Orthodoxy and Cartesianism," 70.

true, certain, and universal ("*veritas, certitudo & . . . universal*"); it must be sound ("*integritas*"), meaning free from corruption ("*per singularem Dei providentiam, immunis existit, ab omni corruptione*"); holy and pure ("*sanctitas ac puritas*"); clear ("*perspicuitas*"); perfect ("*quâ ei nihil omnino deest*"); necessary; and efficacious.[40] All of this meant nothing to Descartes and Spinoza; but it meant the world to Christianized Europe.

The Cambridge Platonists

A middle ground between Puritanism and Spinozan rationalism was struck by a vocal minority of English thinkers known as the Cambridge Platonists (1630–1680). At the heart of the movement were Henry More (1614–1687), Ralph Cudworth (1617–1688), John Smith (1618–1652), Nathaniel Culverwel (1618–1651), and their leader, Benjamin Whichcote (1609–1683). These thinkers laid a greater emphasis on the use of reason in determining issues of faith.

Cambridge Platonism began in reaction to political instability and Puritan dogmatism.[41] Culverwel and Smith were under Whichcote's tutelage, and Cudworth—following Whichcote—was also a fellow and tutor. For Whichcote and his students, human reason is the "the candle of the Lord" and a necessary tool for reining in unfettered dogmatism placed on Scripture by Puritan views of biblical authority and interpretation, while simultaneously avoiding Spinoza's rejection of special revelation. For these thinkers, Platonism is more about Plotinus than Plato himself and, though philosophical idealism comes into the discussion, it is less about the metaphysics as much as its "religious spirit."[42]

As the country went during this time, so did Cambridge; while one might presume a small, tightly knit group within the confines of a university to exist beyond the radar of politics, such was not the case. Laudian policies and the suppression of lecturers at Cambridge, along with Puritan suspicions of their teachings, left the band of Cambridge men trapped between the two. Politically, Cambridge "was engulfed by the upheavals of the time," as Gerald Cragg puts it.[43] When Cromwell's

---

40. Van Mastricht, *Theoretico-Practica Theologia*, 1.2.3–21.

41. As exemplified in the debate between Puritan divine Anthony Tuckney (1599–1670) and his student Benjamin Whichcote, discussed in Roberts, Sr., *From Puritanism to Platonism*, 42–65.

42. Powicke, *Cambridge Platonists*, 21.

43. Cragg, *Cambridge Platonists*, 8.

troops passed through, attempts were made to remove those believed to be sympathetic to the crown.[44] During the tumultuous years of 1643 to 1660, the Cambridge Platonists held their own *via media* between the Puritans and the Anglicans, seeking toleration.[45] "The situation at Cambridge," writes G. A. J. Rogers, "especially in 1643, when the parliamentary troops of the Earl of Manchester took over the University and removed paintings and imprisoned members, was one that must have left a very deep impression on Cudworth, and no doubt confirmed his horror of war and militant confrontation generally."[46] The ups and downs of the times fostered a search for something different and better balanced, leading the Cambridge Platonists to emphasize the roles of Scripture *and* reason. Spinoza, for them, was the resurgence of materialism, and More resolutely attacked his writings as atheistic.[47] At the same time, they did not exclude the obligation to understand Scripture in conjunction with solid and sane reason, a facility that appeared to them to be lacking in the day's conflicts.

Reason is essential, argues Culverwel in *The Light of Nature*, because, based on his reading of Prov 20:27, reason is the "candle of the Lord."[48] Whichcote agrees, writing, in "Think on These Things," that "religion exercises, teaches, satisfies, that which is the height and excellency of human nature":

> Our reason is not laid aside nor discharged, . . . but awakened, excited, employed, directed, and improved by it; for the mind and understanding of man, is that faculty, whereby man is made capable of God, and apprehensive of him, receptive from him, and able to make returns upon him, and acknowledgments to him. Bring that with you, or else you are not capable receivers: unless you drink in these moral principles; unless you do receive them by reason, the reason of things by the reason of your mind, your religion is but shallow and superficial.[49]

44. Ibid., 8; Roberts, *From Puritanism to Platonism*, 7.

45. Cragg, *Cambridge Platonists*, 11; Cudworth was raised Reformed but later became Arminian on the will, providence, and responsibility. This was seen as a "gentler theology" (Colie, *Light and Enlightenment*, 38).

46. Rogers, "Other-Worldly Philosophers and the Real World," 7; Spurr, *Restoration Church of England*, 1991.

47. For a helpful analysis of More's critique of Spinoza see Colie, *Light and Enlightenment*, 66–93.

48. Culverwel, *Elegant and Learned Discourse*, 1.

49. Whichcote, *Works*, 4:139–40. All subsequent citations are abbreviated *WW*, with volume number and page.

Scripture verifies the light of nature that God provides through his creation using the so-called candle of the Lord, that is, the human mind. "A man has as much right to use his own understanding in judging of truth," argues Whichcote in his *Aphorisms*, "as he has a right to use his own eyes to see his way."[50] Unlike Spinoza, this approach does not strip revelation of its authority; but unlike many of the Puritans (according to the Cambridge Platonists), neither does it strip reason of its capacity. Human reason can go only so far, they argue, as God ultimately transcends it, leaving the human being to believe where reason cannot prove; nevertheless, the emphasis found in Reformed theology on first being spiritually transformed goes too far.[51]

This concept of transcendence emerges from their Neoplatonic idealism and Plotinus's understanding of ascetic contemplation of the divine.[52] As Plato wanted to turn the mind away from the material to the immaterial, so did these Cambridge theologians. Being their primary philosophical influence, Plotinus provided them with a hermeneutical tool. Plotinus argues that reality, which is spiritual, is also called Intelligence; this Intelligence corresponds loosely to Plato's World of Forms or Ideas, in which forms are merely emanations of that Intelligence. By adding the element of Intelligence to Ideas, Plotinus is speaking of the mind of "the One," making it the ultimate source of all Ideas. This is closer to the Cambridge Platonists' conception of God: "divine intelligence is the ultimate reality."[53] Human reason (the candle of the Lord) reflects this divine intelligence; it is godlike.[54] Reason allows one to see beyond the material world and into the immaterial. "Reason," writes Whichcote, "is the divine governor of man's life, it is the very voice of God." The connection of reason with the divine makes reason a moral venture. Reason is a spiritual exercise and "nothing is more spiritual than that which is moral."[55] Biblical interpretation, then, is not

---

50. *WW* 4:147; Whichcote, "Moral and Religious Aphorisms," 423 (*Aphorisms*, 40). Subsequent references will be to *Aphorisms* and number.

51. Roberts, *From Puritanism to Platonism*, 75.

52. Copleston, *History of Philosophy*, 56.

53. Cragg, *Cambridge Platonists*, 22.

54. Powicke, *Cambridge Platonists*, 23.

55. Whichcote, *Aphorisms*, 76, 969.

based simply on a whim. Their middle ground and pleas for toleration are essentially founded on reason, which had to be free from duress.[56]

The Levellers, an English political party advocating complete religious freedom, wanted to purge the House of Commons and establish a free democratic Parliament.[57] Their plan, whose text is found in "Agreement of the People," proposed a government of the people, one that included religious toleration and rights guaranteed in a constitution. The Putney Debates, held in October and November 1647 over a new constitution for England and the "Agreement of the People," was at the heart of the fight. The discussions were a powder keg, as Cudworth was well aware when he preached before the House of Commons, and he had no plans for taking one side or the other.[58] "The scope of this sermon," writes Cudworth, "was not to contend for this or that opinion." Rather, it is the dogmatist that Cudworth cautions against. "The sons of Adam," he says, "are now as busy as ever himself was about the tree of knowledge of good and evil, shaking the boughs of it, and scrambling for the fruit; whilst, I fear, many are too unmindful of the tree of life." Rather than clamoring after knowledge as an object, Cudworth's sermon calls them to recognize that it is but a shadow, a mangled and disfigured picture of God. One has to be released from "cold theorems and maxims" and "lean syllogistical reasonings" because one never gets the least "glimpse of the true heavenly light."[59] Cudworth's sermon, delivered in this charged political context, is a call to free the mind to be what God made it to be.

It is this light of reason that lays the foundation for certain hermeneutical principles argued for by the Cambridge Platonists. First, Scripture confirms, and is not contrary to, reason. Therefore, reason as an important tool in biblical interpretation must be set free, and not be bound by the institution. Binding up the free use of reason is, for Cudworth, a source of England's political instability. Second, the biblical interpreter is more humble when he or she realizes that Scripture is nei-

---

56. Cragg, *Cambridge Platonists*, 21.

57. See chapter 13 of Brailsford, *Levellers and the English Revolution*; Haller and Godfrey, *Leveller Tracts*; Frank, *The Levellers* (1955); Pease, *The Leveller Movement* (1965); Robertson, *Religious Foundations of the Leveller Democracy*; Wolfe, *Leveller Manifestoes of the Puritan Revolution*; Sharp, *English Levellers*; Pearse, *Great Restoration*.

58. Cragg, *Cambridge Platonists*, 369.

59. Cudworth, "Sermon Preached Before the Honorable House of Commons," 370, 373, 383, 375.

ther plain nor simple. Reason must be brought to bear upon it in order to make sense of the divine language. John Smith, in his *Of Prophesie*, argues that "*Divine Truth* hath its *Humiliation* and *Examination*, as well as its *Exaltation*. *Divine Truth* becomes many times in Scripture *incarnate*, debasing itself to assume our rude conceptions, that so it might converse more freely with us, and infuse its own Divinity into us . . . *Nos non habemus aures, ficut Deus habet linguam*."[60] Scripture is not, as Smith says, written in the "language of *Eternity*"; rather, it wears "our mantles," learns "our language," and conforms "itself as it were to our dress and fashions." For the exegete to understand Scripture is "not rigidly to examine it upon Philosophical Interrogatories, or to bring it under the scrutiny of School Definitions and Distinctions. It speaks not to us so much in the tongue of the learned *Sophies* of the world, as in the plainest and most vulgar dialect that may be."[61]

Smith takes note of the vulgar attributions to God, the imperfections describing him. His eating, drinking, and riding "upon the wings of the Wind," have less to do with God and more to do with his accommodation of our limitations. Hell is described as a "great valley of fire like that of *Hinnom*" and heaven is described as a "place of continual banqueting," all of which are for our understanding rather than descriptions of actual places or events. "We are not always rigidly to adhere to the very Letter of the Text," Smith argues. "We must not think that it always gives us Formal Definitions of things, for it speaks commonly according to the Vulgar apprehension: as when it tells us of the *Ends of the heaven*, which now almost every Idiot knows hath *no ends* at all."[62] Smith heavily warns the reader against taking too literal an interpretation of Scripture. What is revealed in prophecy, for example, is not always an actual historical event. Often the events of prophecy detailed in Scripture, though seeming to be a part of actual history, are really effective stage props for dreams or visions and have greater meaning symbolically.

Third, since the literal message is not always the most practical, prompting one to look beyond the letter, the Cambridge Platonists made biblical interpretation largely a moral enterprise. Scripture has the greatest authority, but its role is "to confirm natural truth," which

---

60. Smith, *Select Discourses*, 171.
61. Ibid., 171, 172.
62. Ibid., 173, 174.

is primarily a moral message.⁶³ Far from being dry, Scripture is understood to deliver vibrant instruction in godly living. The exegete is not to be fooled into looking strictly for the literal interpretation. "The *Philosophical* or *Physical* nature and Literal veritie of things cannot so reasonably be supposed to be set forth to us," argues Smith, "as the *Moral* and *Theological*."⁶⁴ The light of reason could pull these moral messages from nature, but revelation is needed to confirm their truth. Whichcote writes: "unless you drink in these moral principles; unless you do receive them by reason, the reason of things by the reason of your mind, your religion is but shallow and superficial."⁶⁵ To insist on strict dogma is to miss the heart of biblical interpretation; interpreters are to agree on the clearest principles of morality rather than kill each other over the use of a prayer book.

The latitude in interpretation allowed by the hermeneutics of Smith and his fellows gave them the name *Latitudinarian*, a name that stuck with the second generation of Cambridge Platonists. Like most titles given to a movement, the term was intended to be derogatory.⁶⁶ While the Cambridge Platonists brought a great deal to the stage of biblical interpretation, they did primarily focus on truth as philosophy, as demonstrated by Cudworth's *The True Intellectual System of the Universe*; the next generation put the emphasis on morality.⁶⁷

The Latitudinarians

The term *Latitudinarian* first appeared in print in 1662 when Simon Patrick (1625–1707) wrote *A Brief Account of the New Sect of Latitude-Men*. The movement, if it could be called that, sported names such as John Wilkins, Lord Bishop of Chester (1614–72); John Tillotson (1630–

---

63. Powicke, *Cambridge Platonists*, 31.

64. Smith, "Of Prophesie," 171.

65. *WW* 4:139–40.

66. Colie, *Light and Enlightenment*, 6; see also, Passmore, *Ralph Cudworth*. For more on the relationship between the Cambridge Platonists and the next generation of Latitudinarians, see Griffin, *Latitudinarianism in the Seventeenth-Century Church of England*.

67. Henry More, more so than Cudworth, used philosophy over the biblical text. Joseph M. Levine writes that "More's final source of inspiration, then, was 'from either the open Expression, or else more secret Interpretations of Holy Scripture.' He had not forgotten revelation, though in emphasizing reason and nature he had nearly lost the need for it" (Levine, "Latitudinarians, Neoplatonists, and the Ancient Wisdom," 97).

1694), the popular Archbishop of Canterbury and a student of Benjamin Whichcote; Edward Stillingfleet (1635–1699), Bishop of Worcester; and John Locke (1632–1704). The Latitudinarian name was originally derogatory and about as hard to define as Puritanism.[68] Patrick's book on the movement appears on the heels of the Restoration of 1660, when the monarchy was restored under Charles II and the Church of England was politically restored as Episcopal. Like their earlier Cambridge Platonist teachers, these "polite" thinkers emphasized toleration based on the light of reason and Scripture, and were promoted to high positions in the church.[69]

This second generation continued to interpret Scripture as primarily a moral document (necessary for toleration)—they were dedicated ministers and "practical."[70] Dogmatism tended to divide, they thought, and reason knew no such thing.[71] Often criticized as theological minimalists, they were actually heavy hitters, whose theological musings centered in different areas. Following William Chillingworth (1602–1644), they complemented their understanding of reason with a sophisticated presentation on epistemological issues, such as "certainty," and as a result they approached their interpretation of Scripture cautiously and openly.

What made Chillingworth—an important Laudian in the Church of England who left Protestantism for the Church of Rome—so appealing? His story is a crisis of epistemological certainty. Henry G. Van Leeuwen explains that Chillingworth's surprising exit from Anglicanism was due to "the lack of continuity of Protestantism with the early Church and the need for a living infallible judge to decide controversies concerning the fundamental articles of faith."[72] With coaxing he was convinced to return, but his return then led to a reexamination of his epistemology. In a drawn-out debate with Matthias Wilson (who used the pseudonym Edward Knott), Chillingworth wrote his famous *The Religion of Protestants, a Safe Way to Salvation*.[73] He went to the heart of Wilson-

---

68. Patrick, *Brief Account of the New Sect of Latitude-Men*, 5; Marshall, *John Locke*, 39.

69. Edward Stillingfleet's (1635–99) *Irenicum* (1662), for example, promoted understanding between Episcopalians and Presbyterians.

70. Reventlow, *Authority of the Bible and the Rise of the Modern World*, 223.

71. Roberts, *From Puritanism to Platonism*, 228; Spellman, *Latitudinarians and the Church of England*, 3.

72. Van Leeuwen, *Problem of Certainty*, 16.

73. Ibid., 17.

Knott's charge that there is no salvation outside of the Catholic Church, an infallible source of truth, leaving Protestants in a precarious predicament. Chillingworth no longer demanded infallibilism in interpreting Scripture; rather, he writes:

> I do heartily acknowledge and believe the articles of our faith to be in themselves truths as certain and infallible, as the very common principles of geometry and mathematics. But that there is required of us a knowledge of them, and adherence to them, as certain as that sense of science; that such a certainty is required of us under pain of damnation, so that no man can hope to be in the state of salvation, but he that finds in himself such a degree of faith, such a strength of adherence; this I have already demonstrated to be of a great error, and of dangerous and pernicious consequence.[74]

Chillingworth rejects an absolute infallible certainty and maintains both conditional infallible certainty and "moral certainty." The first, absolute infallible certainty, belongs only to God; the second, "conditional infallible certainty," belongs to mathematics and logic; and the third, "moral certainty," is, as Van Leeuwen describes, "the certainty a sane, reasonable, thoughtful person has after considering all the available evidence as fully and impartially as is possible and giving his assent to that side on which the evidence seems strongest."[75] According to Chillingworth, no human institution has had the first category of certainty, though they may believe fallibly that they do. Because this category is exclusive to deity, humans approach Scripture with fallible reason and, therefore, must approach each other with charity.[76]

This is an important hermeneutical principle for Latitudinarians like John Wilkins, John Tillotson, and Edward Stillingfleet, as it says something about their approach to Scripture in the context of the life of the Christian.[77] "There may be an *indubitable* Certainty where there is not an *infallible* Certainty," wrote John Wilkins in his *Natural Religion*.[78] The evidence for "Moral Certainty may be so plain, that every man whose judgment is free from prejudice will consent unto them. And though there be no natural necessity, that such things must

---

74. Chillingworth, *Works of William Chillingworth*, 317 (see Part 1, Chapter 6).
75. Van Leeuwen, *Problem of Certainty*, 22, 23.
76. Shapiro, *Probability and Certainty*, 81.
77. See Tillotson, *Rule of Faith*; Wilkins, *Natural Religion*; see also, Wilkins, *Ecclesiastes*.
78. Wilkins, *Natural Religion*, 95.

be so, and that they cannot possibly be otherwise, without implying a Contradiction; yet may they be so certain as not to admit of any reasonable doubt concerning them."[79] John Tillotson puts forward a similar argument, noting that not all things require the same amount of proof. "None can demonstrate to me, that there is such an Island in *America* as *Jamaica*," he writes, "yet upon the Testimony of credible persons, and Authors who have written of it, I am as free from all doubt concerning it, as from doubting of the clearest Mathematical Demonstration." In other words, humans, because of their inherent imperfection, are not capable of perfect knowledge. Even when it comes to interpreting Scripture, not all agree as to its meaning. Knowing the pitfalls of certitude, he calls for a belief that is reasonably warranted by the facts, an idea he sees as "moral certainty," the kind of certainty that satisfies "a prudent man."[80] As a result, Latitudinarian sermons are not dogmatic theologies but rather are overwhelmingly centered on morality, and so, not surprisingly, were well received by laypeople wherever they were preached. By many Calvinist academics, however, they were accused of being Arminians, rationalists, or deists in disguise.

While Scripture remained important for these ministers, dogmatic discussions or Athanasian creedal formulations were none of their concern. And not all Calvinists saw them as the enemy. Even in Tillotson's day, high Calvinist and Anglican John Edwards (1637–1716) wrote in *The Preacher*—his how-to manual for young ministers—of the prominence of moral messages coming from the pulpit. Far from discouraging moral preaching, he argues that ministers who preach morality are helping to reform England's "scandalous" and immoral society, and it is John Tillotson who comes to his mind as the greatest of these ministers. Preaching the morality of Christianity "hath been excellently performed by some eminent Preachers of late," writes Edwards, "and by none perhaps better than by the late Archbishop of *Canterbury*."[81]

The Latitudinarian view of the Scriptures was a "halfway" point between traditional Protestant doctrine of Scripture and rationalism.[82] "Tillotson," as Gerard Reedy points out, "never forces his readers to choose between reason and revelation"; rather, "he published four ser-

---

79. Ibid., 7–8.
80. Tillotson, preface to *Works* (1696), preface (unnumbered).
81. Edwards, *Preacher*, 1:65, 69.
82. Cragg, *Church and the Age of Reason*, 71, 72.

mons on the divinity and incarnation of the Word" and other sermons "on the sacrifice of Jesus Christ and on the unity and trinity of God." Because Scripture works in concert with reason, Reedy says of Tillotson that "these doctrinal interests counter the charge that he was a rationalist concerned only to build a morality of nature."[83] Scripture remains the core of all spiritual knowledge. Tillotson's sermon, "The Necessity of the Knowledge of the Holy Scriptures" (taken from Matt 23:13 and Luke 11:52), for example, preaches a return to "the knowledge of the *Holy Scriptures*, which is necessary to our eternal Salvation."[84] Scripture is the "*Rule of Faith*," argues Tillotson. It is in the plain sense of Scripture that "numerous Commentators do generally agree." There are obscure passages over which commentators argue, but that is acceptable "so long as all necessary Points of Faith and matters of Practice are delivered in plain Texts."[85] Tillotson's practicality stood for decades as a model for aspiring ministers. It also took the sting off the theological dogmatists, presenting a gentler side of Christianity to the soul offended in a manner reminiscent of Spinoza.

John Locke

No Latitudinarian stands out as much as John Locke, and it is he, after all, who is often credited—albeit unwillingly—with supplying the rational tools for the formidable deist John Toland (1670–1722). Locke was also charged—inaccurately—with maintaining a modified version of Spinoza's philosophy. But among Latitudinarians, Locke's philosophy contains some distinctive enhancements and fine-tuned clarifications, as found in his *Essay Concerning Human Understanding*. The *Essay* was written to engage in the subtle and not-so-subtle distinctions on the topic of morality and revelation.[86] Central to this discussion are the roles and limitations of faith and reason, and Chillingworth's *Religion of Protestants*, in the context of the growing prominence of infallibilism,

---

83. Reedy, "Interpreting Tillotson," 84; for a look at the background to Tillotson's sermon style, see Mitchell, *English Pulpit Oratory from Andrewes to Tillotson*.

84. Wilkins, *Works*, 343.

85. Tillotson, *Rule of Faith,* 94, 86, 106.

86. Snyder, "Faith and Reason in Locke's *Essay*," 197; for a good look at other influences on Locke's understanding of the relation of knowledge to science, see Osler, "John Locke and the Changing Ideal of Scientific Knowledge," 3–16; see also Rogers, "Boyle, Locke, and Reason," 205–16.

was an important background text for developing his argument.[87] In doing so, Locke set out to "lay down the Measures and *Boundaries between Faith and Reason*."[88]

> Reason therefore here, as contradistinguished to *Faith*, I take to be the discovery of the Certainty and Probability of such Propositions or Truths, which the Mind arrives at by Deductions made from such *Ideas*, which it has got by the use of its natural Faculties, *viz.* by Sensation or Reflection.
>
> *Faith,* on the other side, is the Assent to any Proposition, not thus made out by the Deductions of Reason; but upon the Credit of the Proposer, as coming from GOD, in some extraordinary way of Communication. This way of discovering Truths to Men we call *Revelation*.[89]

Reason is a natural faculty using "Sensation or Reflection" to unite different, but connected ideas into what is recognized as knowledge.[90] Faith cannot be certain and does not rise to the level of knowledge. "For matter of Faith being only Divine Revelation and nothing else," writes Locke, "*Faith*, as we use the Word, (called commonly, *Divine Faith*) has to do with no Propositions, but those which are supposed to be divinely revealed."[91] Reason tests the world empirically, but faith trusts in the testimony, which may or may not be true. The witnesses of the resurrection had knowledge because, as the Apostle Thomas demonstrated, they could see and feel the wounds. But subsequent generations, not present at the resurrection, must trust (without definite knowledge) in the testimony of others.

While sharing a high regard for the faculty of reason as did other Latitudinarians, Locke's great divide between reason and faith does not leave any room for the concept of "moral certainty." Moral Certainty for other Latitudinarians is knowledge of religion to degrees of certainty, but for Locke it is of the utmost importance to keep reason and faith in their respective roles. This places Locke between the worlds of Spinoza and the Puritan Calvinists.[92] While Locke sees natural law as fully assessable to the human mind, he sees Scripture as something more than

---

87. Brown, "Edwards, Locke, and the Bible," 362.
88. *Essay*, 4.18.1.
89. Ibid., 4.18.2.
90. Snyder, "Locke's *Essay*," 203.
91. *Essay*, 4.18.6.
92. Marshall, *John Locke*, 29.

Spinoza since its value is based upon the value of the proposer himself, making it more than just a book and, therefore, not included in the natural sciences.

What does this do for the assurance of the authority and interpretation of the biblical text? Locke proposes a form of assurance when it comes to faith, despite his assertions that faith cannot be certain. Matters of faith are "above Reason," according to Locke, but not contrary to it. "*Faith* gave the Determination, where *Reason* came short," he argues. Faith is not the enemy of Reason, but it is given a different "Dominion," which does not offer any "violence, or hindrance to *Reason*," in that reason "is not injured, or disturbed but assisted and improved, by new Discoveries of Truth, coming from the Eternal Fountain of all Knowledge."[93] In his approach to Scripture, then, Locke proposes a system that seems insistent upon letting the inevitable contradiction remain. One cannot know for sure that the Scriptures are truly God's word, yet the Old and New Testaments are "infallibly true," even if their interpreters are certainly not.[94] Scripture is infallible, but one can know what the infallible Scripture is teaching only via less-than-certain faith. Therefore, the humble man will tolerate others in society, understanding that all fall short of the certainty of reason. Of course, as Snyder points out, one cannot argue with certainty that the Scriptures are infallibly true either.[95] John C. Biddle writes in "Locke's Critique of Innate Principles and Toland's Deism":

> Locke's confidence in the truth of the biblical revelation rested not only on the high probability of its divine origin, which he thought reason could provide from external evidence. His assurance also rested upon reason's ability to confirm certain aspects of the content of Scripture, for he maintained that reason could and must judge the content or parts of a revelation as well as the whole.[96]

Biddle argues that John Toland's Deism "did borrow, but subtly changed, the epistemology and views on the relation of reason and revelation that Locke had set forth in the *Essay*."[97]

93. *Essay*, 4.18.9, 10.
94. Ibid., 3.9.23.
95. Snyder, "Locke's *Essay*," 209, 212.
96. Biddle, "Locke's Critique," 416.
97. Ibid., 418.

Despite the ability of the Deists to accommodate Locke's ideas into their system, and despite the rhetoric blaming Locke for supplying the tools necessary for the rejection of Scripture, Locke himself approaches biblical interpretation with complete confidence in the text. However, true to form, he does not approach the text with complete confidence in himself as its interpreter.[98] This comes out clearly in *A Paraphrase and Notes on the Epistles of St. Paul*, where Locke declares, "I am far from pretending Infallibility."[99] Many commentators, he says, approach the interpretation of Scripture by imposing their opinions on the text and pretending that Paul has spoken through them. Yet, despite their confidence in their ability to interpret Scripture, there is far more obscurity than they are willing to admit. As long as the commentator cannot exist in the day of Paul, there is little actual knowledge to work with. What a commentator can do, Locke says, is take current knowledge and apply it

---

98. Toland does use a rhetoric similar to Locke's. "For as 'tis by *Reason*," writes Toland in *Christianity Not Mysterious*, "we arrive at the Certainty of God's own Existence, so we cannot otherwise discern his *Revelations* but by their Conformity with our natural Notices of him, which is in so many words, to agree with our common Notions" (Toland, *Christianity Not Mysterious*, 31). While Locke was finishing up his *The Reasonableness of Christianity* (1695), he received in advance a manuscript, possibly of *Christianity Not Mysterious*, from a friend of Toland. Upon reading Toland's ideas, Locke directed *Reasonableness* toward the end of converting Deists to Christianity. Locke was insistent that he was not responsible for Deism, meaning that he did not recognize himself in that system (see Locke, *A Letter to the Right Reverend Edward Lord Bishop of Worcester* [1697]). For more on the relationship of Locke to Toland and the difficulties with naming Toland's sources see Weinsheimer, *Eighteenth-Century Hermeneutics*. Toland's concept of reason relies more on Spinoza or other early Deists such as Herbert of Cherbury (*De Veritate*, 1695) or Charles Blount (Blount, *Miscellaneious Work*, 1695); see Colie, "Spinoza and the Early English Deists," 30–31; Cragie, "Influence of Spinoza in the Higher Criticism of the Old Testament," 23–32; Champion, *Pillars of the Priestcraft Shaken*; and Sandys-Wunsch, "Spinoza—The First Biblical Theologian," 327–41 for more on this discussion.

99. Locke, *A Paraphrase*, xix. "The Matters that St. Paul writ about, were certainly Things well known to those he writ to, and which they had some peculiar Concern in; which made them easily apprehend his Meaning, and see the Tendency and Force of his Discourse. But we having now at this Distance no Information of the Occasion of his Writing, little or no Knowledge of the Temper and Circumstances those he writ to were in, but what is to be gathered out of the Epistles themselves, it is not strange that many Things in them lie concealed to us, which, no doubt they who were concerned in the Letter, understood at first sight" (ibid., iii–iv).

to the text, leaving the obscure as it is.¹⁰⁰ He prefers the paraphrase for this reason, as it limits human commentary to a minimum.¹⁰¹

The Edwardsian Theological Genome

As these last two chapters show, confidence in both the biblical text and the interpreter historically progresses from bold to skeptical. The *Quadriga* felt the first blow in the Reformation and then a major upset in post-Reformation and Enlightenment periods. Spinoza dismisses any special providence in the Bible and any need for the Spirit and therefore a spiritual sense of the interpreter in understanding the Bible. Generations following him continue this agenda, even building on it, or trying to find a middle ground.

The thinkers examined in this chapter found their way into Edwards's record of reading and reading interest, including those of the Puritan, Cambridge Platonist, and Latitudinarian traditions.¹⁰² All serve as possible contributors to his intellectual evolution. For example, John Smith's *Discourses* (1660) helped Edwards develop his understanding of the emanation of the divine nature into the world, as well as his understanding of sensation and beauty. In *The Religious Affections*, Edwards refers to Smith's "The Shortness of a Pharisaic Righteousness" as "remarkable."¹⁰³ Cambridge Platonism helps Edwards map out the relationship between heaven and earth. And Ralph Cudworth's *The True Intellectual System of the Universe* (1678), from which Edwards heavily cribs his Miscellanies, is one of his go-to resources in his later years of combat with Enlightenment naturalism.¹⁰⁴ Cudworth's vast knowledge of ancient philosophers and Christian theologians opens a door to the past for Edwards. Of the Latitudinarians widely read in New England, John Tillotson's sermons are notably listed in Edwards's Catalogue;

---

100. Locke, *A Paraphrase,* ix. Paul's epistles cannot have "two contrary meanings," says Locke; yet one could read two commentators, both respected in their fields, who offer differing interpretations of the text (ibid., x).

101. Ibid., x, xi.

102. To date, the most thorough resource on the relation of Edwards to the Cambridge Platonists remains Watts, "Jonathan Edwards and the Cambridge Platonists."

103. Lee, *Philosophical Theology of Jonathan Edwards*, 162; *WJE* 65–6; 217–19; Fiering, *Jonathan Edwards's Moral Thought*, 124.

104. *WJE* 23:15–16 ("Misc" 1343, 1358, 1359); Sweeney notes that Edwards copied over twenty-five thousand words from Cudworth (*WJE* 23:16); Lee, *Philosophical Theology of Jonathan Edwards*, 103–4.

though he often disagrees with the archbishop, Edwards finds him to be "one of the greatest divines," and appeals to him as an authority in his sermons on justification in discussing the believer's union with Christ.[105] As Amy Plantinga Pauw notes, Edwards often appeals to the so-called liberal Anglican divines because he shares "their desire to defend both the reasonableness of Christianity and the need for divine revelation" and is "willing, as always, to borrow good arguments."[106]

Lastly, as many have recognized, Locke's *Essay* is a significant philosophical resource for Edwards. And beyond the *Essay*, Edwards also owned and used copies of Locke's commentaries.[107] But to argue, as Bebbington seems to do, that the lion's share of Edwards's idea of the "spiritual sense" is derived from his extension of Lockean empiricism is difficult to sustain. Locke is an important contributor to Edwards's theological world, but he hardly single-handedly lays the foundation for his thought. The evolution of the spiritual sense (or senses) finds important roots in antiquity, that is, in the Christian interpreters before Edwards, including those examined in the last two chapters.

It may be said, then, that in 1703, Edwards was born into the Puritan world of his father and grandfather and identified himself with his Reformed heritage. But as Part Two of this book will develop, he is far more complex than the "typical" Reformed pastor in New England. The web of knowledge available to him and his unmitigated curiosity provide the necessary elements for the flexing of his theological and philosophical muscles. As a result, his reading of Scripture is lively, benefiting from the discussions that precede him and reflecting the spirituality of an ancient past.

---

105. *WJE* 26157, 263 (entries 206, 568); *WJE* 19:155. For more on Edwards and Tillotson, see Fiering's discussion on Edwards's doctrine of hell in *Jonathan Edwards's Moral Thought*, 227–32. Edwards selectively refers to Tillotson, but he clearly keeps Tillotson as a resource in his studies. For other examples see *WJE* 15:421; *WJE* 18:346–8 ("Misc." 716); *WJE* 20:273 ("Misc." 972); Edwards, "Eternity of Hell Torments," 275.

106. *WJE* 20:13.

107. *WJE* 26:193 (entry 353); for example, *WJE* 20:116, 343, 421, "Misc." 874, 1011, 1060; *WJE* 23:149, "Misc." 1217.

PART TWO

Jonathan Edwards's Spirituality in His New England World

3

The Seeds of Spirituality in the Young Edwards, 1703–1723

> For when a man has the liveliest sense of the spiritual world, he sees best what is congruous to the spiritual world.
>
> —Jonathan Edwards, "Miscellanies," 138 (1724)[1]

> Then they shall see him as he is. Their light, which now is but a glimmering, will be brought to clear sunshine; that which is here but the dawning, will become perfect day.
>
> —Jonathan Edwards, "The Pure in Heart Blessed" (1730)[2]

DURING THE SPRING TERM of 1722, whispers circulated among Yale students, surmising that Timothy Cutler, then rector of the institution, was a closet Arminian. At the commencement that September, the trustees, awaiting confirmation or denial of this rumor, were stunned to hear their esteemed rector end the ceremony by quoting directly from *The Book of Common Prayer*: "and let all the people say, Amen." With these words, Cutler boldly identified himself with Anglican Latitudinarianism and, therefore, in the eyes of many of the students and trustees, with Arminianism.

Over a quarter of a century earlier, as the Latitudinarians infiltrated the power base of the Church of England (rising as high as the Archbishop of Canterbury), accusations of Arminianism were in no

---

1. *WJE* 13:296 ("Misc." 138).
2. *WJE* 17:65.

short supply. The moralism of the Latitudinarians offered what appeared to Calvinists as a works-based justification. So when a leader as prominent as Timothy Cutler took such a position in 1722, the fear of a rising Arminian threat in the colonies appeared to be justified, and the future of Yale College was called into question.

New England Puritan Culture

In this unsettled climate, the young Jonathan Edwards, a student at the college starting in 1716, began an intense quest to understand his own conversion. His beliefs on conversion are, as scholars recognize, "crucial" for getting at the core of his theology.[3] A confluence of persons, events, and ideas provided a significant challenge for Edwards. The pressure to find salvation was a central component of both family life and intellectual society in New England, and Cutler's controversial disclosure moved the Yale trustees to search out his student supporters: who else was a secret Arminian? Edwards was among those under scrutiny. But more personally troubling for the budding theologian was that his conversion experience—when it finally happened, as he understood it—did not have the hallmarks his father and grandfather had taught him to expect. This irregularity led him to question his salvation, setting up a double crisis: how could he assure the trustees and his father that he was of the orthodox Reformed persuasion, contra Cutler, when he could not even convince himself that he was a true Christian?

With an unquenchable desire to comprehend the true nature of conversion and determine whether he had experienced it, Edwards embarked on a study of the Bible that filled notebooks, sermon texts, and eventually his *Quaestio* (masters thesis). Informed by the texts of the day—Puritan and Latitudinarian, scientific and philosophical—his campaign for answers became a rigorous self-exploration. He found answers in a revised concept of conversion based squarely on the idea of union with Christ in justification.

Edwards came to believe that the Christian lives in a new and all-important capacity and status that is made possible by the work of justification in conversion. But, as will be developed elsewhere, his understanding of justification is finely integrated with his view of the

---

3. Zakai, *Jonathan Edwards' Philosophy of History* 81; Zakai, "Conversion of Jonathan Edwards," 127–38.

Christian's union with Christ. While some Reformed Christians were interested in avoiding any hint of so-called earned salvation—placing justification purely within the legal and forensic—Edwards, due to his concept of union with Christ and divine participation, understands justification to be a transaction with teeth. He hones in on some specific points of his Calvinist tradition and amplifies them, giving them meaning reminiscent of the ancient Christian concepts of deification. In short, he came to believe that as Christians are united to their head, Christ, then as one body with him, whatever he possesses, they posses, including the universe and even the very Trinity. For a young theologian in distress, this was a life-changing realization.

Ichabod

From its inception in Saybrook in November of 1701, the Collegiate School (as Yale was called before moving to New Haven) found itself racked with difficulties, including a poor location, insufficient facilities, and inadequate resources—not entirely unlike many schools today. The first rector, Abraham Pierson, refused to leave his church in Killingworth, keeping his home there and his duties divided, arguably stunting the growth of the fledgling school. After Pierson's death in 1707, the trustees called Samuel Andrew, a minister in Milford, as the next rector. Like Pierson, Andrew's duties were divided between church and college, with the senior students studying with him at Milford.[4] While the school continued to suffer from lack of organization, the trustees pushed on.

In 1708, two-thirds of the Yale trustees participated in the Saybrook Synod. From this meeting, the Savoy Confession of 1658 found new acceptance in the form of the Calvinistic Saybrook Confession, the theology of which was to be the backbone of the young college. It was generally well received, with a few exceptions; Timothy Edwards's congregation and several others did not sign on to the statement. But Cutler's commencement surprise some years later would prove how little sway, in fact, the Saybrook Confession held over the school.[5]

Achieving stability at the College required more than a doctrinal confession. Founding members pledged to donate books, but a substantial library was slow in coming. Disgruntled undergraduates

---

4. Kelley, *Yale*, 15.
5. Warch, *School of the Prophets*, 55–58; Miller, *New England Mind*, 266–67.

complained about the quality of their youthful tutors, and the financial support was stretched thin. Fortunately, 1713 offered some relief to these affairs when Jeremiah Dummer, Harvard graduate and representative of Massachusetts and Connecticut to England, donated his personal library of over eight hundred volumes to the school.[6] This acquisition gave students a reason to stick with the fledgling college. But the lack of student housing scattered them into homes throughout the region, dividing the student body and making the library inaccessible for many. Whatever advantage they gained from Dummer's library was removed by its inaccessibility.

In 1715, the trustees saw a glimmer of hope when Connecticut received a settlement of one hundred thousand acres from Massachusetts. Vowing to give £500 to the College from the sale of the land, the trustees began looking for the ideal location for a building. But in a vote to build a home for the school and hire a rector in residence, the trustees also permitted senior students to finish their studies elsewhere. Some junior students, Brooks Mather Kelley remarks in his *Yale: A History*, "chose to interpret this as applying to all classes, and they too departed for more pleasant places. Thus it may have appeared to some observers that the Collegiate School was well on the road to complete disintegration."[7]

The trustees soon divided over a proper location. With the prospective income, the towns of Saybrook, Hartford, and New Haven contended for the honor of becoming home to the new school. Two of the trustees, Timothy Woodbridge and Thomas Buckingham, continued to stoke the coals of dissension, as the history is told, intending to move the school to Hartford. But even without their cooperation, a decision finally was reached to move the school to New Haven, where the first commencement was held in 1717.[8] After Elihu Yale, a wealthy merchant and former governor of Fort St. George, India, made a substantial contribution to the college (at the request of Cotton Mather and Jeremiah Dummer), the trustees renamed the school in his honor, and the college's future in New Haven was secured.[9]

---

6. Pratt, "Books Sent from England by Jeremiah Dummer to Yale College," 7. For another look into Edwards's reading, see Johnson, "Jonathan Edwards's Background of Reading," 193–222.

7. Kelley, *Yale*, 18.

8. Warch, *School of the Prophets*, 87.

9. Watson, "Yale, Elihu," *ODNB*. Yale's contribution included "417 books, a portrait

Unfortunately, the library was also secured—in the home of disgruntled trustee Buckingham, who refused to recognize the new name and location of the school and therefore to release the books, leading to a riot and a face-off with the sheriff.[10] Buckingham's resistance, along with the students' dislike for their tutor Samuel Johnson, remained a thorn in the side of Yale College. Jonathan Edwards, in a letter to his sister Mary in March of 1719, records that Johnson's presence was "the cause of our coming away."[11] But that problem was resolved when Johnson was relieved of his post in the same year, making room for a new resident rector, Timothy Cutler.[12] So students regrouped in New Haven; Yale moved forward. For the time being, the trustees breathed more easily. The library contributions of both Dummer and Yale supplied the students with a window into the issues of the day, including the renowned Deist theologians and Latitudinarian Anglicanism. These important resources supplied the new resident rector with controversial ideas and fortified his silent but slowly adjusting theological commitments. These commitments were apparently in embryonic form when he arrived, and he was not yet confident or articulate enough to take a stand on them, as he would do publicly a few years later.

So for a time, Cutler obtained a respectable reputation with all. On March 11 and 13, 1719, at the meeting of the Governor and Council of Connecticut, it was noted that Cutler "was a person of those qualifications that they could not but think him very proper to take charge of the tuition and government of the students in Yale College." Having a man with Cutler's reputation as a resident rector was understood as "a good means to put an end to the contentions" that racked the school.[13] "Mr. [Timothy] Cutler is extraordinary courteous to us," writes Edwards in a letter to his father on July 24, 1719, "has a very good spirit of judgment, keeps the school in excellent order, seems to increase in learning, and is loved and feared by all that are under him . . ."[14] When Cutler found his authority tested by a student mutiny over the poor quality of the

---

of King George by Sir Godfrey Kneller, and a quantity of textiles to be sold to benefit the college . . . The total value of these donations was some £1162 pounds" (ibid.).

10. Warch, *School of the Prophets*, 92.
11. *WJE* 16:31.
12. Kelley, *Yale*, 28.
13. Dexter, *Documentary History of Yale University*, 190, 191.
14. *WJE* 16:33 (Jonathan Edwards to Timothy Edwards, New Haven, July 24, 1719).

Commons' food, he immediately settled the issue. Admiring Cutler's authoritarian leadership, Edwards writes to his father on March 1, 1720:

> Mr. Cutler, as soon as he was apprised of this cabal, sent on the same day for Mr. [Samuel] Andrew and Mr. [Samuel] Russel, who came on the next, and with the rector ordered all to appear before them; where the rector manifested himself exceedingly vexed and displeased at the act, which so affrighted the scholars that they unanimously agreed to come into the commons again.[15]

Despite the high praise many had for him, once Cutler came out of the Anglican closet, some suspected that he had conspired all along to lead the entire school astray.[16] The Anglo-American culture of the day was veering closer to what many believed was Latitudinarian indifference, the root of Deism itself, as they understood it. Rumors spread throughout New England that the school had been spiraling toward Anglicanism for some time. John Davenport and Stephen Buckingham lamented that within three and a half years under Cutler, the school "should groan out [or declare] Ichabod," referring to the dreadful proclamation of the departure of the glory of the Lord in 1 Sam 4:21.[17]

Davenport and Buckingham were convinced that Cutler had been "of this persuasion" for years and that it was for this reason he was so willing to leave the pastorate for the rectorate. Cutler assured all that he had no intention of leading Yale into Anglicanism, and that he had only shared his changing doctrine with one other person. But Davenport and Buckingham were not convinced, and began to look for Cutler's converts; and they were not the only ones with such a suspicion. An anonymous letter surmises that this "secret Episcopalian" was engaged in a private "plot," intended to "destroy" the Reformed educational goals of Yale, the churches with which he had once been friendly.[18] Poetry appeared in the *New England Courant* bemoaning the apostasy of the

---

15. *WJE* 16:37.

16. Even after the affair of the September 1722 commencement, Ezra Stiles found it hard to write unfavorably of Cutler, taking note of his reputation as a scholar. Stiles even noted that Cutler's change of heart may have been less about a conspiracy or "dishonest dissimulation" than it was about a personal "struggle" between his "convictions and his prospects" (Woolsey, *An Historical*, 102–3).

17. Dexter, *Documentary History of Yale University*, 227, 228.

18. Ibid., 228, 230.

rector.[19] Fallout from Cutler's theological switch left Yale suspect in the eyes of all New England.

Soon after the controversial commencement of October 17, at the next meeting of the trustees, measures were taken to assure the school's reputation and theological safety. Among other decisions, the trustees agreed that anyone elected as rector or tutor at Yale would not be accepted without first publicly confirming his agreement with the Saybrook Confession, including a positive statement in opposition to Arminianism. This decision also set the standard for all future graduations. Any "Officer or member" of Yale who was suspected of Arminianism was subject to similar examination.[20] By 1723, no graduation was secure, and each student who was not as yet thoroughly devoted to the Saybrook Confession would have to tiptoe.

Among these students was Edwards, silently facing his own theological crisis. From childhood, he had found himself confronted with all matters of spiritual and theological distress (including Arminianism), which now seemed to have followed him to Yale. Here, amid the controversy, he would find resolution to his crisis in a statement on justification.

A Case of Miserable Seeking

From childhood, Edwards was constantly mindful of his eternal state. Reminders of mortality, the responsibility of the national covenant, and proof of preparation were an intimate part of his life. "I had a variety of concerns and exercises about my soul from my childhood," he writes in his *Personal Narrative*, "but had two more remarkable seasons of awakening, before I met with that change, by which I was brought to those new dispositions, and that new sense of things, that I have since had."[21] Not for any lack of interest in conversion, Edwards repeatedly found it just out of reach, and he visited and revisited the question in his formative years, hoping to discover why it seemed so elusive.

---

19. Daggy, "Education, Church, and State," 43, 48; Warch, *School of the Prophets*, 113.

20. Dexter, *Documentary History of Yale University*, 233, 235, 236.

21. *WJE* 16:790.

Mortality Fears

Young Edwards was not unique in his distressed search for salvation; his parents' generation, as George Marsden points out in *Jonathan Edwards: A Life*, still remembered King Philip's War of 1675–1676, and Indian and French threats were still feared. Death and its accompanying awareness of mortality often call a person toward self-examination, and Edwards was no exception. He heard constant reminders of eternal things from his father Timothy Edwards, who served as a chaplain during Queen Anne's War. "Remember my love to each of the children, to Esther, Elizabeth, Anne, Mary, Jonathan, Eunice and Abigail," writes Timothy to his wife Esther from Albany, August 17, 1711:

> The Lord have mercy on and eternally save them all, with our dear little Jerusha! The Lord bind up their souls with thine and mine in the bundle of life. Tell the children, that I would have them, if they desire to see their father again, to pray daily for me in secret; and above all things to seek the grace and favor of God in Christ, and that while they are young.[22]

With high mortality rates, as Marsden writes, "parents nightly reminded their children that sleep was a type of death." As illustrated in the *New England Primer*, even teaching children the alphabet was an opportunity to remind them (on the page for *T*) that "*Time* cuts down all both great and small" and (on the page for *X*) that "*Xerxes* the great did die, and so must you & I." The letter *T* in the *Primer* is accompanied with an illustration of the grim reaper, the *X* with Xerxes in a coffin. For the letter *Y*, the rhyme "*Youth* forward slips, death soonest nips," is accompanied again by a skeletal reaper stabbing a child in the head with an arrow.[23] Even the youngest New Englanders were under no delusions of immortality.

The National Covenant

Adding to the personal pressures of mortal awareness were the high expectations of the national covenant. While not as formal as the Scottish National Covenant of 1638, the ideal of having a covenant relationship between the church and God remained a prominent hope of many

---

22. Marsden, *Jonathan Edwards*, 12; Timothy Edwards to Esther Stoddard-Edwards, 17 August 1711 (The Claghorn Collection, unpublished letters).

23. Ford, *New England Primer,* 67. For another detailed discussion of the *Primer* see Marsden, *Jonathan Edwards*, 27.

New England ministers. A covenant-keeping God blesses his covenant-keeping people, as they understood it, but when a community turns toward sin, God does not hesitate to bring judgment, with the intention of also bringing repentance. Perry Miller once argued that Edwards "put aside all this sort of thinking," becoming "a new point of departure in the history of the American mind."[24] But this assertion has been corrected, as Stout writes: "Throughout his career as pastor and teacher he adhered exactly to the logic and tenets of the national covenant," as did his predecessors, including both his father and his grandfather, Solomon Stoddard, the "Pope of the Connecticut Valley."[25]

The concept of a national covenant came from first-generation Puritans, who emphasized the converted soul and required some kind of proof of conversion for obtaining full membership in the church. Puritan covenant theology added to this full membership an additional benefit: these Christians could baptize their children, making the children members of the covenant also. The nation in covenant would therefore consist of numerous churches whose members were personally committed to, and in covenant with, the God they worshipped. This affirmation of the covenant between God and the people meant that they could hope for his blessings on the nation as a whole, so as long as the people did not forsake the church. This seemed to work for the first generation, but a problem arose for the national covenant with the second generation; the children baptized into the covenant became adults and were either uninterested in the church or did not testify to explicit conversion experiences. The position of the second generation was perhaps understandable; they had been raised in the church, after all, and not converted into it like their parents. Puritan ministers needed to know what to do when this second generation brought their own children to be baptized. Was a category of membership available for this group? Could "unregenerate" adults (as they were understood, lacking a conversion experience) baptize their children?

During the 1650s the highly influential Richard Mather proposed a solution dubbed the *half-way covenant*. In this proposal, these "unregenerate" adults were allowed to bring their children for baptism, but unless these parents experienced a genuine conversion, full membership was not open to them. This allowed for persons to be in the church and un-

---

24. Miller, *Jonathan Edwards*, 76.
25. Stout, "Puritans and Edwards," 143.

der its authority, partaking of some of the blessings, while also limiting their influence in its policy until full members. This solution was implemented for a few years by many congregations. But Richard Mather's more conservative son, Increase, opposed his father's solution, and at the beginning of the eighteenth century, he and Solomon Stoddard entered into a decade-long controversy on the subject. With declining membership in Massachusetts churches, maintaining an organized church as a strong influence in New England depended upon the looser standards of the half-way covenant. Though participants in this informal half-way covenant were barred from taking the Lord's Supper or having a voting membership, Stoddard understood it as having the benefits of bringing one under church discipline, of retaining the church's strong influence in society as a whole, and of maintaining a national covenant with the divine being.[26]

Many New England ministers seemed to have a sincere theological conviction that the nation—being a Christian nation—was in covenant with God and therefore duty-bound to that covenant. God creates persons to exist in societies and societies to become nations or kingdoms that worship him, argues Solomon Stoddard in his *The Doctrine of the Instituted Churches* (1700). A nation could be "Christian," he believes, and a nation that had a good relationship with God as a whole would worship him. Congregational churches are like synagogues, says Stoddard; they are "Members of the National Church" and "Subordinate" to it. There is a "Publick Covenant that is between God and a professing People," he writes, ". . . wherein he engages publick Prosperity unto them, upon the condition of their obedience." This covenant was first made with Israel, and represents the manner in which God intends all countries of this world to subsist "unto the end of the World."[27]

In light of this underlying theology, Stoddard insisted that a better congregational church government would look more like a Presbyterian parish system. "In this work," writes Thomas A. Schafer, "Stoddard blithely discarded a fundamental doctrine of the congregational way, that the particular church covenant is the form of the church." Rather,

---

26. Stout, *New England Soul*, 58; Walker, *Creeds and Platforms of Congregationalism*, 278ff. For more background on this, see Mather, *Defense of the Answer and Arguments of the Synod*; Mather, *First Principles of New-England*; Davenport, *Another Essay for the Investigation of the Truth*; Pope, *Half-Way Covenant*; Holifield, *Covenant Sealed*.

27. Stoddard, *Doctrine of the Instituted Churches*, 25, 26.

Stoddard proposes "that to ensure the keeping of that covenant the 'national church' be governed by synods of elders after the manner of Scotland."[28] "Members of a Congregation," he continues, "are bound to carry on the Worship together, this is God's appointment, that his People that live together should carry on his Worship together."[29]

All citizens of a town were to be under the rule of the local church and therefore the ministry of preaching. "If a Christian live in a Town, where there is a Church," he writes, "he is immediately bound to joyn with that Church; and that Church is bound to him to govern him, and give him Christian Priviledges . . ." Expanding the boundaries of the half-way covenant, Stoddard argues that this allows all not only to be baptized, but also to enjoy full covenant privileges, including the Lord's Supper. But this argument opened him up to criticism from Edward Taylor of Westfield and Increase Mather, who feared that anyone drinking the Lord's cup "unworthily" would be drinking damnation upon themselves. Stoddard, on the other hand, sees the cup differently, as a "converting ordinance" or an evangelistic message with the power to move individuals to embrace the covenant for the greater good (local and national).[30]

While Timothy Edwards, Jonathan's father, appears to embrace the concepts of the half-way covenant and a national covenant, he rejects his father-in-law Stoddard's push for a national church. Concerned with preserving the purity of the church, he insists upon true evidence of conversion before one be allowed to partake of the sacraments. Each individual must make a personal covenant with God, Timothy Edwards argues, but those individuals, as part of a church, are also in covenant with each other.[31] Therefore, his sermons repeatedly remind his congregation of the need for true conversion and obedience. In a fast day sermon in 1695, for example, he recounts the many ways a "great & holy God" will "mercifully" bring his disobedient children that "great and reasonable duty of obedience unto his holy Just and good commands . . ." But by what means does God bring his people to repentance? From

---

28. Schafer, "Solomon Stoddard and the Theology of Revival," 332; see also Stein, *Jonathan Edwards's Writings*.

29. Stoddard, *Doctrine of the Instituted Church*, 8.

30. Ibid.; Mather, *Order of the Gospel Professed and Practised*.

31. Minkema, "Edwardses," 31, 38.

the time of Israel, he says, God always moved from kindness to severity in the discipline of his people:

> Sometimes ye L^d follows em with—expressions of his goodness & bounty Loving Kindness & tender mercy causes his paths to drop fatness before em. Draws with ye cords of Love & with ye bands of man. Yea take em by ye arms and gently Leads em along as a Father doth his child as in ye 11th of Hosea. & in ye 4: I verses. &. if this course fails he takes another, if mercy and ye cords of Love will not do, he try^s afflictions & ye Rods of anger.[32]

"Judgments afflictions and calamitys" were sent by God as a sign that "he is angry with e'm," argues Timothy, so that his people may forsake their sinfulness. These judgments could include "Famine. Wars. & Pestilence or some grievous wasting sickness," as well as, according to his fast day sermon of 1709, victories by the French and Indians. And years later, in 1741, at the death of the son of parishioner Enoch Morris, Jonathan Edwards too considers the possibility that God is angry.[33]

As fearful as this worldview may seem, Stout notes, calamities were considered divine "calls to reformation"; one could take comfort in the idea that God cared enough to discipline his children.[34] This same covenantal view will be echoed with clarity later on in Jonathan Edwards's fast day sermon in April of 1738:

> They are a people that have been the visible worshippers of this God; a people that have in profession accepted of the covenant offers that God has made; that have laid hold on his covenant, and have on their part obliged themselves in covenant to him to be his people, to worship him, and be in subjection to him, and cleave to him as their God.[35]

His father's sermons exhorting congregants to obey their God and keep their covenant supplied the context for the "remarkable seasons of awakening" that Jonathan experienced as a child. In May of 1716, he enthusiastically writes to his sister Mary about the movement of revival in their father's congregation, saying that there was a "very remarkable stirring and pouring out of the Spirit of God" but that he had "reason to

32. Timothy Edwards, sermon on Isa 9, quoted in Stoughton, *"Windsor Farmes,"* 122.
33. Stoughton, *"Windsor Farmes,"* 124, 132, 135.
34. Stout, "Puritans and Edwards," 145.
35. *WJE* 19:751.

think it is in some measure diminished."³⁶ Despite having all of this divine blessing so close to home, it still felt as if it was out of his reach. He recalls being "affected for many months, and concerned about the things of religion," and his "soul's salvation." He prayed five times a day and discussed theology and prayed with the neighborhood boys. But despite all his religious fervor as a youth, he later concluded that this part of his spiritual journey was driven by "self-righteous pleasure." He writes in his *Narrative* that "many are deceived with such affections, and such a kind of delight, as I then had in religion, and mistake it for grace." He then recalls returning to his sin "like a dog to his vomit." Each such occasion would be followed by yet another conviction via his father's sermons or some reminder of mortality, and the cycle would repeat.³⁷

Preparationism

This cycle of conviction and returning to sin was not entirely unexpected for those raised within the world of the Puritans. Timothy Edwards stood in the long line of Puritan ministers who taught preparationism: that is, that conversion is a process that one hopes will lead to the grace of justification. Timothy's "gradualism" of conversion, writes Kenneth P. Minkema, "was instrumental in shaping his son's views."³⁸ A threefold process, conversion (in this view) begins with "conviction," or an awakening, a sense of one's eternal condition. This is followed by "humiliation," or "a realization of God's anger against sin," which hopefully ends in the third state of "repentance"; but Marsden reminds his readers that for the Puritans, "An 'awakening' was no guarantee of salvation."³⁹

Preparationism is also a central feature of Stoddard's twofold conversionism, consisting of "awakening" and "humiliation." "The very cornerstone of Stoddard's doctrine of conversion," writes Thomas A. Schafer, "is the idea that the sinner can and must do something to prepare himself for conversion."⁴⁰ The tone of Schafer's description may imply that Stoddard sees the work of preparation as in the hands of the sinner. But though the sinner's heart and mind are involved in each step,

36. *WJE* 16:29.
37. *WJE* 16:790, 791.
38. Minkema, "Edwardses," 82.
39. Marsden, *Jonathan Edwards*, 26.
40. Schafer, "Solomon Stoddard and the Theology of Revival," 335; see also Miller, "Solomon Stoddard," 277–320; Coffman, *Solomon Stoddard*.

Stoddard sees the sinner as a passive recipient, acting as acted upon. In his own words:

> There are *two degrees* of this preparation. The *first* is a *work of awakening*, whereby the sinner is convinced of a present necessity of peace and reconciliation with God; whereby he is put upon a diligent use of all means in order to his salvation. The *other* is *Humiliation*, whereby the sinner is brought out of himself, and off from all his *carnal confidences*, to yield himself a Prisoner to God. Until the soul be thus humbled he is not capable of Faith; Men will not come to Christ, till they are convinced of an *absolute necessity* of Christ.[41]

To be saving, awakening and humility must be followed by faith in Christ. Some have faith, says Stoddard, but their faith is not saving; justifying grace is only infused into the heart of one who completely relies on Christ's work as mediator.

So though the Calvinist society of Edwards's youth preached that true conversion was a gift from God, outside of the sinner's unaided capacity to act, this society also emphasized mortality and the drastic social consequences of not keeping the national covenant. Thus from all sides of young Edwards's environment, he experienced acute pressure to find assurance of salvation, an assurance that long eluded him.

A Conversion Crisis

Given this environment, it is no wonder that Edwards was so concerned with the nature of true conversion. Marsden writes that he "was undergoing the most intense spiritual journey of his life."[42] And while he sought to define his conversion in a manner congruent with that described by his father and grandfather, Edwards's experience in the spring of 1721 did not conform to his expectations. His search for conversion was, at first, an act of "miserable seeking."[43] But the occasion he came to see as his genuine conversion was entirely different, leaving him without "terror," a word that David Laurence points out is equal to the second step of Stoddard's preparationism: humiliation. "We learn by experience," writes Stoddard, "that men's hearts are generally set for carnal things

---

41. Stoddard, *Safety of Appearing at the Day of Judgement*, 205; Stoddard, *Guide to Christ*, xv; see also Stoddard, *Treatise Concerning the Nature of Saving Conversion*.
42. Marsden, *Jonathan Edwards*, 39.
43. WJE 16:791.

before they are terrified, and for their own righteousness before they see their own hearts. Generally, such men who have not had the terrors of God in them don't much mind eternal things." But, as Laurence writes, "This was precisely the lesson that Edwards' experience had not taught him and he seems to have heard this strong voice of Stoddard's before all others in his anxiety about the steps of conversion."[44] His childhood pressures, high mortality rates, a strong doctrine of preparationism, and the national covenant all kept Edwards diligently seeking eternal life. The unexpected nature of his conversion, when it occurred, would render a new understanding of God and grace beyond his previous experience.

Conversion was more than surprising for Edwards; it was inspiring. Prior to his conversion, Edwards was "full of objections against the doctrine of God's sovereignty." To believe that God chose and rejected whom he willed was a "terrible doctrine," he wrote. But after his conversion, he saw this doctrine differently. He did not know "how, or by what means" he changed his mind, but his entire outlook on Scripture had changed. Upon reading 1 Tim 1:17, shortly after his conversion, Edwards saw the being of God in a new, less-than-frightening way. For the first time he read the words "Now unto the King eternal, immortal, invisible, the only wise God, be honor and glory forever and ever" with a "sweet delight in God."[45]

> From about that time I began to have a new kind of apprehensions and ideas of Christ, and the work of redemption, and the glorious way of salvation by him. I had an inward, sweet sense of these things, that at times came into my heart; and my soul was led away in pleasant views and contemplations on them.

He speaks of being raptured by thoughts of the beauty of the divine, as if "being alone in the mountains." Whether his eyes gazed on the "blue sky," the sun, moon, flowers, or trees, he only saw the "divine glory." Even thunderstorms, which previously had terrified him, now led him to "sweet contemplations" of his "great and glorious God."[46] In his conversion he found security and beauty, neither of which he had anticipated, being conditioned to think of conversion in terms of mortal terror. And

44. Stoddard, *Guide to Christ,* xvii; Laurence, "Jonathan Edwards," 269.

45. *WJE* 16:792. When referencing Scripture passages that Edwards is engaging in his work, I will cite the King James Version to remain faithful to his thinking process and historical context.

46. *WJE* 16:793, 94.

this new attitude toward conversion became a mystery of its own, one he was driven to solve by the pressures of his academic program, family, and new pulpit responsibilities. So from late 1722 to the fall of 1723, Edwards pursued a better understanding of redemption, finding his fulcrum point in the integrated work of union and justification.

Academically, the removal of Cutler in the fall of 1722 provided plenty of reason to establish a sounder view of salvation. While Edwards was embracing Calvinism, Cutler was running headlong toward Arminianism. But no one could have known the direction Edwards was taking, and any new graduate was a potential convert of Cutler. In a letter Cutler wrote to Timothy Edwards on June 30, 1719, he congratulated Timothy on his son's "promising ability and advances in learning." "He is now under my care," continues Cutler, "and probably may continue so, and doubtless will so do, if he should remain here, and I be settled in the business I am now in."[47] As Minkema points out, Edwards's undergraduate valedictory address included high praise of Rector Cutler and the tutors under him, but "he, and many in the audience, would come to regret the truth and praise they had lavished on the college's leader." With all eyes on Edwards and the others previously supportive of Cutler, they now had to dispel any ideas of "lingering heterodoxy."[48] That this inquisition created enormous pressure on Edwards is clear from his diary entry of July 29, 1723, where he expresses concern about an upcoming public performance—his Master's *Quaestio*, then only a month and a half away.[49]

His family also questioned his conversion. Wilson H. Kimnach has demonstrated from Edwards's Resolution 46, in the Spring of 1723, and his Diary entries of July 19 and August 12 and 13, that his father and mother differed with Edwards on "the validity of conversion which did not follow in 'those steps,'" that is, the steps laid out by Timothy, Stoddard, and other divines. Edwards (like his parents) could not overlook this discrepancy between the traditional Puritan order of conversion and his own experience. "I do not remember that I experienced regeneration, exactly in those steps, in which divines say it is generally wrought," writes Edwards in his Diary on December 18, 1722. He feared

---

47. Timothy Cutler to Timothy Edwards, 30 June 1719 (The Claghorn Collection, unpublished letters).

48. Minkema, "Jonathan Edwards," 4, 5.

49. *WJE* 16:777.

that he did not "feel the Christian graces sensibly enough" or that his affections were "hypocritical." He thus dedicated himself to understanding the salvation experience. "And my mind was greatly engaged," he reflects years later in his *Personal Narrative*, "to spend my time in reading and meditating on Christ; and the beauty and excellency of his person, and the lovely way of salvation by free grace in him."[50]

It was during this period that Edwards accepted a nine-month position (August 1722 to April 1723) ministering to a small Presbyterian congregation in New York City. While trying to understand the nature of what had transpired in his soul, he was now trying to care for the souls of others. From the number of Miscellanies entries and sermons on conversion, justification, holiness, and other similar subjects written at this time, it appears that Edwards devoted himself to killing two birds with one stone: he was preparing for his upcoming *Quaestio* on the doctrine of justification while also immersing himself in self-discovery: "I found no books so delightful to me," he says in his *Personal Narrative*, "as those that treated of these subjects."

Edwards embarked on a significant campaign to discover the nature of conversion and thus the truth about his own experience. He could not resist the engrained suspicion that he was self-deceived; the voices of his father and grandfather, among others, echoed in the back of his mind. And so the irony of his experience is that while his conversion brought about this surprising joy, the fact that he felt joy, rather than terror, immediately produced a fear that challenged his joy every step of the way. "Decayed. I am sometimes apt to think, I have a great deal more of holiness than I have," he writes in January of 1723. "I find now and then, that abominable corruption which is directly contrary to what I read of eminent Christians . . . How deceitful is my heart!" A few days later, he took notice of the rigor he put himself through for the sake of mortification and sanctification: "This week . . . it is suggested to me, that too constant a mortification, and too vigorous application to religion, may be prejudicial to health. But nevertheless, I will plainly feel it and experience it, before I cease, on this account. It is no matter how much tired and weary I am, if my health is not impaired."[51] The pressure to formulate a better theology fueled much of his earliest exegetical writings and notes. It is in this context that he writes his 28th resolution:

50. *WJE* 16:793.
51. *WJE* 16:761, 763.

"Resolved, to study the Scriptures so steadily, constantly and frequently, as that I may find, and plainly perceive myself to grow in the knowledge of the same."[52] Over the next several months he lived out this commitment, embarking on the study that would result in his masters *Quaestio*.

His search for answers drove him to amass a stockpile of weaponry, including a menagerie of notebooks. In 1992 Wilson Kimnach demonstrated the intricate relationship between Edwards's various notebooks and his sermon development. In the notebooks he labeled "Miscellanies," Edwards traces every significant theological thought that catches his attention, connecting the dots between Scripture, philosophy, and science. No two sequential entries are on the same subject, so he numbers and cross-references them, and even creates indices. These Miscellanies are the maps of his thought experiments.

Another notebook, "Notes on the Apocalypse," is directly aimed at an exposition of the book of Revelation. It is one of Edwards's early ventures into the commentary system he had come to know through his Puritan tradition. His motive for starting this notebook, however, may be bound up in—and tells us something about—his personal crisis.

What could Edwards find in biblical apocalyptical material that might explain his own crisis? For much of his life Edwards used this notebook to develop a full-fledged eschatology. Concern about the end times was not unusual in his era. By the time of the Great Awakening, many saw the Reformation as more than just an historical event; for Edwards, it was also the beginning of the end of what he identified as the antichrist's kingdom, the "fifth vial" judgment of the New Testament book of Revelation. Early in his musings on the future, Edwards identified the Reformation as the second vial of the apocalypse, but after reading Moses Lowman (ca. 1679–1752), Edwards's scheme for the end of the world changed dramatically and the Reformation became the historical fulfillment of the fifth vial of Revelation (16:10–11).[53] The Reformation is, for Edwards, the beginning of a work "to weaken . . . and to diminish" the so-called kingdom of the antichrist, which for him equaled the Church in Rome.[54] He came to see his own day and context as playing

---

52. *WJE* 16:755.

53. *WJE* 5:199; I have also published on Edwards's views of the future. The interested reader may wish to see Withrow, "Future of Hope," 75–98 and Withrow, "Empty Threat," 69–92.

54. *WJE* 5:199, 193.

an important role in this cosmic drama. In later years, and during the Great Awakening in which he plays a role, he connected this conclusion to America. "And 'tis worthy to be noted that America was discovered about the time of the Reformation, or but little before," he writes in 1742:

> ... [the] Reformation was the first thing that God did towards the glorious renovation of the world, after it had sunk into the depths of darkness and ruin under the great antichristian apostasy. So that as soon as this new world is (as it were) created, and stands forth in view, God presently goes about doing some great thing to make way for the introduction of the church's latter-day glory, that is to have its first seat in, and is to take its rise from that new world.[55]

From the time of the Reformation, he argues, God did marvelous things through the Protestant church, protecting it along the way, but the work was not complete.[56] That duty is left to another generation, one that begins in Edwards's time; signs of this new work appear, as he sees it, in the revivals of New England. He sees every sermon preached and every soul converted as contributing to the cause of redemptive history and the struggle against the dogma of Rome.

While American evangelicalism, particularly since the days of the fundamentalist-modernist controversy in the early twentieth century, is primarily premillennial, Edwards is decidedly a postmillennial evangelical. His view of judgment may sound like a fairly pessimistic view of the future, but this cannot be read through the lens of the popular *Left Behind* series. Edwards does not look for the world to get worse, but rather understands it to be improving, leading to a future golden era of light and life, where the world is transformed by the rule of Christ through the church. The world will eventually know peace; but first it may be shaken a bit.

Edwards's fuller vision of the future takes years for him to develop, but his work began in his younger days as he sought answers to what occurred in his conversion. Even in these early years, Edwards writes often in his notebook about the end of the world, perhaps hoping that something new is occurring, something that can make sense of his own experience. His Diary entry of August 12, 1723, shows his mind at work:

---

55. *WJE* 4:353.
56. *WJE*: 5:199, 193.

> The chief thing, that now makes me in any measure to question my good estate, is my not having experienced conversion in those particular steps, wherein the people of New England, and anciently the Dissenters of Old England, used to experience it. Wherefore, now resolved, never to leave searching, till I have satisfyingly found out the very bottom and foundation, the *real reason, why they used to be converted in those steps* [emphasis mine].⁵⁷

One cannot help wondering that if by saying, "they used to be converted in those steps," Edwards is convinced that his unusual conversion experience signaled a new work of God, more specifically, that work he later sees as the sixth vial of Revelation. "I had great longings for the advancement of Christ's kingdom in the world," writes Edwards of his conversion years later in his *Personal Narrative*.

Despite the place these eschatological ideas held for Edwards's understanding of his situation, his apocalyptical notes did not dominate his intellectual pursuits or fill his sermon text. His main source for his sermon notes and masters *Quaestio* at this time was his first "Miscellanies" notebook (entries a–99). In the few notes written before 1723, Edwards speculates on various theological questions, most often on conversion, holiness, and justification (see the end of this chapter), as one might expect, given his search for answers about his own experience.⁵⁸ For example, it is Miscellanies "a," labeled "On Holiness," which is an important description of Edwards's new understanding of conversion. Holiness in the soul, he says, is "a Divine beauty." It is the text of this "Miscellanies" that provides material for his early sermon "The Way of Holiness" on Isa 35:8, and also appears to foreshadow the language he uses to describe his conversion in his *Personal Narrative*.⁵⁹ Through these notes we see the seeds of thought leading to a significant step for resolving his personal crisis.

---

57. *WJE* 16:779.

58. As Thomas Schafer notes in his introduction, many of the "Miscellanies" are the basis for his *Quaestio*. In "Miscellanies" b, s, nn, oo, 2, 27b, 30, 32–33, 35–38, 41, and 45, Edwards works out the details of justification by faith.

59. *WJE* 16:796; *WJE* 13:164 ("Misc." a).

Possessing All Things

Edwards's *Quaestio*, a short piece, largely concerns the role of faith in justification. If he struggled with Arminianism early on, Edwards now places himself firmly within the Reformed tradition in this thesis. His "task," he writes at the beginning:

> is, to defend the truth of the Reformed religion to Protestants and of the Christian religion to Christians. Nor do we consider it to be a slight glory to guard that which is assuredly central, both always for the first Christians and for those more recent who everywhere profess the purity of Reformed Christianity, all of whom agree that the highest glory of the gospel and the delight of the Scriptures is this very doctrine of justification through the righteousness of Christ obtained by faith.[60]

Appealing to the Reformation, Edwards presents the trustees of Yale with an acceptable distillation of doctrine in his Latin text and gives a sincere nod to the Saybrook Confession. What he writes in his *Quaestio*, however, barely represents the total preparation he first worked out in his notebook.

In the *Quaestio*, Edwards describes justification as "an act of divine favor towards the sinner which forgives sins and approves him as righteous." This is twofold righteousness, according to Edwards. It is not enough merely to declare someone not guilty; it is a declaration of someone as righteous as well: "there can be no doubt that justification is a certain act of *positive* favor that not only frees a person from sin but is also understood in fact as the approval of him as righteous through the righteousness of Christ, both active and passive in both obedience and satisfaction."[61] His immediate appeal to the active and passive righteousness of Christ is also the first priority in chapter 11 of the Saybrook Confession, and probably warmed the hearts of the trustees.[62]

Active and passive righteousness are important for connecting the fall of Adam to the work of Christ as the second Adam. If Adam's eternal happiness is based simply on his innocence, Edwards argues, then he never would have been subjected to "probation" in the garden. Eternal life for Adam involved both his "doing ill" and his "doing well."[63] As a

---

60. *WJE* 14:60.
61. *WJE* 14:60.
62. *SC* 13:1.
63. *WJE* 13:173–74 ("Misc." s).

result of Adam's sin, his posterity are "by nature altogether depraved and corrupted . . . children of wrath," says Edwards in his "Miscellanies."[64] Similarly, the Saybrook Confession states that the "first covenant made with man was a covenant of works, wherein life was promised to Adam and in him to his posterity, upon condition of perfect and personal obedience."[65] The first covenant still needs to be satisfied, even after Adam's fall, and requires a second Adam, namely Christ, who can fulfill it by his obedience. Justification requires Christ's active obedience to this covenant. "We are not to be saved merely on the account of being free from guilt . . . by the death of Christ," says Edwards, referring to passive obedience, "but on the account of Christ's activeness in obedience and doing well: he acted Adam's part over again." It is this same traditional parallel between Adam and Christ—a parallel that has captivated Christian theologians for centuries—that finds its way into his sermons, like "True Repentance Required" on Luke 13:5 and "Glorious Grace" on Zech 4:7, and fills his notes over the next decade and a half. He uses this parallel to build a vibrant spirituality with a controlling theology of union and divine participation.[66]

The *Quaestio* is Edwards's explicit statement on conversion, distancing himself from the perceived problems of Cutler's theology: "We assert," Edwards writes, "that a sinner is justified in the sight of God neither totally nor in part because of the goodness of such obedience . . . ."[67] Finite humans and their finite faith are incapable of satisfying that infinite offense.[68] In a "Miscellanies" entry virtually copied into the *Quaestio*, Edwards notes that the "DEMERIT OF SIN" against an infinite God is "of infinite demerit." The high Calvinist clergyman John Edwards, whose *Theologia Reformata* is found in Jonathan Edwards's Catalogue of Reading from this time, spells out sin much the same way: "Finite, and Sinful Men" are, the other Edwards writes, "altogether incapable of satisfying the Infinite Majesty that was Offended and Provoked."[69]

---

64. *WJE* 13:245 ("Misc." 78).

65. *SC* 7.2.

66. *WJE* 13:186 ("Misc." 186); *WJE* 10:512, 391–92; *WJE* 13:217 ("Misc." 30); *WJE* 13:219 ("Misc." 35).

67. *WJE* 14:63, 61.

68. *WJE* 13:187 ("Misc." nn, oo); *WJE* 14:62.

69. *WJE* 13:187 ("Misc." nn.); *WJE* 26:142, 154 (entries 129, 195); Edwards, *Theologia Reformata*, 346.

The finite person's sin against an infinite God creates an "infinite evil" and an "infinitely holy God... hates sin with infinite hatred."[70] Therefore, salvation requires the work of a mediator, namely, the incarnate Christ.

Edwards keeps his tone safe in the *Quaestio* with no significant wavering from the Saybrook Confession; faith earns nothing and the sinner has nothing. Yet behind the scenes in his notes, he is not satisfied making the salvation of the soul simply a matter of a legal statement.[71] Something in his experience convinced him that there must be more than the mere legal; and this is where, for the process of conversion, he begins to look to the idea of union with God in the incarnation. There is a twofold union in the justification process: union with the Spirit, and union with Christ. Union with Christ, made possible by the union (or "bond" as he will also call it) with the Spirit is less about the forensic and more akin to participation in the divine.[72] While Edwards is working out his salvation with fear and trembling—trying to determine whether he is indeed redeemed—he begins to develop a theology that will drive his later, more controversial statements.

The first union (union with the Spirit of God) makes the second (union with Christ) possible. Thus the Holy Spirit plays an imperative role in conversion. He is the bond of the union between the Christian and the God-Human and he prepares the soul for participation in the divine. While an early entry, "INFUSED HABITS," indicates that conversion is instantaneous, leaving the sinner in "a state of damnation" at any moment before, Edwards quickly follows it in "INFUSED GRACE" with speculation that the Spirit infuses a "principle that causes vigorousness and activity in action" prior to conversion.[73] Similarly, in notes on the "Preparatory Work" of the Spirit, Edwards affirms that there is preparation; conversion occurs "in a moment," but "who can believe that the Spirit of God takes a man in his career of sin, without any forethought ... or any preparatory circumstances to introduce it?" But in harmony

---

70. *WJE* 10:426.

71. *SC* 11.1; *WJE* 14:61–62; *WJE* 13:199 ("Misc." 2, see also "Misc." 33, 36).

72. *WJE* 13:164, 165 ("Misc." b).

73. *WJE* 13:169, 171 ("Misc." l, p). There is an intense discussion on infused grace already circulating in the literature, particularly in regards to "Miscellanies" 27b and 77. I cover the relevant material in chapter 5.

with his own experience: "We do not determine how great a difference there may be in this preparatory introduction of Christ in the soul."[74]

In his New York sermon "Life Through Christ Alone," Edwards tells his congregation that the bond of the union with Christ is the union with the Spirit; the two are inseparable: "That Holy Spirit by which Christians are led, and guided to heaven, is the Spirit of Christ; he dwells with them and in them by his Spirit."[75] And because the Spirit unites the soul to Christ, as he writes in his sermon "Christ, the Light of the World" (on John 8:12), graces "spring forth in the soul which are like the sweet flowers that adorn the face of the earth in the spring, and like the sweet melody of singing birds." More precisely, as he says in his sermon "Living to Christ" (on Phil 1:21), Christ dwells "as a principle of life in the soul," and the Spirit "is diffused as new life" throughout the Christian's soul. Edwards's favorite theologian, Peter van Mastricht, also says as much, writing that the "Holy Ghost begets in men . . . the first act or principle of spiritual life . . ."[76]

"Christ himself lives in the soul of a true Christian," says Edwards, "and influences and actuates him by his Holy Spirit." The union of the soul with Christ in justification means the Christian has a real and vital connection to the righteousness of Christ. "The soul is united to Christ, and therefore partakes in his life: he lives in Christ and Christ lives in him, yea, not only lives in him but is his life."[77] This union by faith gives the sinner a new status in Christ. As Edwards makes clear in his "Life Through Christ Alone," Christ, as an infinite person, is loved by the Father with "an infinite love, and therefore whatever he doth is accepted upon his own account" for the sinner who embraces in faith.[78]

---

74. *WJE* 13:173 ("Misc." r). In "True Repentance Required," Edwards says preparation includes contrition and turning from sin. He is careful to write: "I do not say that a true penitent's thoughts always run exactly in this order, but I say that they are of this nature," and "this humiliation, which is the effect of godly contrition, is not always to the same degree; but it is always of the same nature. . . ." For a systematized reading of Edwards's preparationism from the Calvinist perspective, see Gerstner and Gerstner, "Edwardsian Preparation for Salvation," 5–71.

75. *WJE* 10:526.

76. Van Mastricht, *Treatise on Regeneration*, 13.

77. *WJE* 10:570. 71.

78. *WJE* 10:524.

Christians are united to Christ or "ingrafted," finding "vital and spiritual nourishment" communicated to them.[79]

Not only does this real and vital union to the righteousness of Christ stand behind the relatively tame theology of his *Quaestio*, but it also leads Edwards to a conclusion that makes sense of his conversion. When the converted is united to Christ, he says, "he doth really possess all things." And by "all things," Edwards really means all things:

> God three in one, all that he is, and all that he has, and all that he does, all that he has made or done—the whole universe, bodies and spirits, earth and heaven, angels, men and devil, sun moon [and] stars, land and sea, fish and fowls, all the silver and gold, kings and potentates as well as mean men—are as much the Christian's as the money in his pocket, the clothes he wears, or the house he dwells in, or the victuals he eats; yea more properly his, more advantageously, more *his*, than if he [could] command all those things mentioned to be just in all respects as he pleased at any time, by virtue of his union with Christ . . .[80]

Though the Christian possesses all things, he or she does not have to manage the universe, as Christ takes on that responsibility. The Christian, by virtue of this union, can sit back and "enjoy" all of creation "with surprising, amazing joy." God created everything for "intelligent beings," says Edwards; they are the "end of creation, that their end must be to behold and admire the doings of God, and magnify him for them, and to contemplate his glories in them." This makes "religion . . . the end of creation." The Christian, in union with Christ, is united to the righteousness of Christ, and in this new connection, gains a new status as owner (or co-owner) of the universe, whose beauty brings the heart to sing praises to its creator, not fall back in terror, as Edwards had expected to experience during his conversion.[81] The union between Christ and those who love him is closer than that between lovers. The delight he found in his conversion was, therefore, the natural outcome of being united to Christ:

> Christ has a tendency to fill the soul with an inexpressible sweetness. It sweetens every thought and makes every meditation pleasant; it brings a divine calm upon the mind, and spreads a

79. *WJE* 10:525.
80. *WJE* 13:183–84 ("Misc." ff).
81. *WJE* 13:185, 186 ("Misc." gg).

heavenly fragrance like Mary's box of ointment. It bedews the soul with the dew of heaven, begets a bright sunshine, and diffuses the beginnings of glory and happiness in embryo. All the world smiles upon such a soul as loves Christ: the sun, moon and stars, fields and trees, do seem to salute him. Such a mind is like a little heaven upon earth.[82]

These words, mimicking his "Miscellanies," "On Holiness," his sermon "The Way of Holiness," and his *Personal Narrative*, demonstrate that it was his being united to Christ and his benefits that gave his conversion joy. His "inward, sweet sense" found in conversion was, as the last line above describes, "a little heaven upon earth." Like the owner of a new house who simply cannot turn her eyes away from the walls and floors that are now hers, Edwards rejoices over the little piece of heaven he has snatched up in his conversion. He can finally justify his joy.

Seeing God in Everything

Another important discovery that informed Edwards's experience is his use of Christian Platonism as it relates to the science of his day. To possess all that the divine being possesses, via union with Christ, demands a different conversion experience; and for Edwards, this explained a large part of his surprising and amazing joy. But several years after his initial conversion struggle and resolution, Edwards would discover Cotton Mather's 1726 volume *Manuductio ad Ministerium*, which would provide an additional explanation. Mather's advice in this book must have rung true in Edwards's ears, for it typifies his conclusions during the early 1720s. The sciences, according to Mather, carry the mind quickly "into those *Immechanical Principles*, from whence, *The next step is into God!*" Because the sciences connect nature to the divine being itself, the sciences are servants of theology. "The *Gravitation* of Bodies is One of them; For which *No Cause* can be assigned," writes Mather, "but the *Will* of the Glorious GOD, who is the *First Cause* of all." If, in other words, gravitation has no natural cause, then the cause must be God, and if the cause is God, one should see evidence of God in gravitation. "*Child*," urged Mather, "*See* GOD *in every Thing!*"[83] If Edwards understood the relationship between God and nature in this way—and it is clear that

---

82. *WJE* 10:617.
83. Mather, *Manuductio ad Ministerium*, 52.

he did by 1723—then he undoubtedly wondered if he saw God when gazing at the beauty of the natural world.

Edwards was beginning to understand, even before his conversion, that the divine being sustained nature. But at his conversion, Edwards was surprised to find such a close relationship to God through his enjoyment of nature itself. Around January 1721, Edwards began his "Natural Philosophy" notebook, in which he targets materialism. While the materialist insists that the substance of matter is the only thing that exists, Edwards argues in this notebook that matter is the product of the divine will. Following the cue of Cambridge Platonist Henry More, as well as Isaac Newton, Edwards seeks to rebut the materialist claims with a concept of divine being that served as the foundation for all existence. In his "Of Atoms," written between January 1721 and June 1722, Edwards argues that matter is not self-sustaining, independent, and blindly subject to laws, that is, to the motion of other interacting bodies; rather, it requires an infinite, intelligent, and immaterial being to subsist. Matter is the same as "indivisibility and resisting to be annihilated, or the persevering to be of a body," he writes, but ". . . indivisibility is from the immediate exercise of God's power." Therefore, matter or "solidity results from the immediate exercise of God's power, causing there to be indefinite resisting in that place where it is." The unknown substance sustaining all matter is the essence of God's being.[84]

If this is the nature of matter, what might one conclude about space? In his short treatise "On Being," he says it is "utterly impossible" for space to be nothing (an absence), rather it must be something (a presence): "Space is this necessary, eternal, infinite and omnipresent being"; that is, "Space is God." As Henry More wrote in his appendix to his *An Antidote Against Atheism*:

> For if after the removal of corporeal Matter out of the world, there will be still Space and Distance in which this very Matter, while it was there, was also conceived to lye, and this distant Space cannot but be something, and yet not corporeal, because neither impenetrable nor tangible; it must of necessity be a Substance Incorporeal necessarily and eternally existent of itself: which the clearer Idea of a Being absolutely perfect will more fully and punctually inform us to be the Self-subsisting God.[85]

---

84. *WJE* 6:211, 214–15.

85. More, *Collection of Several Philosophical Writings*, 165; see also Cudworth, *True Intellectual System of the Universe*, 769–70.

God's being, infinite and eternal, fills all things and eliminates the possibility of a "nothing."[86] Concurring with Mather and many others, Edwards says even gravity "depends upon the divine influence."[87]

That the divine being is the source of the material is not limited strictly to philosophy. During this period Edwards was also reading Isaac Newton, who personally donated volumes to Yale's Dummer collection.[88] Newton's *Opticks* and *De Principia* became sources for entries in Edwards's "Natural Philosophy" notebook.[89] Current studies in Newton's thought have noted the role theology plays in his concept of absolute time and space. God "is eternal and infinite, omnipotent and omniscient," writes Newton, "that is, his duration reaches from eternity to eternity; his presence from infinity to infinity . . . he is not eternity or infinity, but eternal and infinite; he is not duration or space, but he endures and is present. He endures for ever, and is every where present; and by existing always and every where, he constitutes duration and space."[90] God's constituting duration and space demonstrates the importance that theology plays in the science of Newton.[91] Wallace E. Anderson notes that "the Newtonians whom Edwards read . . . associated the absolute space and time of Newton's theory with the divine Being."[92] There was consensus with Mather that science is the tool of the theologian.

Edwards quickly follows this discussion of nature's dependence upon the divine being with his early thoughts on idealism. It is impor-

---

86. *WJE* 6:202, 203.

87. *WJE* 6:234.

88. Bryant and Patterson, "List of Books Sent by Jeremiah Dummer," 464.

89. For a discussion on Newton and Edwards see *WJE* 6:18, n.5; Tufts, "Edwards and Newton," 609–22. Mather's discussion of gravity is based on his reading of Newton, whom he called "our *Perpetual Dictator, the Incomparable*" (Mather, *Manuductio ad Ministerium*, 50). Newton concluded that he was not able to "discover the cause of those properties of gravity from phenomena" and therefore could "frame no hypothesis" (Newton, *Principia*, 442).

90. Newton, *Principia*, 441.

91. William Lane Craig writes that ". . . Newton here declares explicitly that space is *not* in itself absolute and therefore not a substance. Rather it is an emanent—or emanative—effect of God. By this notion Newton meant to say that time and space were the immediate consequence of God's very being" (Craig, *Time and Eternity*, 46).

92. *WJE* 6:58. In Newton's "On the Gravity and Equilibrium of Fluids," he argues for a corresponding relationship between extension (space) and the divine being, where extension or space exists in the divine being (Kaiser, *Creational Theology and the History of Physical Science*, 241).

tant to say not only that God alone sustains the whole universe, but also to place the existence of the universe squarely in the mind of God. In his essay "Of Being," he reasons that "nothing has any existence anywhere else but in consciousness. No, certainly nowhere else, but either in created or uncreated consciousness."[93] He takes this even further in "Miscellanies pp," writing: "supposing [there is] a room in which none is, none sees the things in the room, no created intelligence: the things in the room have no being any other way than only as God is conscious [of them]; for there is no color there, neither is there any sound, nor any shape, etc."[94] If the solidity of matter is ultimately and finally due to the conscious sustaining mind of the divine being, then when that divine being is no longer conscious of it, it becomes nothingness. The ultimate reality is not here in the concrete material world, for without God's mind, the concrete is nothing. This world is a shadow of the divine, because its cohesive, substantive existence relies on the original conceiving of it by the divine mind.

This is not to say that how human beings perceive the world is meaningless. God created the world for intelligent beings, writes Edwards. Intelligent beings "are the end of the creation," and "their end must be to behold and admire the doings of God, and magnify him for them, and to contemplate his glories in them."[95] The universe exists for these finite minds, but if they do not exist, then the universe only exists by virtue of the divine mind. "Let us suppose for illustration this possibility," writes Edwards in "Of Being," "that all the spirits in the universe to be for a time deprived of consciousness, and God's consciousness at the same time to be intermitted. I say, the universe for that time would cease to be, of itself; and not only . . . because the Almighty could not attend to uphold the world, but because God knew nothing of it."[96]

Thus when the young Edwards saw the shadows of the divine being in nature, he concluded that he was ultimately getting a glimpse into the divine mind itself. Given this striking spirituality, a few historians have perceived strong similarities between Edwards and Eastern theologians such as Gregory Palamas (1296–1359), Archbishop of Thessalonica. The similarities between Edwards and Palamas were addressed in short but

93. *WJE* 6:204; *WJE* 6:76.
94. *WJE* 13:188 ("Misc." pp).
95. *WJE* 13:185 ("Misc." gg).
96. *WJE* 6:204.

significant form by Michael J. McClymond, who writes that "Edwards and Palamas share a common Platonic or Neoplatonic philosophical heritage that they modified in analogous ways under the impact of their understanding of God's grace and the Christian experience of communion with God."[97] While there is little by way of direct exposure between Edwards and Palamas, their shared philosophical tradition, says McClymond, brings the two of them to similar theological conclusions, leaving Edwards speaking in terms of deification and in agreement with Palamas on significant points. In *The Triads*, for example, Gregory Palamas writes, "So, when the saints contemplate this divine light within themselves, seeing it by the divinising communion of the Spirit, through the mysterious visitation of perfecting illuminations—then they behold the garment of their deification, their mind being glorified and filled by the grace of the Word, beautiful beyond measure in His splendour..."[98]

Edwards's language, with its emphasis on union and participation in the divine, is not substantially different. In *Charity and Its Fruits*, Edwards appeals to the great passage on theosis, 2 Pet 1:4, to explain the extraordinary gifts of the Spirit—gifts that, like Palamas, he calls "garments." When the Spirit, as he argues, "bestows saving grace, he imparts himself to the soul in his holy nature . . . and the subject becomes a spiritual being . . ."[99] Writing on 2 Pet 1:4 in his first published sermon, *God Glorified in Man's Dependence*, Edwards says the Christian is given a "spiritual excellency and joy by a kind of participation in God. They are made excellent by a communication of God's excellency: God puts his own beauty, i.e. his beautiful likeness, upon their souls."[100] That beauty in the soul recognizes itself in the surrounding world.

Likewise, if Scripture is the word of this same divine being, one should expect to have a "sweet delight in God" when reading it.[101] The biblical words should, as Edwards understood it, have greater depth for the person whose mind is now lifted beyond the mere natural knowledge of this world and into the mind of God. Much like his ancient and medieval theological ancestors (explored earlier in Part I of this book), this includes understanding the eternal significance and beauty of the

97. McClymond, "Salvation as Divinization,"139–60, 141.
98. Palamas, *The Triads*, 1.3.5.
99. *WJE* 8:158.
100. *WJE* 17:8.
101. *WJE* 16:792.

multiple layers of the text itself, though Edwards prefers to call it—in the language of his Calvinist interlocutors—typology. Calvinist divines, such as Matthew Poole, Matthew Henry, and John Edwards, gave him plenty of reason to look for types within Scripture. For example, in his sermon fragment, "Application on Love to Christ," Edwards (like Poole or Henry) looks to the Song of Solomon and finds images of Christ in its description of the Lily of the Valley and the Rose of Sharon.[102] In his sermon "Christ's Sacrifice" on Heb 9:12 ("Neither by the blood of goats and calves, but by his own blood he entered once into the holy place, having obtained eternal redemption for us"), the Old Testament sacrificial system is compared to, and contrasted with, the work of Christ. "By these types and shadows," Edwards tells his congregation, "they [the Israelites] were led to true faith and a Mediator," that is, Jesus Christ, whom Edwards says is both sacrifice and priest.[103] "The things of the ceremonial law are not the only things whereby God designedly shadowed forth spiritual things," he writes. "Very much of the wisdom of God in the creation appears in his so ordering things natural, that they livelily represent things divine and spiritual, [such as] sun, fountain, vine . . ."[104] It seemed right to Edwards that the creator would leave his divine autograph in both his book of Scripture and his book of nature.

Thus Edwards's conversion experience led him to see Scripture and nature with new eyes. Now assessable by means of conversion, the beauty of the divine mysteries in Scripture and the divine being in nature supply his experience with a sweetness that casts out fear.

Solution: Surprised by Amazing Joy

The origins of, and influences upon, Edwards's Christian Platonism continue to be a source of discussion. Broadly speaking, and as seen in Part I, idealism is part of the spirituality of the Christian tradition. His interest in it at this time, as Anderson argues, seems to be derived largely from his struggle to find conversion.[105] The many volumes he had access to growing up in his father's home or at Yale would have provided the exposure. Cambridge Platonism, for example, gave him an explicit

---

102. *WJE* 10:613. One of the earliest examples of typology is found in the "Miscellanies" note titled "TYPES OF SCRIPTURE" and is very brief ("Misc." m).

103. *WJE* 10:595, 596, 597.

104. *WJE* 13:284 ("Misc." 119).

105. *WJE* 6:78.

philosophical basis for these beliefs. His reading of the Cambridge Platonists would have firmly established the correlation of the physical world to the spiritual (see chapter 6 for more). Divine intelligence, according to the Cambridge Platonists, is the ultimate reality. The "candle of the Lord," namely "reason," can see beyond the material world, into the immaterial. Edwards would eagerly explore this in his notebooks by writing on the spiritual types found in nature.[106] The divine being, as the reason for all existence, must impress itself upon nature, so that natural reflects the spiritual.[107] Others have speculated that there is a connection between Edwards and Bishop George Berkeley's *Alciphron*, or Nicolas Malebranche's *Search After Truth*, or both.[108] There is evidence that Edwards was interested in and later obtained Malebranche's *Search After Truth*, since his "Miscellanies" contains a reference to him; but though Edwards may pull from both Berkeley and Malebranche at a later date, the evidence for his use of these thinkers in his early years is far from concrete.

---

106. Edwards and the Cambridge Platonists would not have been in full agreement on the "candle of the Lord." As Walter Schultz points out, "whereas the Cambridge Platonists understood the 'candle of the lord'—which enlightens the mind—to be natural reason, Edwards's 'divine and supernatural light' is the Spirit-inspired sense of the excellency and reality of the things of God" (Schultz, "Jonathan Edwards's *End of Creation*," 255).

107. His enthusiasm for the spiritual in nature can be found in his *On Sarah Pierpont*. Written when Sarah was around thirteen years old, Edwards could not ignore her fervent religious spirit: "She loves to be alone and to wander in the fields and on the mountains, and seems to have someone invisible always conversing with her" (*WJE* 16:790). For more on Sarah's conversion, see Ellison, "Sociology of 'Holy Indifference,'" 479–95 and *WJE* 4:331–41.

108. Berkeley, *Alciphron, or the Minute Philosopher in Seven Dialogues*; Malebranche, *Search After Truth*. Regarding the question of how early Edwards would have been exposed to Malebranche, in his reading of John Edwards's *Theologia Reformata*, Edwards would have come across a very brief and marginal mention of Malebranche on the human soul (Edwards, *Theologia Reformata* 1:14). For discussion on Edwards's idealism see Lyon, *L'idéalisme en Angleterre au XVIIIe siècle* (1888); Gardiner, "The Early Idealism of Jonathan Edwards," 573–96; Anderson, "Immaterialism in Jonathan Edwards' Early Philosophical Notes," 181–200; Rupp, "The 'Idealism' of Jonathan Edwards," 209–26; Fiering, *Jonathan Edwards's Moral Thought and Its British Context*, 39–45; Fiering, "Rationalist Foundations of Jonathan Edwards's Metaphysics," 73–101; Lee, *Philosophical Theology of Jonathan Edwards*, 59–60; Lowance, "Jonathan Edwards and the Platonists," 129–52; Hall, "Did Berkeley Influence Edwards?," 100–21; Chai, *Jonathan Edwards and the Limits of Enlightenment Philosophy*, 141–42 n. 3; Marsden, *Jonathan Edwards*, 72–74.

On the other hand, as also seen in Part One, Edwards's emphasis on divine light and the spiritual sense has clear precedence in his Reformed tradition, and his union with the divine through the incarnated Christ is an echo of Calvin. The Reformed tradition was his nearest theological antecedent. The fact is, however, that Edwards is pulling from many sources at once and to focus on one figure or factor misses the complexity of it all. For example, while Edwards is strongly influenced by the Cambridge Platonists, the Cambridge Platonists he is reading are regularly discussing ancient and medieval figures. Likewise, while Edwards would see himself as in the Reformed tradition, he also sees himself as improving on it with the newest ideas of the day, including Newton and Locke. Added to this, in the next chapter I will show that while Edwards's understanding of the incarnation likely comes directly from John Owen, Owen finds much of his Christology in the Eastern father Didymus of Alexandria.

Edwards's theology is a complicated web of belief that does not rely on a single strand of thought. This context, contemporary and ancient, provided a young theologian with the first steps to understanding his own conversion. It gave him the ability to respect the culture and context provided by his family, while simultaneously giving him permission to think differently and to build on that world. The surprising and amazing joy that he experienced in his conversion was not a mistake after all, because in that conversion, his sins were not only removed, but he also came to "really possess all things."

4

The Pursuit of Divine Excellencies, 1723–1730

> This is the most excellent knowledge, to understand the Word of God. God's word teaches things of the highest nature . . . those spiritual, heavenly and divine things that earthly things, that other men's knowledge is conversant about, is but dirt and dung to.
>
> —Jonathan Edwards, *Profitable Hearers of the Word*[1]

> So the soul, by a vital union with Christ and by the faculties being as it were swallowed up in Christ, are altered, sanctified and sweetened.
>
> —Jonathan Edwards, *Images of Divine Things*[2]

ON A CHILLY DAY in February 1729, minister William Williams stood before a crowd of mourners in Hatfield, Massachusetts, howling, "*The Crown is fallen from our Heads!*" Solomon Stoddard, "the *Light and Glory, the Strength and Beauty*" of Northampton, was dead.[3] Stoddard was representative of a generation rapidly vanishing from Northampton; and all eyes now were on his assistant and successor, his grandson Jonathan Edwards.

Under Stoddard, the town had experienced numerous revivals or "harvests," but Edwards believed it was now in desperate need of spiritual renewal. His previous ministry experience in New York in 1722–1723 while still a student and his brief time in Bolton, Connecticut

---

1. *WJE* 14:252.
2. *WJE* 11:111.
3. Williams, *Death of a Prophet Lamented*, 27; Murray, *Jonathan Edwards*, 89.

(1723–1724), as well as his time assisting his grandfather, had done much to prepare him for solo ministry. Even with this advance preparation, having nearly thirteen hundred people suddenly under his care, the built-up stress led to health issues. So he and Sarah Pierpont, a young woman he had met shortly before his conversion experience and then married in 1727 (when she was only fifteen), and their daughter (also named Sarah), first took some recuperation time to visit New Haven and his hometown of East Windsor. This trip provided an opportunity to spend time with his younger sister Jerusha, an opportunity he would not appreciate fully until her death in December of that year. After several refreshing weeks away, he returned to the Northampton pulpit eager to lead a spiritual renewal, which to his understanding required a genuine, lasting conversion of his congregants.

To best understand his mind at this time, one must take a closer look at the years leading up to this point, because much of Edwards's mature theology can be traced back in one form or another to the preparatory years beginning in late 1723 to 1730. During these years, as Edwards preached in Bolton, taught at Yale, and eventually took over for his grandfather, a highly sophisticated theologian was emerging. In his notebooks and sermons, he was crafting fine points of doctrine, sometimes spending years on single strands of thought. He was attempting nothing less than an explanation of the very nature of physical and spiritual existence.

Edwards attempts in this early period to develop what might be dubbed *a metaphysical theory of everything*. That there is a connection between the converted sinner and God is not enough to satisfy his understanding of his own conversion; he further seeks to discover how this union between heaven and earth is made. How is the human being—finite and subject to the laws of nature and sin—connected to the infinite, that is, to the supernatural lawgiver and righteous God? As Edwards approaches this question, his understanding of conversion is bolstered by an incarnational analogy, that is, that the Christian is united to Christ in justification in a way that mimics the incarnation itself. This brings an unimaginable quality to conversion, one lost on a purely forensic view of justification. It also helps Edwards cope with his new perspective on the world, one in which he can see God in everything.

For all intents and purposes, the incarnation of Christ solves his theological conundrum. The discord between eternity and time—the gap between heaven and earth—is closed by the incarnated Christ in the bond of the Spirit—the God-Human that participates in both. Conversion is beautiful because conversion is a second type of incarnation.

Light: "One special season of uncommon sweetness"[4]

Edwards delivered his masters thesis in 1723, six years before Grandfather Stoddard would die and leave his legacy in Jonathan's hands. In the days leading up to and following the delivery of his thesis, Edwards pursued spiritual joy and soaked in the divine beauty through long walks in fields and woods and through his scientific observations. On November 11 of that year, he agreed to become the pastor of the church of Bolton, Connecticut, and remained with the church until the following May. His work from his time in New York provided the momentum he needed to get started in Bolton. His sermons from the New York period initially supplied him in the pulpit, and in these and his notes he continued his musings on the divine.

Characteristically, his thoughts outnumbered the sheets of paper available to him, pressing him to take notes in the white margins of any used newspapers he could find. During this time, he started an exegetical outlet in what would become known as his Scripture notebook, and also engaged in philosophical theology in his "Natural Philosophy" notebook.

Also characteristic of Edwards in this period and throughout his life was his tendency to overwork himself, resulting in recurring bouts of extreme stress and depression. He tried to rein in negativity by thinking on the positive aspects of life. George Marsden notes that "his sermons written at Bolton were among his most consistently in cheerful major keys."[5] But this cheerfulness was not easily claimed, considering the relationship troubles that apparently plagued the church. In his sermon *Living Peaceably One with Another*, he tackles this difficulty head on: "We ought to endeavor to live peaceably with all men universally. None are to be excepted." Pulling from his observations on the spiritual side of nature, Edwards says the "Christian's good will" is to be "like the beams of the sun that enlightens the whole world and rejoices all sorts of creatures, shines indifferently on gardens and the wilderness,

---

4. *WJE* 16:798.
5. Marsden, *Jonathan Edwards*, 96.

on fruitful fields and the barren mountains alike, on fragrant fruits and flowers and on the bramble."⁶ In addressing these and other concerns at Bolton, he does not merely rely on what he has already written but aggressively continues his theological exploration on the nature of God and the complexities of redemption.

In June 1724, Edwards left his temporary post at Bolton and returned to Yale, this time as a tutor. Timothy Cutler's defection two years earlier had sent Yale into a tailspin, and the trustees were still performing damage control and searching for a new rector. One candidate, Elisha Williams, the son of William Williams and Edwards's former tutor in Wethersfield, was presented as a good possibility, but the trustees did not believe he could be pulled away from his pulpit. By April of 1724, trustee Eliphalet Adams was elected rector, but his church was unwilling to release him. Other candidates had already cited their duties to their churches or families as the primary reason for not accepting the position. By September's commencement, trustee Samuel Andrew was serving as rector *pro tempore* and continued as such until the following year's commencement.⁷

After receiving a great deal of pressure to find a leader for the school, the trustees again considered Elisha Williams. As Richard Warch notes, beyond Williams's ecclesiastical commitments, the fact that he had trained the Wethersfield students probably made the trustees cautious of bringing him into a more powerful position. But Williams accepted the call, and his church was financially compensated for their loss. The day after the 1726 commencement, Williams signed the Saybrook Confession and assumed his new post. While it would be two more years before an opening appeared on the board and Williams could join the trustees, things began to stabilize for the school. He would stay on as rector for fourteen years, finally providing to Yale the stability it had sorely lacked since its founding.⁸

Arriving amidst these changes and prior to Williams's installment, Edwards was entering into less-than-ideal circumstances. With no rec-

---

6. *WJE* 14:121.

7. Warch, *School of the Prophets,* 130, 131; see also an excerpt from President Stiles' diary in Woolsey, *An Historical Discourse,* 103, and an excerpt of the "Proceedings of the Trustees, April 20, 1725," available in Dexter, *Documentary History of Yale University,* 258.

8. Warch, *School of the Prophets,* 132; Woolsey, *Historical Discourse,* 10; Dexter, *Sketch of the History of Yale University,* 24.

tor yet, the lion's share of the work fell on him and Robert Treat (a Yale tutor in 1724), and later him and his uncle Daniel Edwards (a Yale tutor beginning in 1725); the work included, among other duties, the task of reining in the unruly students, of which there were several. (A school for the privileged Yale was not, in the early days.) Studying at Yale was hard work, and students were known for making the tutors' work even harder. With sixty students becoming scholars during his time as tutor, Edwards had to labor at keeping them in line.[9] His Diary records his efforts and the related struggles with melancholy. "After I went to New Haven," he writes in his *Personal Narrative,* "I sunk in religion; my mind being diverted from my eager and violent pursuits after holiness, by some affairs that greatly perplexed and distracted my mind."[10]

These "affairs," which included spiritual struggles and new duties he received as a tutor, were counted by Edwards as distractions. One such project involved Edwards and his colleague Treat; both were given extra income for organizing and cataloguing the library.[11] This proved to be invaluable to Edwards in the collecting of book titles he wanted to add to his personal library, as well as in affording an opportunity to read books to which he was otherwise unlikely to have access. The Dummer library contained volumes by thinkers like John Tillotson (*Sermons*), Richard Baxter (*Practical Works*), Matthew Henry (various commentaries), Stephen Charnock (volume one of his works), John Owen (*Pneumatalogia*), Bishop Stillingfleet (eight volumes against Socinians), and Henry More (*Enchiridion Ethicum*); many of these make an appearance in Edwards's "Catalogue of Reading."[12] This "Catalogue" shows a variety of interests from astronomy to mathematics, and demonstrates that Edwards's primary interests include bodies of divinity, books on biblical interpretation, philosophy as it relates to religion, histories of the Old Testament, church histories, and questions of epistemology.[13]

---

9. Oviatt, *Beginnings of Yale*, 416.

10. *WJE* 16:798; see also his Diary for June 6, 1724 (*WJE* 16:786).

11. Marsden, *Jonathan Edwards*, 103.

12. Bryant and Patterson, "The List of Books Sent by Jeremiah Dummer," 425, 427, 428, 430, 440, 441, 443.

13. Some of those that interested Edwards include: Nieuwenty, *Religious Philosopher*; Bates, *Harmony of the Divine Attributes*; Cooper, *Characteristics of Men*; Lukin, *Introduction to the Scriptures*; Wodrow, *History of the Sufferings of the Church of Scotland*; and Berkeley, *Treatise Concerning the Principles of Human Knowledge*.

Another significant distraction was of a less intellectual nature. By spring of 1725, Edwards was engaged to ideal Christian, Sarah. As Marsden speculates, this relationship likely supplied sexual tension, as a Diary entry from November of 1725 speaks of suppressing thoughts that distract from religion, such as melancholic, anxious, or passionate thoughts.[14]

Determined to stay the course despite the distractions of books and ideal women, Edwards worked hard, denying himself food and sleep. In September 1725, he set out to visit his parents but became very ill (for "about a quarter of a year") and stopped far short of his destination at the home of Isaac Stiles in North Village (North Haven). After getting some help, he managed to finish his recovery in East Windsor. The trauma of the experience drew his attention back to divine things:

> And in this sickness, God was pleased to visit me again with sweet influences of his spirit. My mind was great engaged there on divine, pleasant contemplations, and longing of soul. I observed that those who watched with me, would often be looking out for the morning, and seemed to wish for it. Which brought to my mind those words of the Psalmist, which my soul with sweetness made its own language, 'My soul waiteth for the Lord more than they that watch for the morning; I say, more than they that watch for the morning' [Psalm 130:6]. And when the light of the morning came, and the beams of the sun came in at the windows, it refreshed my soul from one morning to another. It seemed to me to be some image of the sweet light of God's glory.[15]

Despite this brief resurrection of his passion for understanding the divine being, by the time of his full recovery and return to Yale, his work as a tutor again caused him to sink into despair. The struggle with depression would be relieved only by his new position under his grandfather in Northampton in the autumn of 1726.

Now in his eighties, Stoddard saw Edwards as his successor, and the grandson began to move into another stage of life, one that involved picking up more of his grandfather's duties. His position as assistant became official in November 1726; he was ordained the following February, with his wedding five months later. Life was far less depressing and Edwards

---

14. Marsden, *Jonathan Edwards*, 107; *WJE* 16:788 (November 16, 1725).
15. *WJE* 16:798–99.

was regaining his spirit. On his feelings about his time in Northampton, Edwards writes in his *Personal Narrative*:

> Since I came to this town, I have often had sweet complacency in God in views of his glorious perfections, and the excellency of Jesus Christ. God has appeared to me, a glorious and lovely being, chiefly on the account of his holiness. The holiness of God has always appeared to me the most lovely of all his attributes. The doctrines of God's absolute sovereignty, and free grace, in showing mercy to whom he would show mercy; and man's absolute dependence on the operations of God's Holy Spirit, have very often appeared to me as sweet and glorious doctrines.

Edwards also notes that during this time he found "exalting thoughts of God" and the Trinity, and his heart was concerned with the "advancement of Christ's kingdom" and the future of the world. Moreover, the "way of salvation by Christ" appeared "glorious and excellent" and it "often appeared sweet" to him "to be united to Christ; to have him for my head, and to be a member of his body . . ."[16] It is this last part on union that speaks volumes as to the future trajectory of his theology.

As shown in the previous chapter, Edwards's conversion experience was an unexpected surprise, one that bathed him in a sense of the divine perfection. With new eyes, Edwards saw the world and its beauty as the result of the being of God. In one sense, the divine being is all there is; this has earned Edwards the accusation of being a monist. Given this connection of the divine to nature, it is only natural that, in conversion, the new eyes capable of seeing God would see him in all things material, namely, the beauty of nature. Therefore this new life of holiness is equated with beauty, and the greater the beauty, the greater the conformity to God. "'Tis the highest beauty and amiableness, vastly above all other beauties," Edwards explains, "'Tis a divine beauty, makes the souls heavenly and far purer than anything here on earth."[17]

This sense of the divine excellency or beauty is unlike any other sense "exercised in an [sic] common objects," for nothing can "bear down the mind at such a rate as [do] the divine properties." As Edwards writes, "the notion of God, or idea I have of him, is that complex idea of such power, holiness, purity, majesty, love, excellency, beauty, loveliness,

---

16. *WJE* 16:799.
17. *WJE* 13:163 ("Misc." a).

and ten thousand other things"[18] The universe is created to facilitate this relationship: "intelligent beings are the end of the creation," and as a result they are expected to worship and adore him for eternity. This makes religion "the great end, the very end," of creation: "the harmony of the world is indeed a very true picture and shadow of the real glories of religion," writes Edwards with a Platonic cadence. The objects to behold in this world "are but the shadows of the greatness and are worthless, except as they conduce to true and real greatness and excellency, and manifest the power and wisdom of God."[19]

Unfortunately, the presence of sin in the soul moves the passions to love that which is far less beautiful.[20] To rectify that problem, in conversion one is given eyes to see divine beauty and approve of it. Thomas Schafer has long observed that Edwards's early sermon, *A Spiritual Understanding of Divine Things Denied to the Unregenerate*, paves the way for his first entry on "Excellency" in "The Mind" and his 1734 sermon, *A Divine and Supernatural Light*. "There is no entry in the 'Miscellanies' during the same general period," writes Schafer, "that brings together so many aspects of Edwards' theology of conversion as does this sermon."[21] The sermon tone and content is quintessential Edwards.

The sermon text he chose, 1 Cor 2:14 ("But the natural man receiveth not the things of the Spirit of God: for they are foolishness unto him: neither can he know them, because they are spiritually discerned"), allows him to discourse freely on divine excellencies and spiritual knowledge. The "natural man," says Edwards, does not receive the spiritual things found in Scripture or in "saving illumination." When spiritual things are presented to the unregenerate person, he or she "can see no manner of excellency or beauty or wisdom in them." Spiritual knowledge, for Edwards, is far less about content or quantity of facts, and more about the recognition of excellence and beauty. "The great and learned men of the world perhaps may have a hundred times the notional knowledge of divinity when yet the humble, plain, illiterate Christian really hath an understanding that is above, that he never has reached to and cannot attain." The Christian's eyes are opened to see the divine and to a "certain intenseness and sensibleness in their apprehension of [them], a

18. *WJE* 13:177, 178 ("Misc." aa).
19. *WJE* 13:185 ("Misc." gg); Ibid., 224 ("Misc." 42).
20. *WJE* 13:199–200, 218–19 ("Misc." 3, 34).
21. *WJE* 13:49; see also *WJE* 14:69.

certain seeing and feeling." God is "most excellent of all beings, and has infinite perfection," writes Edwards; he "is the fountain of all excellency and loveliness"—but while the natural person can recognize this, he or she cannot enjoy it any more than a piece of human art.[22] There is a disagreeableness between God and the sinner, whose mind is filled with darkness. Conversion changes this altogether.

Some years later Edwards would give much more attention to this idea in his *A Treatise Concerning Religious Affections*, his greatest analysis of the nature of true religious experience. It is this text that is often the subject of scholarship on his ideas of the spiritual "sense." Edwards noted the idea of a "new sense" in describing his own conversion: "there came into my soul, and was as it were diffused throughout it, a sense of the glory of the divine being; a new sense, quite different from anything I ever experienced before."[23]

This spiritual sense is said to be Edwards's corrective to Locke's empiricism, thus making him the child of the Enlightenment. For example, David Bebbington writes, "Edwards derived his confidence about salvation from an atmosphere of the English Enlightenment."[24] But this is an incomplete picture. "For Locke," writes Bebbington, "knowledge derived from the senses is certain . . . Edwards was simply extending the range of sense available to a human being."[25] Edwards does not simply extend Locke's empiricism, dressing up Locke's conclusions in the Spirit's clothing, however. And contrary to his reputation, neither does Locke exalt empiricism to the exclusion of the spiritual.

When Edwards writes about the spiritual sense in *Religious Affections*, he does use the words "sense" and "idea" and the Lockean phrase "new simple idea," as Bebbington notes.[26] But it could be argued that Locke, despite his empiricism, is not rejecting outright the idea of a spiritual sense. Arguing for a twist on the traditional disparity between Locke and Edwards over a spiritual sense, Norman Fiering writes that Edwards's use of Locke's terminology was to "satisfy empiricist critics," not to imitate Locke.[27] Unfortunately, Fiering takes that argument too

22. WJE 14:71, 72, 74, 75–76.
23. WJE 16:792.
24. Bebbington, *Evangelicalism in Modern Britain*, 48.
25. Ibid.
26. Ibid.; WJE 2:205.
27. Fiering, *Jonathan Edwards's Moral Thought*, 125.

far and concludes that "Edwards's spiritual sense has little resemblance to anything in Locke, and the English philosopher, had he been alive, would undoubtedly have dismissed Edwards's idea of a special sensation of divine things as 'enthusiastic' nonsense."[28]

There is more to Locke than this picture portrays. As seen in the first chapter, Locke indicates that faith is a companion for reason but with a different dominion. Locke's engagement of the biblical text demonstrates that he has little difficulty accepting it. More than that, as Robert E. Brown has argued, Locke does not appear to outright reject the concept of a spiritual sense at all. Locke writes in his *Essay*:

> In what I have said I am far from denying, that GOD can, and doth sometimes enlighten Mens Minds in the apprehending of certain Truths, or excite them to Good Actions by the immediate influence and assistance of the Holy Spirit, without any extraordinary Signs accompanying it. But in such Cases too we have Reason and the Scripture, unerring Rules to know whether it be from GOD or no.[29]

It may be called an inconsistency in Locke's thought or a concession to the tradition from which he was not yet willing to part, but whatever the missing components between faith and reason, Locke seems to have no problem embracing the reality of their coexistence.

Between his early years and the later treatise on religious affections, Edwards's apparent practice was to glean from many sources; no doubt he noted a parallel in Locke's *Essay*, but this was only Edwards's latest discussion on the subject, not his first exposure to it. In any case, his view at this time was that the shadows of this earthly life reflected the reality (the mind of God), and the converted eyes could see that through the spiritual sense. Edwards was interested in reverse-engineering existence itself to find out exactly what bridges the gap between earth and heaven; and for that, he ultimately turns to the subject of union with Christ by the bond of the Spirit.

---

28. Ibid.
29. *Essay*, 4.19.16; see also Wolterstorff, *John Locke and the Ethics of Belief*, 118–33.

Excellency: "God's manifestation of his own perfection"[30]

The spiritual divide between shadow and form, between that which is perfect or the ideal and that which is deformed, is at the heart of Edwards's discourse on "Excellency." That the first entry in "The Mind" on "Excellency" follows naturally from *A Spiritual Understanding of Divine Things Denied to the Unregenerate* there is no doubt. Edwards saw previous discussions of excellency as lacking in substance: ". . . But what is excellency? Wherein is one thing excellent and another evil, one beautiful and another deformed? Some have said that all excellency is harmony, symmetry or proportion; but they have not yet explained it."[31] As the physicist seeks the elusive Theory of Everything, uniting all natural phenomena, so also Edwards seeks to unite the natural and the spiritual under the greater model of "Excellency." Key to understanding this concept is his explanation of beauty and consent. "Edwards was convinced," writes Roland André Delattre in his *Beauty and Sensibility in the Thought of Jonathan Edwards,* "that beauty is the reality in terms of which the Divine Being and the moral and religious life of human beings as well as the order of the universal system of being, both moral and natural, can best be understood." *Beauty* supplies the "objective foundation" for determining whether something is excellent.[32] Remembering that Edwards is working out of an era that did not encounter exploration of the avant-garde in art (where concepts of standards are questioned), but rather is in the transition from the Baroque to Enlightenment periods, he understands beauty in the sense of something objective, displaying harmony, symmetry, and proportion. Harmony or proportion is the amount of agreeableness or *consent* between the parts that make up the beautiful.[33]

---

30. *WJE* 14:147.

31. In 1723 Edwards crossed out entry 78 of his "Miscellanies" notebook, labeled "Excellency," with a large X and began "The Mind." "Miscellanies" 78 became an entry on "Regeneration" and it along with several other entries (many in the immediate vicinity of entry 78) cover topics closely related to his discussion of Excellency in "The Mind" (*WJE* 6:332). When Edwards says "some have said," he is referring to, as Wallace E. Anderson has noted, Anthony Ashley, the Earl of Shaftesbury, and his *Inquiry Concerning Virtue.*

32. Delattre, *Beauty and Sensibility in the Thought of Jonathan Edwards*, 1, 2.

33. *WJE* 6:332.

Consent is like four-part harmony: the tighter the harmony, the more pleasant the sound. Edwards understands this pleasantness as a natural human recognition of consent between the voices in harmony, that is, a recognition of the balance and relational union of the parts to produce such a beautiful sound. It is assumed that all humans are created to recognize the consent of parts by nature or divine design, that is, unless their sinfulness finds pleasure in dissent. "One alone, without any reference to any more, cannot be excellent," writes Edwards.[34] He looks to symbols of perfection, such as lines and circles, to express his understanding of consent. The more complex something is and the greater the consent between its parts, the greater the beauty. While there is an attempt at an objective understanding of beauty for Edwards, there is unavoidably an element of subjectivism. Edwards goes on:

> How exceedingly apt are we, when we are sitting still and accidentally casting our eye upon some marks or spots in the floor or wall, to be ranging of them into regular parcels and figures; and if we see a mark out of its place, to be placing of it right by our imagination—and this even while we are meditating on something else. So we may catch ourselves at observing the rules of harmony and regularity in the careless motions of our heads or feet, and when playing with our hands or walking about the room.[35]

While marks on a floor or wall may appear to Edwards as some sort of shape or figure, this obviously is not objective; another person may see something entirely different, like two persons seeing different animals in passing clouds, or like the Big Dipper being seen as a plough or butcher's cleaver in Europe.

Based on this perception of consent and beauty, Edwards understands consent as agreement of parts, whether they occur on either a *natural or lower level* or on a greater scale, rising into the *spiritual level* of an agreement or harmony of spirit between persons. Lower beauty can be found in the simple balance between two lines in art.[36] It may also be found in the complex symmetry and harmony of Bach.[37] Baroque period poetry, for example, stunned readers by sheer size and powerful

34. *WJE* 6:337; "Mind," 1.
35. *WJE* 6:336; "Mind," 1.
36. *WJE* 6:333: "Mind," 1.
37. For a comparison to Bach, see Marsden, *Jonathan Edwards*, 475.

complexity. Parts, even in a complex form, consent when they form a coherent whole, and so it is no wonder that Edwards places John Milton's *Paradise Lost* among many works of "great genius," which possess "*natural* excellencies," but which, he notes, fall infinitely short in their complex beauty from God's excellency.[38] "The more the consent is, and the more extensive," states Edwards, "the greater is the excellency."[39] God's beauty is perfect, infinitely extensive, and spiritual. Nothing on earth can match it, though it can reflect it on the scale of beauty.

Spiritual and Higher Beauty

Understanding simple beauty and complex beauty is really only the beginning; it is only a natural shadow of the spiritual beauty which contains far more consent and therefore more excellency. Spiritual beauty occurs between living beings: "Spiritual harmonies are of vastly larger extent; i.e., the proportions are vastly oftener redoubled, and respect more beings, and require a vastly larger view to comprehend them, as some simple notes do more affect one who has not a comprehensive understanding of music."[40] The regenerate, as he noted in his sermon *A Spiritual Understanding of Divine Things Denied to the Unregenerate*, consent to divine excellencies, for they can sense its agreeableness spiritually, while the unregenerate find it worthless. Consent for spiritual beauty is, as Edwards will call it later, "cordial consent"; that is, consent determined by an act of a being's will (or cordiality). Art and music have consenting parts, but not a consent driven by will. It is, essentially, only a shadow (as Plato might call it) of the true consent of spiritual beings: "for so far as a thing consents to being in general, so far it consents to him [God]. And the more perfect created spirits are, the nearer do they come to their creator in this regard." For this reason, love is one of the "highest excellencies," the "consent of spirits consists half in their mutual love one to another, and the sweet harmony between the various parts of the Universe is only an image of mutual love."[41] As he explores the subject over the years, this element of *will* and *love* will transform the concepts of consent or agreeableness into the terms of conversion (e.g., faith

---

38. *WJE* 2:299.
39. *WJE* 6:336.
40. *WJE* 6:336.
41. *WJE* 6:337, 338.

and union). These connections are instrumental for his understanding of what occurs when the sinner is justified by faith in Christ.

Beauty and excellency exist, therefore, on a scale. From normal consent found in the examples above, beauty can be found in inanimate objects. But on a higher level of existence—the spiritual level—beauty is found in the cordial consent (i.e., love) between persons. It is a union or agreement between wills. The greater one's love for or consent to God and his will, the greater the excellency and therefore beauty. At the highest level of this scale, then, would be the Trinity. There can be no "consent" without a "plurality," and since God is love of the greatest kind, and love is one of the "highest excellencies," the divine being must be a "plurality."[42] Even more, since "the more perfect created spirits are, the nearer do they come to their creator," and since "excellency consists in the similarness of one being to another," the divine plurality must also be equal to one another. The Trinity is the epitome of excellency itself, that which all other lower excellencies are but shadows of and to which they must conform. When one is converted, one has all that God has, including the Trinity, and in this sense, "excellency."

In his sermon *Nothing on Earth Can Represent the Glories of Heaven* (1724), Edwards preaches on Rev 21:18 (". . . and the city was pure gold, like unto clear glass").[43] He reminds his congregation that Scripture uses phrases such as "like unto clear glass" to describe the New Jerusalem as a reminder to humans that the things of this world are imperfect representations, shadows, or types of the perfect excellencies of the Godhead and heaven. They are meant to communicate something of God himself: "therefore the motive of God's creating the world must be his inclination to communicate his own happiness to something else," namely, human beings. "The creation of the world," says Edwards, "is nothing but God's manifestation of his own perfection and excellency." Human beings were "created to behold the manifestations of God's excellency . . . and to be delighted . . ." or to have cordial consent.[44] Based on this understanding of the relationship between God's being and creation, creation as the manifestation of "God's excellency" is therefore the manifestation of the Trinitarian image. Conversion, for Edwards, is not merely the acquisition and acceptance of certain notions or doctrines, but rather the

42. *WJE* 6:337.
43. *WJE* 14:137–60.
44. *WJE* 14:146, 147.

bringing together of creature and creator, or eternity and time. The soul consents to the divine being, and in so doing, conforms in some divinized way to the excellency and beauty of that being as it is in the Trinity.

The excellency of the Trinity is the highest beauty, the ultimate measure against which all beauty is examined. Intellectual historians often discuss the Trinitarian traditions in terms of the division between Eastern and Western Christianity. The East, led by the Cappadocians, emphasized the "threeness" of the Trinity, known today as the social Trinity. The West, according to this line of thinking, followed Augustine's psychological analogy of the Trinity, thereby emphasizing its "oneness." Understanding Christian traditions on the Trinity, for these historians, is to apply these two categories of either threeness or oneness. The question then becomes, to which tradition does Edwards belong?

In her book *The Supreme Harmony of All: The Trinitarian Theology of Jonathan Edwards*, Amy Plantinga Pauw argues that Edwards refuses "to take sides in the debate." In the West, notes Pauw, Augustine employs the psychological analogy to explain the Trinity. Because of the doctrine of *vestigia Trinitatis*, one has reason to look for shadows or images of the Trinity that exist in creation, notably in the human psychology. According to Augustine in his *De Trinitate*, the human soul has oneness, but it also is the plurality of three things: 1. the *mind*; 2. the mind's generating of "self-knowledge"; and 3. its "self-love" of its self-knowledge.[45] The *mind* is as the Father (the originator), the mind's *knowledge of itself* is as the Son, and the *love of the mind for self-knowledge* is as the Holy Spirit. When the mind "knows its whole self and nothing else together with itself, its knowledge exactly matches itself," says Augustine, "and when it perceives its whole self and nothing else, it is neither less nor greater," and therefore, "when these three are complete they are consequently equal" and one.[46]

Alternatively, the social model of the East, says Pauw, emphasizes the "love and intimate fellowship among the members of the Trinity by likening them, not to a single human soul, but to a family, a society, or a communion of friends." This is the tradition of the Cappadocians and Richard of St. Victor. Edwards is said to see no reason to choose between either model, but is happy to live with the tension of both.[47]

45. Pauw, "Supreme Harmony of All," 10; WSA 5:259.
46. WSA 5:275, 273.
47. Pauw, "Supreme Harmony of All," 14, 11.

The tension, however, may not be all that dramatic. Disagreeing with Pauw, Steve Studebaker argues that historical paradigms along the lines of East versus West are flawed and "overgeneralized." In consequence, argues Studebaker, "the paradigm reduces the theological history of trinitarianism to the conceptual idioms of threeness and oneness." Studebaker suggests that Edwards's Trinitarianism and its social aspects come from another analogy Augustine offers for the Trinity called the "mutual love" model. This model (from *De Trinitate* 15) is the source for Edwards's Trinitarianism and where he finds the balance between threeness and oneness.[48] In this way, Augustine's mutual love model reflects the social aspects of the Eastern theologians, but remains distinctly Western in that the Spirit is proceeding from both the Father and the Son. It may be worth noting, however, that to connect the Spirit so strongly to both the Father and the Son in this way is not entirely a product of the West. One particularly important Eastern theologian, Didymus of Alexandria (ca. 313–398), whom I will discuss in more detail later, lays the groundwork for some of Augustine's own thinking.

Edwards is making use of Augustine's mutual love model in these early years. According to "Miscellanies" 94, "God is infinitely happy from all eternity in the view and enjoyment of himself, in the reflection and converse love of his own essence, that is, in the perfect idea he has of himself, infinitely perfect."[49] In "God's reflecting on himself the Deity is begotten," he writes; "there is a substantial image of God begotten." For God to reflect on anything less than himself is, for God, to not reflect on himself but a poor representation. Christ is called "the express image of his person" (Heb 1:3) because this deity "begotten" would be the Son of God. But begetting an image is not the same as delighting in it. For God to delight perfectly in himself is to give himself entirely in love. "The Holy Spirit," continues Edwards, "is the act of God between the Father and the Son infinitely loving and delighting in each other." More to the point, "the delight of God is properly a substance . . . even the essence of God."[50] By having a perfect understanding of himself, God generates himself over again. Edwards's emphasis on the Trinitarian community is

---

48. Studebaker, "Jonathan Edwards's Social Augustinian Trinitarianism," 268 (*SJT*); Studebaker, "Jonathan Edwards' Social Augustinian Trinitarianism," 90–91; 272 (PhD diss.).

49. *WJE* 13:257 ("Misc." 94). See also "Misc." 96, 117, 143, 144, 151, 157.

50. *WJE* 13:258, 261 ("Misc." 94).

easily found in this mutual love model. This is the "plurality" or Trinity of harmony, perfection, and cordial consent known as love and therefore the highest of excellencies.[51]

God as Trinity is the highest of spiritual beauty, but Edwards insists that God created the world "to communicate" this "happiness to something else."

> ... God, who was thus happy in himself, has a natural propensity and inclination to communicate happiness to some other beings ... And 'twas because of this inclination that he created the world, and especially that he created men and angels in it. 'Twas not that he might be made more happy himself, but that [he] might make something else happy; that he might make them blessed in the beholding of his excellency, and might this way glorify himself.[52]

Just as the Trinitarian family is a sharing of excellency, beauty, happiness, and delight, so too, God wants his creatures to experience all that he has. "Yea, he is nothing but excellency; and all that he does, nothing but excellent."[53] God seeks to raise the person from a lower spiritual beauty to the true form of beauty, himself.

This is what Edwards discovered in his conversion. Suddenly, the world appeared strangely different, and the divine being, the Trinity itself, could be seen everywhere in creation. The internal love of the Trinity is expressed in the sustaining of creation. Edwards found "happiness" in his conversion because he could see the love of the Trinity in creation and he participated in that love—the Holy Spirit—that binds the Trinity together. From his perspective, he *possessed* the Trinity itself, and could now spiritually see its image and excellencies shadow forth in nature's lower beauty. His new status as a justified sinner provided him through grace the rights and privileges of the Godhead. In other words, the justification of the sinner in conversion is the gifting of the very excellency of the Trinity to the sinner.

The lesson taken from *A Spiritual Understanding of Divine Things Denied to the Unregenerate* is that only those converted human beings can truly enjoy God's happiness and joy. If the end of creation is reli-

---

51. Edwards was at this time reading John Edwards's *Theologia Reformata* (1:323). This source is definitely one from which Edwards would have picked up the mutual love model.

52. *WJE* 14:153.

53. *WJE* 13:252 ("Misc." 87).

gion, then *only* those creatures worshipping in true religion can partake. Through Christ, the sinner can "consent" with the divine: "that object which God infinitely loves must be infinitely and perfectly consenting and agreeable to him."[54] Redemptive history, then, is the realigning of cordial consent between the creature and the creator—a restoration of excellency made possible by Christ and therefore a reflection of the Trinity. The end of creation, due to the inherent goodness or excellency of God, must include the restoration of justice.[55]

> All excellency, when perceived, will be agreeable to perceiving being, and all evil disagreeable. But God, being omniscient, must necessarily perfectly perceive all excellency, and fully know what is contrary to it; and therefore, that all excellency is perfectly agreeable to his will, and all evil perfectly disagreeable; and therefore, that he cannot will to do anything but what is excellent.

For this reason, a relationship of a fallen creation to its creator requires a restoration to that which is excellent through justification: "justice is an excellency," writes Edwards.[56]

Christ maintains a status of rightness, harmony, and cordial consent (or love) with the Father and the Christian obtains Christ's status when united to him. Some years later, Edwards would elaborate on this in his famous discourse on justification: "the love, honor, and obedience of Christ towards God, has infinite value, from the excellency and dignity of the person in whom these qualifications were inherent."[57] His righteousness or excellency are acts of will and in cordial consent with the Father, and it is that which the Father sees on the sinner's account in justification.[58] Furthermore, the Spirit changes the soul of the sinner, making the person capable of having cordial consent with Christ, also known as having faith. In that faith, the Christian is united or in harmony with Christ and his excellencies.

The world is a mere shadow of the real excellencies, but it is created to give a "glimpse of his excellencies." When Christ created the world, he ultimately did so "to communicate himself in an image of his own

---

54. *WJE* 13:283 ("Misc." 117).
55. *WJE* 13:251 ("Misc." 87).
56. *WJE* 13:253 ("Misc." 89).
57. *WJE* 19:162.
58. *WJE* 19:199.

excellency" to spiritual beings.[59] The closer this relationship becomes, the greater their happiness. Edwards finds this especially true for the Christian in eternity. "It appears that they shall be thus exceeding blessed and glorious," writes Edwards, "because they shall enjoy God as their own portion, and shall fully enjoy the possession of all things."[60] Their union with Christ that begins in justification carries on and grows increasingly closer into eternity.[61] Christians are united to Christ in heaven as "near as our hands and feet are to our head," as "one spirit, as near as the body is the soul," insists Edwards.[62] He now could see that his happiness had a theological justification. As the Trinity is united by the bond of the Holy Spirit, seen as the divine love, this same love is the bond between the person and Christ. At this point, Edwards still wants to understand how close the bond is and how it works. What he finds is that the Spirit plays an intimate role in uniting the natures of Christ in the incarnation, and conversion is a second sort of incarnation.

Spirit-Christology: "The bond of perfectness"

The idea that the Holy Spirit is the bond of unity (or cordial consent) between the persons of the Trinity remained important for Edwards throughout his entire life.

> It was more especially the Holy Spirit's work to bring the world to its beauty and perfection out of the chaos, for the beauty of the world is a communication of God's beauty. The Holy Spirit is the harmony and excellency and beauty of the Deity . . . therefore 'twas his work to communicate beauty and harmony to the world, and so we read that it was he that moved upon the face of the waters (Gen 1:2).[63]

The Holy Spirit, says Edwards, is the "perfect act" of God, the "activity, vivacity, and energy of God," and it is his duty "to actuate and quicken all things, and to beget energy and vivacity in the creature."[64] As the Holy Spirit is responsible to communicate the excellencies and beauty within the deity to creation, that is, the higher beauty to the lower, so also, the

---

59. *WJE* 13:279 ("Misc." 108).
60. *WJE* 14:154.
61. *WJE* 13:275 ("Misc." 105). See also "Misc." 108, 112, 114.
62. *WJE* 14:155.
63. *WJE* 13:384 ("Misc." 293).
64. *WJE* 13:261 ("Misc." 94).

Spirit is responsible to communicate these excellencies to the very heart of the justified sinner in conversion who possesses "all things."

Christ's incarnation bridges heaven and earth, but the Spirit is the one who maintains that bridge. According to Edwards, it is the Spirit who unifies the two natures of Christ (to make one person) and also Christ to the minds or spirits of the saints (to make one body).[65] The union of the two natures of Christ in the incarnation is a model for the union of Christ to the Christian. The details of this union are especially drawn out in one of the last "Miscellanies" of this period, entry 487, labeled: "INCARNATION OF THE SON OF GOD AND UNION OF THE TWO NATURES OF CHRIST." "There is a likeness between the union of the Logos with the man Christ Jesus and the union of Christ with the church," he writes. It is likely that this speculation on the nature of the incarnation is driven by a reading of John Owen's *Pneumatalogia* (and other works) at this point. By the time of this entry (1730), there is no explicit evidence that he possesses this work of Owen's, but in earlier "Miscellanies" he appears to have read Owen on Hebrews, and around this time, in his "Catalogue of Reading" he mentions Owen's works (entries 47 and 455).

Stephen Holmes notes this connection to John Owen in his *God of Grace and God of Glory*. The communication between the two natures was left to the role of the Holy Spirit, says Owen, who is "the immediate operator of all divine acts of the Son himself, even on his own human nature." Holmes calls this particular Christology a "radicalisation of the basic Reformed position" which "introduced doctrinal innovation."[66] In the incarnation, the Spirit plays a central role in the communication between the human and divine natures. According to Owen, the Spirit created the human nature of Christ, sanctified it, and filled it with grace "according to the measure of its receptivity."[67]

---

65. *WJE* 13:330 ("Misc." 184).

66. Trueman, *Claims of Truth*, 177; Holmes, *God of Grace*, 136–38. Holmes notes that Edwards had definitely read Owen's *Pneumatalogia* by "Miscellanies" 1047 (Holmes, *God of Grace,* 136 n. 35); *WJO* 3:162; my thanks to Carl Trueman for pointing out that Owen's Spirit-Christology is probably derived from his reading of Didymus of Alexandria. See Didymus of Alexandria, *De Spiritu Sancto*, PG 39:1068–69. Didymus's work *On the Holy Spirit* is quoted throughout Owen's work on the Spirit. For more on Didymus see Studer, *Trinity and Incarnation*. Didymus "depended" on and developed the works of the Cappadocians, and his work was widely distributed (ibid., 152).

67. *WJO* 3:168.

Differences exist, of course, between Edwards and Owen on the nature of this relationship between the Spirit and the incarnate Christ. Pauw believes that Holmes "overplays the similarities" between Edwards and Owen.[68] "Owen insisted that the Logos is in union with the man Jesus not immediately," writes Holmes, "as traditional Christologies had taught, but mediately, through the Spirit."[69] According to Pauw, however, Owen sees the assumption of the human nature proper as an act of the Logos, but the creation of the human nature and the communion of attributes as belonging to the role of the Spirit. Edwards, on the other hand, sees the Holy Spirit as having the primary role in the entire process, even in the union of the Logos with the human nature.

This does seem to be a major difference between Edwards and Owen on the issue of Spirit-Christology.[70] The Logos was responsible for bringing the anhypostatic human nature into hypostatic union, for Owen, but the Spirit was responsible for the mediation of natures.[71] The importance of this distinction—that is, whether the Logos directly forms the union with the human nature or whether it is the role of the Spirit—is found in figuring out exactly how the God-Human remained free of sin and corruption. "In Owen's theology," writes Pauw, "this emphasis on the role of the Spirit helped protect the genuine humanity of Jesus Christ: by the power of the Spirit, Jesus' humanity was gradually perfected over the course of his earthly life."[72] This small discussion is one that will be reserved for chapter 6, but it is sufficient to say here that there are more important similarities than differences for this conversation and that Edwards is indeed gleaning from this theological perspective.

Edwards gained a great deal from Owen's appropriation of this Spirit-Christology. Owen's argument for the Spirit's role in the incarnation is derived from the context of his response to the Socinian question: if Christ is God, how is it that he grew in wisdom and stature (Luke 2:52)? After all, would he not know all things? How could Christ be one person, both God and human, without a co-mingling of attributes, or in this case, omniscience? Following the *extra Calvinisticum*, that is, the principle of *infinitum non capax finite*, Owen utilizes the Spirit-

68. Pauw, "Supreme Harmony of All," 146 n. 127.
69. Holmes, *God of Grace*, 136.
70. See *WJO* 3:160–63.
71. Trueman, *John Owen*, 93.
72. Pauw, "Supreme Harmony of All," 146–47.

Christologies supplied by Calvin and the early Greek father Didymus of Alexandria to answer such objections from Socinians like John Crellius.[73] For Owen, the answer is found in the role of the Holy Spirit in the incarnation; the Spirit is an agent of communication between the two natures, preserving the integrity of both.

Owen's greatest resource for *Pneumatalogia* was Didymus of Alexandria's classic book *De Spiritu Sancto*. After examining 1 Pet 1:11, which states that the Spirit is the Spirit of Christ, the famous Eastern theologian, appointed head of the school of Alexandria by Athanasius, engages in a discussion about the "union, which the Holy Spirit has to God, and to Christ," and concludes that "it is clearly pointed out, that the Holy Spirit is inseparable from Christ," so that where one is or goes, so does the other.[74] The Spirit, for Didymus, plays an important role in maintaining the integrity of Christ's incarnation:

> In operation the Spirit is one with the Father and the Son, and this oneness of operation involves oneness of essence. He is the Finger of God; the Seal which stamps the Divine image on the human soul . . . He is a Divine Person. He goes forth from the Father, He is sent by the Son . . . as indivisibly one with the Person who sent Him . . . He is not separated from the Father or the Son.[75]

Moreover, communication between the two natures of Christ, according to Didymus, is secured by the role of the Holy Spirit in maintaining the union of the two natures in one person. Owen capitalizes on this conclusion. The Socinian argument is based upon the presupposition that the communication of attributes between natures was of necessity, rather than voluntary. Owen is arguing for a more controlled understanding of the interaction between natures. Thus, at times, Christ's human nature cried out "for light and consolation" upon the cross and at times did not possess, as to the human nature, certain knowledge (e.g. Matt 5:25–34; 24:36; 27:46; Luke 22:42).[76] "The human nature, therefore," writes Owen,

---

73. Crellius, *Touching One God the Father*, 164.

74. Pelikan, *Christian Tradition*, 1:214 (PG 39:1069; *De Spiritu Sancto* 40). The Apostle Peter writes, "the prophets . . . seeking to know what person or time the Spirit of Christ within them was indicating as He predicted the sufferings of Christ and the glories to follow" (1 Pet 1:10–11). For background see Louth, "Fourth-Century Alexandrians," 275–82.

75. *De Spiritu Sancto* 34–37 quoted and translated in Swete, *Holy Spirit in the Ancient Church*, 224.

76. *WJO* 3:161.

"however inconceivably advanced, is not the subject of infinite, essentially divine properties; and the actings of the Son of God toward it, consequential unto its assumption, and that indissoluble subsistence in its union which ensued thereon, are voluntary."[77]

The desire to uphold the Chalcedonian definition is what fueled Owen's emphasis on the role of the Spirit in the incarnation, particularly in reference to the communio idiomatum.[78] The communication between the two natures was left to the role of the Holy Spirit, who is "the immediate operator of all divine acts of the Son himself, even on his own human nature." The works of the Son were not simply a result of the union of the two natures; rather, "whatever the Son of God wrought in, by, or upon the human nature, he did it by the Holy Ghost, who is his Spirit, as he is the Spirit of the Father."[79] When Christ grew in knowledge and power, it was also by the design of the Holy Spirit:

> His divine nature was not unto him in the place of a soul, nor did immediately operate the things which he performed, as some of old vainly imagined; but being a perfect man, his rational soul was in him the immediate principle of all his moral operations, even as ours are in us. Now, in the improvement and exercise of these faculties and powers of his soul, he had and made a progress after the manner of other men; for he was made like unto us "in all things," yet without sin. In their increase, enlargement, and exercise, there was required a progression in grace also; and this he had continually by the Holy Ghost: Luke ii.40, "The child grew and waxed strong in the Spirit."[80]

Christ's human nature was capable of having "*new objects* proposed to its mind and understanding" and "in new trials and temptations he *experimentally* learned of the new exercise of grace," yet "this was the constant work of the Holy Spirit" in his human nature. The work and ministry of Christ was therefore under the constant guidance and dispensation of the Holy Spirit. The Holy Spirit necessarily "anointed him with all those *extraordinary powers and gifts,*" but all actions of the Spirit were consistent with the abilities and limitation of his growing human nature.[81]

---

77. *WJO* 3:161.
78. Ferguson, "John Owen and the Doctrine of the Person of Christ," 90.
79. *WJO* 3:162, 167.
80. *WJO* 3:169.
81. *WJO* 3:170, 171.

It was by the Spirit that Christ was "*guided, directed, comforted, and supported*, in the whole course of his ministry, temptations, obedience, and sufferings."[82] Though a Christian is perpetually being sanctified by the Spirit due to human imperfection, the Spirit's sanctification of Christ is that of maintaining his already perfect state, which the Spirit ensured at his conception and maintained by a *donum superadditum*.[83] Through the Spirit he was able to suffer on the cross, and even while his human body lay in the grave it "continued under the especial care of the Spirit of God" to fulfill the promise that "'his soul should not be left in hell, nor the Holy One see corruption'" (Ps 16:10; Acts 2:31).[84] Even in the resurrection the Holy Spirit was responsible for the glorification of his human nature and Christ's ascension to the right hand of God.[85]

In his notebooks, Edwards picks up on Owen's understanding of the incarnation and applies it to his own theology. "As the union of believers with Christ be by the indwelling of the Spirit of Christ in them," reasons Edwards in "Miscellanies" 487, "so it may be worthy to be considered, whether or no the union of the divine with the human nature of Christ ben't by the Spirit of the Logos dwelling in him after a peculiar manner and without measure."[86] The Holy Spirit, according to Edwards, unites the Logos and the human nature in the incarnation. "If 'tis by the Spirit of God that the human nature of Christ was conceived, and had life and being, why should we not suppose that 'tis also by the Spirit that he has union with the divine nature?"[87]

Owen, as will be seen in the next chapter, also sees Christ's incarnational existence as paralleling what happens in conversion, that is, between the role of the Spirit in the union of Christ's natures and the union of the person to Christ in justifying faith. Edwards agrees with the incarnational analogy, but gives a greater role to the Spirit in the initial forming of a union. "The Spirit of Christ's dwelling in men causes an union," writes Edwards, "so that in many respects [they may be] looked upon as one: perhaps the Spirit of the Logos may dwell in a creature after such a manner, that the creature may become one person [with the

82. *WJO* 3:174.
83. *WJO* 3:168; Owen, *Exercitations on the Epistle to the Hebrews*, 315.
84. *WJO* 3:180.
85. *WJO* 3:183.
86. *WJE* 13:528 ("Misc." 487).
87. *WJE* 13:528, 531 ("Misc." 184).

Logos], and may be looked upon as such and accepted as such." He then concludes:

> In Jesus who dwelt here upon earth, there was immediately only these two things: there was the flesh, or the human nature; and there was the Spirit of Holiness, or the eternal Spirit, by which he was united to the Logos. Jesus who dwelt among us, was as it were compounded of these two; the one from earth, which he received of the Virgin Mary, the other from heaven, which descended on the Virgin at his conception.[88]

The Spirit unites the Trinity in love, he unites the two natures of Christ as one person, he unites Christians in Christ as one body, and in all of this he unites heaven and earth, the higher beauty or excellency and the lower, infinity and the finite.

> All divine communion, or communion of the creatures with God or with one another in God, seems to be by the Holy Ghost. 'Tis by this that believers have communion with Christ, and I suppose 'tis by this that the man Christ Jesus has communion with the eternal Logos. The Spirit of God is the bond of perfectness by which God, Jesus Christ, and the church are united together.[89]

When Edwards writes, as seen in the last chapter, that the Christian possesses all things, including the Trinity, it is this idea that is percolating in his mind. The incarnation closes the gap between God and humanity and by the power of the Spirit makes all one.

As Christ could be considered one person, because of the work of the Spirit, but still have two natures, so also Christians are united to Christ as one body with him. He is their "head," says Edwards, and they are his "members," but they are nevertheless "one."[90] And if they are one with Christ, and in Christ "dwells the fullness of the Godhead bodily" (Col 2:9), then it stands to reason that the Christian is one with the Trinity in some sense. Edwards writes in "Miscellanies" 376 that Christian communion with the Trinity "consists" in their communion with the Holy Spirit. This is "the bond of perfectness."[91]

---

88. *WJE* 13:530, 531, 532 ("Misc." 184).
89. *WJE* 13:529–30, 528 ("Misc." 487).
90. Ibid.
91. *WJE* 13:448 ("Misc." 376). The language is very close to "Miscellanies" 487.

By the strength of this union, Christians share in the death of Christ: "this is done by the union of the persons with Christ's person: they are made so much one that his death belongs to them; they own it, it is their death, in as proper a sense as Adam's sin is their sin—they sin in Adam and they die in Christ."[92] According to this same line of thought, Edwards concludes that if the grave could not hold Christ, it cannot hold the saint either. By virtue of their union, they must be resurrected.[93] Part of Christ's body, after all, cannot remain in the grave. "Union or oneness with God is requisite in order to a person's righteousness being accepted by God for another that has no righteousness," says Edwards in his sermon *The Threefold Work of the Holy Ghost* (1729). But Christ has "the divine nature and excellencies," he continues, "he had an infinite worthiness, and so was worthy not only to be accepted for himself, but for others."[94] The distinction between Christ and his people is one of paradox; Edwards's incarnational language as applied to the Christian and discussions of the possession of Christ's righteousness by the sinner are inherently Chalcedonian (as will be seen in the next chapter), affirming both distinction and union between the individual and Christ.

At his conversion, Edwards discovered the beauty and love of God. He felt his mind opened to the divine being and he finally began to connect the dots. The sinner is cut off, unable to see the beauty of this excellency by virtue of a sinful nature inherited from Adam. When the person is regenerated, he or she can see and embrace the beauty of the eternal God through Christ and enjoy it. Spirit-Christology leads to Spirit-Conversion; the incarnation serves as an analogy for Edwards's conversion.

It makes sense to Edwards why, when he was converted, he would see the divine being emanating in creation and sustaining it. It also makes sense as to why he reads Scripture differently. The human and divine in Christ were joined together as one personality, one mind. The Christian is also united to the mind and being of God; he or she truly possesses all that the divine being possesses. As he writes:

> The man Jesus becomes one person by a communion of knowledge and will; but as in believers all divine knowledge is by the Spirit—'tis by the Spirit that the knowledge of inspiration and

---

92. *WJE* 13:380 ("Misc." 281).
93. *WJE* 13:304 ("Misc." 155).
94. *WJE* 14:401.

> prophecy is given, and 'tis by the Holy Ghost that the spiritual knowledge of all believers is given: "The Spirit searcheth all things, even the deep things of God" [1 Cor 2:10]—so, I suppose, 'tis by the Spirit that divine knowledge and consciousness is given to the man Jesus.[95]

Thus, if Edwards understands himself as directly united to that being, how could he ignore it? How could the young, energized theologian not approach nearly everything differently? Whether he walked through the fields, soaking in the warmth of the sun, the sound of wind whistling between the branches, or whether he picked through the words of Scripture, Edwards believed he saw it through divine eyes. His soul was raised from mere earthly shadows into the beauty and consent of the heavenly and divine. He understood that there were limitations—some, like Christ, were natural due to his human nature—yet his Spirit-Christology provided an incarnational answer.

Moving Forward to Maturity

In 1730, following years of intensely studying conversion and Scripture, Edwards would consider pulling these themes and notes into one book. He would jot down a short outline of a potential book, titled "A Rational Account of the Main Doctrines of the Christian Religion":

> 1. The being and nature of God
> 2. Of created minds, free will, etc.
> 3. Of excellency
>   Trinity, and God's attributes
>   God's decrees; necessity, contingency, etc.
> Creation: the ends of it.
>   Things made in analogy to spiritual things. Treat the fall of angels after the fall of man.
> Faith, or a right believing of divine truths
> Faith in Christ
> Free Grace
> Justification[96]

The pattern of this outline, reflecting the development of his thought, leads curiously into the topic of justification. Justification, which became the focus of his *Quaestio* in the 1720s, will be an inevitable highlight

---

95. *WJE* 13:530 ("Misc." 487).
96. *WJE* 6:397, 398.

just a few years later in 1734–1735, during which Edwards preaches a series of revival sermons on the subject, capping it off in 1738 with his now famous treatise, *Justification by Faith Alone*. In this work, the crafty theologian comes full circle with his early crisis. Moreover, during this time, Jonathan Edwards will become the premier American theologian and an international icon.

5

The Incarnational Spirituality of the Mature Edwards

> They have spiritual excellency and joy by a kind of participation in God. They are made excellent by a communication of God's excellency: God puts his own beauty, i.e. his beautiful likeness, upon their souls.
>
> —Jonathan Edwards, *God Glorified in Man's Dependence* (1730/31)[1]

> Christ is not only the legal head of the saints. As their head, he is their representative, and their head of government, but also their virtual head, their head of influence and communication, and that both of holiness and happiness . . . so that they enjoy all things in him . . . partaking with him.
>
> —Jonathan Edwards, "The Terms of Prayer" (1738)[2]

ON A BUSY DAY in Boston in July 1731, Jonathan Edwards stood before a packed crowd of clergy and Harvard graduates to deliver what would eventually become his first published sermon, *God Glorified in Man's Dependence*. Its message was the culmination of a decade of his theological musings and foreshadowed the eventual Arminian scare that would soon fill the towns surrounding Northampton. Fears of Arminian sympathizers within the pulpits, like Cutler, were solidified by perceptions of Harvard as a Latitudinarian school. Yale also continued to be the subject of constant scrutiny. Given this, Edwards's choice of

1. *WJE* 17:208.
2. *WJE* 19:779.

subject—emphasizing human dependence on God—was pointed, and with its timely publication he became a national figure.[3]

In the immediate years following this sermon, Edwards returned to the study of justification by faith alone, the same subject that he was drawn to in his years at Yale under Cutler. This became his preemptive measure against a possible Arminian surge in the region and led to a new stage in his public career; he was now a revivalist. By 1734–1735 he developed a series of sermons on justification that led to a revival in Northampton and hurled Edwards from the national scene into the who's who of international theologians. The success of the revival was so great that shortly before what would be called the Great Awakening, he republished the justification sermons in a revised discourse under the title *Justification by Faith Alone*.

In *Justification by Faith Alone* Edwards engages in a difficult theological dance undoubtedly indebted to his evolving conclusions on union with Christ or participation in the divine being. On the one hand, he argues (as classic Reformed theologians often do) that the sinner has nothing to bring to the table; on the other hand, he insists that the sinner has everything possessed by God. Moreover, while many Reformed theologians were more comfortable using only forensic and imputational terms when speaking about justification by faith, Edwards was willing to allude to much more. "'Tis in and by Christ that we have righteousness," he writes, "'tis by being in him that we are justified, have our sins pardoned, and are received as righteous into God's favor. 'Tis by Christ that we have sanctification: we have in him true excellency of heart, as well as of understanding; and he is made unto us inherent as well as imputed righteousness."[4]

Edwards's return to, and fascination with, justification demonstrates just how connected it was to his overall understanding of faith and what makes or breaks a doctrine of salvation. Justification is, in the words of Ava Chamberlain, "the central organizing concept of his soteriology" during this period (stretching loosely from 1731–1742).[5] That he returned to justification in both sermon and book form is a testimony

---

3. Marsden, *Jonathan Edwards*, 140; Murray, *Jonathan Edwards*, 107–9; *WJE*: 17:196; Goodwin, "Myth," 213–37; Chamberlain, "Theology of Cruelty," 335–56.

4. *WJE* 17:201.

5. *WJE* 18:37, 38.

to the lasting internal impact of his conversion crisis and theological conclusions.

Though published two and half centuries ago, his *Justification* discourse still drives significant scholarly interest, particularly in the area of Edwards's most controversial statement, found therein: "What is real in the union between Christ and his people, is the foundation of what is legal, that is, it is something really in them, and between them, uniting them." What has yet to be shown is the way his conversion experience and historical context inform this bold statement.

Edwards has in mind at least three important factors when discussing union with Christ. First, the redeemed soul's spiritual union with Christ, the second Adam, follows an incarnational analogy. Second, there is a strong parallel between this union with Christ and the union that exists between the unredeemed sinner and the first Adam of Genesis. And third, the Christian has nothing to bring to his or her salvation despite possessing everything—including the justifying righteousness of that salvation—due to union with Christ and the resulting participation in the total divine being.

In the *Justification* text, Edwards formalizes many of the ideas he ruminated on in his notes in previous years resulting from his conversion crisis, and for the first time, he publicly portrays in some form the importance of divine participation or union with Christ as it relates to the concerns of justification and spiritual experience.

Historical Setting

From 1730 on, Edwards continued his theological development with significant strength. While his intellectual accomplishments up to this time were noteworthy, his mind showed no signs of slowing down. He was seriously concerned with two potential threats: an incipient Arminianism and a lax antinomianism. As had occurred during his time at Yale, Arminianism was rumored to be invading congregations in New England. By 1734, this fear—a typical Reformed concern—materialized in substantive ways. If in the 1720s Cutler was the symbol of the devil's handiwork, in the 1730s the devil's name was Robert Breck.

Arminianism and Robert Breck

The Latitudinarian Arminianism or Anglicanism of the Timothy Cutler years continued to grow in New England in the 1730s.[6] This is a theology that emphasized the "candle of the Lord." While not a full-breed Arminianism, the type of synergism that marked the Arminianism of the Remonstrance is all the New Englanders needed to be concerned. It is to this Arminian Anglicanism that Cutler defected and to which Edwards was exposed, as Anglican books such as those by John Tillotson began to fill the libraries of Yale and Harvard.

From his early years, Edwards (like others in New England) read John Tillotson's sermons and, as seen before, found them insightful at times but also occasionally flawed. For example, when Edwards discusses the union of the believer to Christ in his published edition of *Justification by Faith Alone*, he quotes Tillotson favorably, even if he is said also to be "one of the greatest divines on the other side of the question in hand."[7] Not all of Edwards's contemporaries were as nuanced. Jonathan Parsons, a Yale graduate, recalled how at one time he was enamored with "Arminian principles" under the influence of his reading of Archbishop Tillotson.[8] Books always have been feared by some as a potential source of corruption, and New England ministers never hesitated to warn their congregations about those books they found disagreeable.[9] When Edwards wrote his *Quaestio*, Arminian emphasis on faith and repentance as a requirement for God's work of salvation took center stage. Much the same, he is concerned with countering this type of Arminian

---

6. Early discussions on Arminianism in New England concluded that it was hybrid of Calvinism and Arminianism (see Miller, "Preparation for Salvation," 253–86), but by the 1970s it became apparent that it was in fact a popular form of Anglican Latitudinarianism (see Goodwin, "Myth," 215–37).

7. *WJE* 19:155; see also Norman Fiering's discussion on Edwards's response to Tillotson's sermon on hell. "Tillotson," writes Fiering, "is a representative of a trend toward the general softening of Calvinist teaching insofar as it had a grip on the Anglican church . . ." (Fiering, *Jonathan Edwards's Moral Thought*, 227).

8. Quoted in Goodwin ("Myth," 219) and originally from a letter of Jonathan Parsons to Thomas Prince written on April 14, 1744.

9. See, for example, White, *New England's Lamentations*, which warns of books on free will. Berkeley's collection of books given as a gift to Yale in 1732 was considered a potential attempt to tip the scales toward Latitudinarian Arminianism at the school (Marsden, *Jonathan Edwards*, 139).

synergism in his *Justification* discourse, not by dismissing faith, but by narrowly defining its role as a condition of salvation.

In the 1730s, synergism was considered a key Arminian trait, and it was also believed to be a type of gateway doctrine, leading to a slippery-slope of theological errors. Edwards was socially active in keeping Arminianism out of the New England pulpits. New England was behind the times, as George Marsden notes: "That Deism and antitrinitarianism should be beyond the New England pale was understandable, but to be still fighting against 'Arminianism' in this age of high moral ideals could be seen as pitifully provincial."[10] The New England fixation on Arminianism, however, may not be as "provincial" as it may seem; a living, local example seemed to underscore the implied connection between Arminianism and Deism. In the 1730s, the church of Springfield called Robert Breck to be their pastor. The situation drew furor from other ministers, who cautioned against Breck's unorthodox opinions. It is the Breck case that Edwards has foremost on his mind when he gives his sermons on justification by faith alone in Northampton in 1734–1735.[11]

Around 1733 to 1734, when Breck was asked to pastor the Springfield congregation, the Williamses, most notably William Williams, quickly opposed it. Breck had reportedly rejected the idea that God would condemn those who had not heard the gospel.[12] It was reported that he spoke approvingly of Thomas Chubb, an English Arian, but he also was willing to agree to the Westminster Confession. Breck denied all accusations, but he was still challenged by the Hampshire Association, a gathering of Hampshire County ministers who believed it was their responsibility (among many others) to promote the purity of New England theology. As a member of this association, Edwards, too, joined the voices against Breck, and the affair led to a long and intense fight. A series of letters back and forth from the Association to Breck seek a show of evidence for Breck's orthodoxy or for an answer to their concerns.[13] Springfield

10. Marsden, *Jonathan Edwards*, 139.
11. Jones, "Impolitic Mr. Edwards," 64–79.
12. *WJE* 12:6.
13. *WJE* 16:58–64. See letters from Edwards to the Association (e.g. to "Col. John Pynchon et al," on August 7, 1735; to "Capt. William Pynchon, Jr." on August 14, 1735; to "Col. John Pynchon" on August 14, 1735; to "Capt. William Pynchon, Jr." on August 26, 1735; and to "The Reverend Samuel Hopkins (of Springfield)" in November of 1735).

Church ignored the concerns and called Breck to their pulpit. It was Edwards who was asked to write the Hampshire Association's official letter of defense of their position against Breck in 1737.

Edwards's biographers have largely understood this scene to represent a reaction to Arminianism, but Robert Brown has argued that there is also the added element of deistic fears in the Breck case.[14] Brown notes that Thomas Clap, a Windham, Connecticut minister, vowed to block Breck's ordination: "Clap's letter concerning his own conversations with Breck asserts that Breck had denied two passages in the New Testament (John 8:1–11 and 1 John 5:7–8) were inspired because they were spurious additions to the text."[15] Clap argued that Breck rejected God's ability to preserve the biblical text. In a pre-critical period, challenging the biblical text was a sign of Deism.

How important this aspect of Deism was to Edwards at this time is unknown. What is clear, however, is that he was thoroughly disturbed by the assertions that Breck was Arminian, and wanted to ward off any rising Arminianism before it had its expected nefarious effect. When writing his *A Faithful Narrative of the Surprising Work of God*, an account of the revival that occurred under his preaching in Northampton, Edwards accounts for the factors leading up to the revival, especially "the great noise that was in this part of the country about Arminianism."[16] The ministers of the area were disturbed by the thought of the competing theological system and what it might do to the orthodoxy of the church. Writes Edwards:

> The friends of vital piety trembled for fear of the issue; but it seemed, contrary to their fear, strongly to be overruled for the promoting of religion. Many who looked on themselves as in a Christless condition, seemed to be awakened by it, with fear that God was about to withdraw from the land, and that we should be given to heterodoxy and corrupt principles; and that then their opportunity for obtaining salvation would be past; and many who were brought a little to doubt about the truth of the doctrines they had hitherto been taught, seemed to have a kind of a trembling fear with their doubts, lest they should be led into bypaths, to their eternal undoing: and they seemed with much concern and engagedness of mind, to inquire what was indeed

14. Brown, *Jonathan Edwards and the Bible*, 20.
15. Ibid., 21.
16. *WJE* 4:148.

the way in which they must come to be accepted with God. There were then some things said publicly on that occasion concerning justification by faith alone.[17]

When Edwards responded to this incipient Arminianism with his lectures on justification by faith, a revival broke out in Northampton. He attributed the revival to God's approval of his teaching on the doctrine and, consequently, God's rejection of Arminianism.[18] Justification by faith alone would therefore continue to have an appeal for him, and he would revise these sermons in 1738 under the title of his *Justification by Faith Alone* discourse.

The Antinomian Ghost of Anne Hutchinson

In the 1730s, Edwards's main concern was primarily Arminianism, but as Samuel T. Logan writes, "in the shadows of the Northampton meetinghouse lurked another threat, a threat of almost exactly one hundred years duration in New England Puritanism," namely, antinomianism.[19] Both Arminianism and antinomianism were concerns for Edwards in developing his doctrine of justification by faith alone. If Arminianism represented a works-earned salvation for Edwards, antinomianism was the other extreme; that is, it resisted works as evidence of salvation in favor of the inner-light of the Spirit only.

In the 1630s, Anne Hutchinson, a member of John Cotton's Boston church, had been the face of antinomianism and was tried as a heretic for her views. Her views were based on her understanding of Cotton's teachings, though he rejected that connection. Recording the nature of the theological disagreement in his journal (though undoubtedly not without bias), John Winthrop writes:

> One Mrs. Hutchinson, a member of the church of Boston, a woman of a ready wit and bold spirit, brought over with her two dangerous errors: 1. That the person of the Holy Ghost dwells in a justified person. 2. That no sanctification can help to evidence to us our justification.—From these two grew many branches; as, 1. Our union with the Holy Ghost, so as a Christian remains dead to every spiritual action, and hath no gifts or graces, other

---

17. *WJE* 4:148.
18. *WJE* 4:116; Jonathan Edwards, *Five Discourses*, ii.
19. Logan, "Doctrine of Justification," 27.

than such are in hypocrites, nor any other sanctification but the Holy Ghost himself.[20]

In an attempt to emphasize the dependence of the person on God and to remove any potential attribution of salvation to the ability of the person, Hutchinson and her followers argued that other ministers were making too strong of a connection between justification and works of sanctification. To argue that the works of sanctification were evidence of salvation, she believed, served as a form of legalism and ignored the necessity of grace.[21]

For the Puritan, works of sanctification were a necessary evidence of one's conversion by grace, a belief that finds its roots in John Calvin's teaching on the twofold grace or *duplex gratia*. "Christ was given to us by God's generosity, to be grasped and possessed by us in faith," according to Calvin. "By partaking of him, we principally receive a double grace: namely, that being reconciled to God through Christ's blamelessness, we may have in heaven instead of a Judge a gracious Father; and secondly, that sanctified by Christ's spirit we may cultivate blamelessness and purity of life."[22] Both justifying and sanctifying graces are Christ's and are applied to a person by the Holy Spirit. The person's union with Christ not only makes justification possible, but sanctification inevitable; both are the result of grace.[23] Without works, objected the Puritans who agreed with Calvin, individuals are left without any means of knowing if they are truly saved.

Ministers do not need to look for evidence of sanctification, responded Hutchinson. The Holy Spirit abides in the person, acting directly on the soul, indubitably confirming whether someone is truly a Christian or not.[24] Regeneration is a spiritual transformation that gives the soul a God's-eye view of one's spiritual state.[25]

Antinomianism was still alive in the 1730s. In 1734, William Rand, a friend of Breck and a minister of Sunderland, promoted antinomian

---

20. Winthrop, *Winthrop's Journal*, 195–96.
21. Hall, *Antinomian Controversy*, 6.
22. *ICR* 3.11.1.
23. Stoever, "Nature, Grace and John Cotton," 25, 26.
24. *WJE* 12:34; see Winthrop's *Short Story*, in Hall, *Antinomian Controversy*, 238–39.
25. Stoever, "Nature, Grace and John Cotton," 31; Stoever, *Faire and Easie Way to Heaven*, 162.

views, though some confused his antinomianism with Arminianism.[26] Edwards's sermons on justification in 1734–1735 were now more complicated than during his younger years at Yale as he had both so-called heresies to resist. In order to combat Arminianism, he had to remove the necessity of works, but in order to fight antinomianism, he had to maintain their necessity.

In a culture of suspicion, finding that balance requires walking an intellectual tightrope. Edwards's emphasis on the great role of the Spirit in conversion, for example, could have resulted in an antinomian-like, inner-light conclusion. As seen before (in "Miscellanies" 487), Edwards paralleled the role of the Spirit in incarnation with the role of the Spirit in the believer's union with Christ. As the "man Jesus" was one person by "a communion of knowledge and will," so also believers have direct access to spiritual knowledge by the Spirit.[27] In 1733, two years after preaching *God Glorified in Man's Dependence*, he preached his *A Divine and Supernatural Light* on Matt 16:17 ("And Jesus answered and said unto him, Blessed art thou, Simon Barjona: for flesh and blood hath not revealed it unto thee, but my father which is in heaven"). The content of *A Divine and Supernatural Light* is heavy on the internal testimony of the Spirit, and because of this Ava Chamberlain suggests that Edwards's theology contains a "latent antinomianism."[28]

In Edwards's day, this latent antinomianism did not go unnoticed. Charles Chauncy, a popular minister at the First Church in Boston, was deeply concerned that the New England revivalism found in Edwards's own church would lead to antinomianism. The revivalist "mistakes the workings of his own passions for divine communications," wrote Chauncy, "and fancies himself immediately inspired by the SPIRIT of GOD, when all the while, he is under no other influence than that of an over-heated imagination."[29]

While Edwards most likely did not intend antinomianism to be the result of his theology, within little time after the revivals at Northampton he at least recognized a form of practical antinomianism emerging in his church, and this drove him to new conclusions.[30] His congregation

26. The diary of minister Stephen Williams, quoted in *WJE* 4:17.
27. See nos. 489, 540, 628, 630.
28. *WJE* 18:24.
29. Chauncy, *Enthusiasm Described*, 3.
30. *WJE* 18:20.

no longer demonstrated good works as they did during the height of the revival, as Edwards sees it. The decrease in conversions and commitment to religion in general in the years following 1734–1735 led him to emphasize the inseparable connection between justification and sanctification (also called perseverance). "Happy would it be for us," writes Edwards in his original preface to *Justification by Faith Alone*, "if God should bless what is here printed, so to revive the Memory of the past great Work of God amongst us, and the lively impressions and Sense of Divine Things that persons then had on their Minds, and to cause us to lament our Declensions. . . ."[31] Demonstrable good works provided evidence of the Spirit's work in revivals, as he was beginning to see it, and left less to, in the words of Chauncy, the "over-heated imagination."

The perceived threats of Arminianism and antinomianism in the late 1730s helped set the stage for Edwards's revamped and published *Justification by Faith Alone* discourse in 1738. In it he continues his tightrope walk over difficult theological territory, hoping to avoid landing in either of these camps by formulating several theological nuances that lead to an inevitable incarnational analogy.

Justification Comes Full Circle

Edwards's first balancing act comes in discussing the role of faith. "But to him that worketh not, but believeth on him that justifieth the ungodly, his faith is counted for righteousness," says Rom 4:5 in Edwards's King James Version. This text, the focus of Edwards's *Justification by Faith Alone* discourse, appears to leave Paul with an inevitable contradiction. Justification does not include works, yet "faith is counted for righteousness." Is faith a work? For Edwards, as seen in the previous chapter, *faith* is equal to *cordial consent*. It is essential for union with Christ. But is it a work?

Understanding the nature of faith is a first step in getting at Edwards's concept of union with Christ. Immediately appealing to his Reformed tradition, he argues against any implication that God accepts faith as a work by insisting that faith is first accomplished by God's work and that God cannot accept an "imperfect righteousness."[32] As he says

---

31. Edwards, *Five Discourses*, vi.

32. As Edwards writes: "the phrase, as the Apostle uses it here, and in the context, manifestly imports, that God of his sovereign grace is pleased in his dealings with the sinner, to take and regard, that which indeed is not righteousness, and in one that has

about this passage in his "Blank Bible," God has no "respect to any goodness or righteousness at all in faith."[33]

As far as seeing faith as a work, then, Edwards is classically Protestant. Throughout the *Justification by Faith Alone* discourse, he eagerly divests the person of any power or merit, including the act of faith. While the "by" before "faith alone" implies faith is a condition, Edwards is only willing to accept that faith is a sort of "condition." Faith according to Edwards is something simpler; "faith in this Mediator is that which renders it a meet and suitable thing, in the sight of God, that the believer rather than others should have this purchased benefit assigned to him."[34] This perspective is driven by Edwards's discussion on *excellency* and *consent* (discussed in the previous chapter):

> God in his constitutions, doubtless appears much in the fitness and beauty of them, so that those things are established to be done that are fit to be done, and that these things are connected in his constitution, that are agreeable one to another: so God justifies a believer according to his revealed constitution, without doubt, because he sees something in this qualification, that as the case stands, renders it a fit thing that such should be justified . . .[35]

Consent between parts of a thing or consent of will between persons is a form of beauty or symmetry and makes up excellency. Faith is such consenting. Without such symmetry, there can be no union between the Christian and Christ and, therefore, no divine participation.

Edwards's word for this type of symmetry in his *Justification* discourse is "fitness," particularly in two categories of *natural fitness* and *moral fitness* that help make his point:

> There is a two-fold fitness to a state; I know not how to give them distinguishing names otherwise than by calling the one a *moral*, and the other a *natural* fitness: a person has a moral fitness for a state, when his moral excellency commends him to it. . . . A person has a natural fitness for a state when it appears meet and condecent that he should be in such a state or circumstances, only from the natural concord or agreeableness there is between such

---

no righteousness, so that the consequence shall be the same as if he had righteousness" (*WJE* 19:148). See also Logan, "Doctrine of Justification," 36, 39.

33. *WJE* 24:993; see also his comments on Rom 4:3–4 in *WJE* 15:90.

34. *WJE* 19:153.

35. *WJE* 19:154.

qualifications and such circumstances; not because the qualifications are lovely or unlovely, but only because the qualifications, and the circumstances are like one another, or do in their nature suit and agree or unite one another.[36]

In other words, with *moral fitness*, there is something excellent in the person alone that demands to be regarded as righteous, in and of itself. With *natural fitness*, there is nothing in the person that demands that regard; rather it is a matter of two things belonging together by nature. For example, a stone ball may fall to the ground because it is on a planet with a significant gravitational field. When one drops the ball, it is only the nature of things that it should fall, but there is nothing in the ball that demands it fall; take away the relationship to the planet and it floats weightlessly. The two by nature are suitable for a certain outcome (i.e., the ball falling to the ground).

When discussing natural fitness, Edwards has in mind the agreeableness of consent, that is, two persons that consent mutually are united together by it; and for God, faith as consent unites the person to Christ. "And thus it is that faith is that qualification in any person," writes Edwards, "that renders it meet in the sight of God that he should be looked upon as having Christ's satisfaction and righteousness belonging to him, viz. because that *in* him, which, on his part, makes up this union between him and Christ."[37] Faith unites the person to Christ and therefore his righteousness, but only as a matter of natural fitness. "God," says Edwards, "don't give those that believe, an union *with*, or an interest *in* the Savior, in reward for faith, but only because faith is the soul's active uniting with Christ, or is itself the very act of union, on their part."[38]

All of this seems fairly benign, and in light of what Edwards is writing, when he makes his now infamous aforementioned statement ("what is real in the union between Christ and his people, is the foundation of what is legal; that is, it is something really in them, and between them, uniting them, that is the ground of the suitableness of their being accounted as one by the Judge") it should naturally be understood as coming from this context of consent making persons one.[39] And because of this understanding of faith, Edwards can safely insist that all humans

36. *WJE* 19:159.
37. *WJE* 19:156.
38. *WJE* 19:158.
39. *WJE* 19:158.

are justified and in union with Christ without any contribution of their own.[40] Yet there is a sense in which, while Edwards is eliminating the idea of justification as the result of righteousness possessed by the sinner, he nevertheless is allowing for some righteousness really abiding "in" and "between" both Christ and his people. It is a righteousness that the Christian possesses.

Reformation-era Protestants rejected any theology in which the justifying righteousness of Christ is *infused* or *inherent* in the person being justified. Righteousness is understood by the Reformers as being imputed and alien to the person being justified. Edwards's famous statement that *what is real is the foundation of what is legal* between the person and Christ, however, seems to imply more than a mere declaration of righteousness by God.

To make matters more complicated, in this same discourse Edwards understands the "etymology" of being "justified" as "*to make righteous, or to pass one for righteous in judgment*."[41] The words "make righteous" were removed from subsequent editions, likely by editors who fretted that such wording endorsed a form of infused righteousness; the inclusion of an infused righteousness would imply some form of inherent good on the part of the one justified, sounding too Catholic for comfort. Justification, as Edwards sees it, is more than the mere forgiveness of sins; it is being "admitted to communion in, or participation of the justification" of Christ.[42] Similarly, in Edwards's sermon series on 1 Cor 13, *Charity and Its Fruits*, he speaks of the "infusion" of grace. Like his *Justification by Faith Alone* discourse, in *Charity and Its Fruits*, Tryon Edwards (Edwards's grandson) is known for having removed his grandfather's references to *infusion* because of the implications of inherent righteousness or making righteous.[43]

Edwards establishes a very complicated relationship between the person and Christ when he writes that "what is real is the foundation of what is legal." Since justification is based on faith, and faith makes the sinner and Christ *one* in every sense of the word, then the sinner

---

40. *WJE* 19:149.

41. *WJE* 19:150 (emphasis mine). Other editions have "which signifies to pass one for righteous in judgment, but also manifestly agreeable to the force of the word as used in Scripture" (Edwards, *Works*, 1:623 [Dwight edition]).

42. *WJE* 19:151.

43. *WJE* 8:739–50.

is swimming in the glory of Christ and participating in everything that is his. In that sense, when God declares the person righteous based on Christ, it is because, in some way, he or she possesses the righteousness of Christ that brings justification.[44]

The Missing Incarnational Connection

Returning to Edwards's incarnational parallel made in the previous chapter—that as the divine and human are united in Christ to form one person, so also the human Christian is united to the divine Christ to form one body—the nature of the phrase "what is real is the foundation of what is legal" in his *Justification* discourse can now be explored. What amounts to a passing statement in his justification discourse has led to a good deal of spent ink and debate in the last few years. Unfortunately, the focus of scholars on the nature of what Edwards means by "what is real" has led most to miss an important connection to the incarnation.

While the literature on the subject is extensive and there is no need to go into every contribution here, some brief background of the discussion is necessary.[45] The serious questions surrounding the above statement were first raised by Thomas A. Schafer in his 1951 article, "Jonathan Edwards and Justification by Faith." Schafer writes:

> What, then, of the "legal union" of the soul with Christ which is concerned with the imputation of Christ's righteousness? Faith, says Edwards, by constituting a vital natural union, renders it "fit" and suitable that Christ and the believer should be treated as one "legally" and that the righteousness of one should be imputed to the other. But the natural creates the legal, not vice

---

44. *WJE* 14:402–3.

45. For a more thorough reading, I point the reader to the current literature. Leading this discussion is McDermott, in his book *Jonathan Edwards Confronts the Gods*. Other engagements of this subject include Morimoto, *Jonathan Edwards and the Catholic Vision of Salvation*; McDermott, "Possibility of Reconciliation," 173–202; Withrow, "Jonathan Edwards as a Resource"; Gilbert, "Nations Will Worship," 53–76; McDermott, "Response to Gilbert," 77–80; Withrow, "Jonathan Edwards and Justification," 93–109 (Part One); Withrow, "Jonathan Edwards and Justification," 98–111 (Part Two); Bombaro, "Jonathan Edwards' Vision of Salvation," 45–67; Caldwell, "Holy Spirit as the Bond of Union," 162–68; McDermott, "Jonathan Edwards on Justification," 119–38; Hunsinger, "Dispositional Soteriology," 107–20; Bombaro, "Dispositional Peculiarity, History, and Edwards's Evangelistic Appeal to Self-Love," 121–57; Waddington, "Jonathan Edwards's 'Ambiguous and Somewhat Precarious' Doctrine of Justification?," 357–72.

> versa; something really existing in the soul precedes the external imputation . . .⁴⁶

According to Schafer, Edwards insists that something real is in the person and forms the basis for the forensic declaration of justification. Edwards is presenting sanctification before justification and, writes Schafer, insists on an element of "holiness" in the soul before holiness is in action. Faith must flow from something; therefore there is something in the soul before justification, namely, love. Love is an infused virtue in the soul that leads to faith, according to Schafer's interpretation; it is God's "irresistible regenerating grace."⁴⁷ Schafer believes that this implies that this love alone is acceptable for God.⁴⁸

> God therefore takes real delight in the good principles and acts of the saints; not because there is "merit" in them (that is really beside the point), but because the love wherewith they love him is simply his own love reflected and returned to him. It is not, therefore, by the doctrine of imputed righteousness that Edwards prefers to safeguard human dependence and divine glory; rather it is by the doctrine of "infused grace."⁴⁹

Schafer offers the necessary theological qualifications about faith not being a work and recognizes Edwards's distinction between natural and moral fitness.⁵⁰ Nevertheless, he concludes that Edwards "was evidently not worried about making inherent states and qualities in the soul conditions of salvation so long as they were relieved of all meritorious connotations," and therefore went beyond the doctrine of the Reformers "to the 'real' acts and relations which underlie it."⁵¹

Scholars have wondered about Schafer's "inherent states and qualities in the soul." The highly praised work by Sang Hyun Lee, *The Philosophical Theology of Jonathan Edwards*, opened the door for this continued discussion.⁵² To get at this "state" of being, Lee's book centers

---

46. Schafer, "Jonathan Edwards and Justification by Faith," 58.
47. Ibid., 64.
48. Ibid., 67–68.
49. Ibid., 61.
50. Ibid., 58.
51. Ibid., 59, 64.
52. In recent years a few scholars have challenged the conclusions of Lee. While any theory is open for revision, for purposes of this book—and as a full evaluation of Lee is outside the scope of this book—I plan to argue from the premise that Lee's

on Edwards's understanding of the nature of a disposition, also known as a habit in medieval philosophy. The "real that is the foundation of the legal" is, according to Lee, a gracious disposition.

What is a gracious disposition? According to Lee, a disposition is something akin to a natural law. As seen earlier, Edwards believes that matter has no inherent solidity; it receives solidity from the power of God. That all existence coheres by the power of God, namely, the Spirit, could lead one to conclude that God is all there is. Given this, what keeps Edwards from becoming pantheistic or panentheistic? According to Lee, a disposition or habit is what separates creation from Creator.

Edwards is borrowing from his contemporary, the scientist Isaac Newton, whose mechanistic universe was driven by absolute laws.[53] "Dispositions or habits," writes Lee, ". . . take on the character of laws for Edwards in that they actively and prescriptively govern the occurrences and characters of events and actions."[54] A habit or disposition, writes Edwards, is "only a law that God has fixed, that such actions upon such occasions should be exerted."[55] According to Edwards, while matter's solidity is "from the immediate exercise of divine power," the permanence of matter is "according to certain conditions which we call the laws of motion."[56] By God's established and permanent "laws of nature" we can trust that if the moon orbits Earth today, it will tomorrow as well. This gives the moon and Earth, despite cohering by the power of God, a sense of their own separate and stable existence. They avoid the possibility of simply becoming, pantheistically speaking, the same as God.

As there are dispositions or laws for the physical universe, there are also dispositions or laws at play in the spiritual domain. Laws, says Edwards in "The Mind," "constitute all permanent being in created things, both corporeal and spiritual."[57] A spiritual disposition is the law of one's spiritual nature to be inclined to act one way or another in any particular circumstance. A spiritual law or disposition for an unregenerate person, as Edwards sees it, is to flee from God and toward sin. In

---

essential points are valid. For those interested in more, I suggest reading Holmes, "Does Jonathan Edwards Use a Dispositional Ontology?" 99–114.

53. Lee, *Philosophical Theology of Jonathan Edwards*, 49; WJE 21:6.
54. WJE 21:7.
55. WJE 13:358 ("Misc." 241).
56. WJE 6:216.
57. WJE 6:391.

order for the soul to embrace Christ in faith, be united, and justified, it must have a disposition or spiritual law of *believing* in place prior to the exercise of faith. This law is what Edwards calls a believing disposition, grace, or the Holy Spirit. The real that is the foundation of what is legal is such a gracious disposition or law in Edwards's theology. Faith is therefore the presence of a disposition to believe, a disposition which has no substance of its own, but must be upheld by God through the abiding presence of the Holy Spirit.

Following Lee, Anri Morimoto added significant fuel to the fire with his highly controversial *Jonathan Edwards and the Catholic Vision of Salvation*, which portrays Edwards as a very Catholic Protestant. "By 'what is real,'" writes Morimoto, "he means not the reality of sanctification, but the reality of the union 'between Christ and his people' established by this active consenting of the believer."[58] Morimoto understands Edwards to not relinquish forensic justification; this is his nod to Edwards's Protestant background. Nevertheless, as his title suggests, he is interested in pointing out areas in which Edwards's vision of salvation is Catholic. In doing so, Morimoto suggests that what is "real" is established by faith, and faith is a "virtuous disposition" or "habit" that exists in the soul prior to justification.

This debate functions much like the medieval discussion of *gratia increata* (uncreated grace) and *gratia creata* (created grace). The first, *gratia increata*, is the conclusion of the medieval theologian Peter Lombard, and implies that there is nothing intrinsically worthy in the person being justified. The presence of a gracious habit or disposition (or in this case, law) in the person is the Holy Spirit himself. The second option, according to Thomas Aquinas, is that grace is both *gratia increata* and *gratia creata*. By adding *gratia creata*, the person possesses the grace in the soul; grace does not simply belong to another party, such as the Holy Spirit. This means that the person experiences a real change ontologically, and that is the "real" in union that is the basis of the "legal." To conclude that Edwards intended *gratia creata* causes significant problems for his Protestant friends. If one is justified due to nothing of one's nature, as Protestants insist, then to have justifying grace infused into one's soul, as a law of spiritual nature possessed by the person and not belonging only to God, is not the justifying of the ungodly found in Romans.

58. Morimoto, *Jonathan Edwards and the Catholic Vision of Salvation*, 90.

According to Morimoto, there is a goodness prior to justification and that goodness is a newly created disposition in the soul of the individual:

> Edwards put strong emphasis on the active role of faith in justification, and he did not deny the existence of goodness and holiness even prior to justification. Ultimately, however, his scheme of justification is a new rendition of the Augustinian concept of God rewarding his own gifts. All the virtuous dispositions, including faith, are nothing but God's antecedent gift given with the intention to reward afterward.[59]

In regeneration, the Spirit infuses grace—known as a new disposition or habit—which is only capable of being exercised due to the presence and moving of the Spirit. According to Morimoto, this "functions in justification as the ontological ground of the forensic imputation."[60]

On the other side of the discussion, others have sought to protect Edwards's Protestant reputation. According to this other side, dispositions or laws are a by-product of the Holy Spirit's presence. What is real in the union does not truly belong to the person, but is an uncreated grace. Edwards's *Treatise on Grace*, which followed his *Justification* discourse, takes center stage in this argument.[61] In this treatise, Edwards explicitly says that "there is no other principle of grace in the soul than the very Holy Ghost dwelling in the soul and acting there as a vital principle." If the Spirit was removed, says Edwards, "all habits and acts of grace would of themselves cease as immediately as light ceases in a room when a candle is carried out."[62]

In "Miscellanies" 471, Edwards writes that "the Holy Ghost influences the godly as dwelling in them as a vital principle, or as a new supernatural principle of life and action" and implies faith. The Spirit of God "communicates and exerts itself in the soul" and "operates in the minds of the godly by only being in them, uniting itself to their souls, and living in 'em and acting itself."[63] When the saint acts in faith, says Edwards in "Miscellanies" 614, he or she acts "by the Spirit, or rather it

---

59. Ibid., 101.
60. Ibid., 158.
61. *WJE* 21:150, written sometime between 1739–43.
62. *WJE* 21:196. See also Waddington, "Jonathan Edwards's Doctrine of Justification," 365–71, and Caldwell, "Holy Spirit as the Bond of Union," 142.
63. *WJE* 13:513 ("Misc." 471).

is the Spirit of God that acts in them."[64] The disposition infused into the soul is the Spirit and contains faith because, as Jeffrey C. Waddington writes, "the Holy Spirit ... *is* the exercise of faith and love in the life of the believer."[65] When believers consent or have faith and are one with Christ, it is, properly speaking, the Spirit that is acting.[66] This eliminates the possibility of the sinner contributing anything to his or her justification. That which is "real in the union between Christ and his people" is the consenting of wills that unites them in faith and that, in turn, is the Spirit.[67] Nothing belongs to the person proper from this perspective, leaving Edwards's Puritan wig firmly attached.

The problem with the debate, in part, is that scholars are trying to make Edwards more consistent that he really is. To be fair, Edwards does not make it easy for scholars, and it would have helped if he pulled more of his private thoughts into his public works. At times, even his semi-private notebooks harbor musings that are not entirely clear.

For example, in questioning the traditional preparationism passed on to him by his father and grandfather, Edwards's earliest "Miscellanies" ponder the nature of the soul prior to justification, resulting in several entries on the nature of a disposition or habit. In one entry titled "INFUSED HABITS" he concludes that conversion is instantaneous, and that during the moment prior to a person's salvation he or she was in "a state of damnation."[68] This appears to eliminate any contribution by the person. However, in a 1723 entry shortly after this one, Edwards continues the discussion of "INFUSED GRACE," this time adding that prior to faith, the Spirit infuses a "principle that causes vigorousness and activity in action . . ."[69] With this addition of infused grace, he now appears to shift his perspective.

By entries 27b, 77, 241, and 393, this change in perspective appears to move forward. In 27b on "CONVERSION" Edwards questions the idea that "a man can't be saved before he has actually believed." Edwards

---

64. *WJE* 18:146 ("Misc." 614).

65. Waddington, "Jonathan Edwards's Doctrine of Justification," 362.

66. *WJE* 18:146 ("Misc." 614).

67. Bombaro writes that "for Edwards, there is no distinction: the Spirit is a personal disposition of holiness given immediately by God and grace can only be grace if God is the only and immediate source, medium and result of grace . . ." ("Jonathan Edwards' Vision of Salvation," 54).

68. *WJE* 13:169 ("Misc." l).

69. *WJE* 13:171 ("Misc." p).

appears to attribute a certain saving significance to the disposition. A person "may have the disposition in him for some time before he ever sensibly feels them, for want of occasion and other reasons"; therefore, "'Tis the disposition and principle is the thing God looks at. Supposing a man dies suddenly and not in the actual exercise of faith; 'tis his disposition that saves him; for if it were possible that the disposition was destroyed, the man would be damned and all the former acts of faith would signify nothing."[70] Likewise, in entry 77, Edwards asks whether, as "held by some, that none can be in a state of salvation before they have particularly acted a reception of the Lord Jesus Christ for a Savior, and that there cannot be sanctification one moment before the exercise of faith." He insists that there must be a principle "before there can be the action, in all cases." The soul of the sinner must be changed "before this act of faith in nature (as the cause before the effect)." Further, he writes that "a person . . . may be in a state of salvation, before a distinct and express act of faith in the sufficiency and suitableness of Christ as a Savior."[71]

Morimoto's argument capitalizes on passages like these.[72] If a person has a believing disposition intrinsically, and if the disposition is a law, then what happens if that person suddenly dies between the moment of receiving the believing disposition and that moment of having faith? "The person is saved on account of his disposition," says Morimoto, "without regard to its exercise at the time of death."[73] One could be saved by the disposition without having any knowledge of Christ at all. "They may not as yet manifest their saving disposition into a faith that is specifically Christian," says Morimoto, "but they might as well be given the disposition and counted as saved because of that disposition." Further, "they may remain non-Christian for their whole lifetime, and still be saved; if the conditions and circumstances do not arise, their saving disposition will remain unexercised."[74] In other words, the "real" that is the foundation of the "legal" is substantive disposition in the possession of the one who is justified, a grace in the soul that belongs to the individual, and by which one can be saved even without faith. An inactive, believ-

---

70. *WJE* 13:214 ("Misc." 27b).
71. *WJE* 13:458 (Misc." 393).
72. Morimoto, *Jonathan Edwards and the Catholic Vision of Salvation*, 46.
73. Ibid., 33.
74. Ibid., 66.

ing disposition in the soul is the only thing required for salvation, as Morimoto understands Edwards, and no act of faith or content of faith itself is required.

However, by 1729, Edwards seems to be singing a different tune (at least publicly) in his sermon *None Are Saved by Their Own Righteousness*. The disposition is not described in the terms he freely uses in his "Miscellanies."

> That is, there are none saved upon the account of their own moral or religious excellency or goodness, or any qualification of the person, any good disposition of the heart, or any good actions, either sincere or not sincere.
>
> There are none saved upon the account of any habitual excellency, either the excellency of the natural temper or any good qualification obtained by education, or any moral or religious habit obtained by frequent acts or any truly gracious habit. Nor upon the account of any labor, diligence, devotion or affection in religion, or any exactness or brightness of morality, any justice or charity, though they should give all their goods to feed the poor. Men are not saved at all upon the account of any such habits or works of righteousness.[75]

That a created habit or disposition of grace—belonging solely to the person in question—saves a person, is explicitly denied here.

What is one to make of this? Since Edwards is concerned with defeating any so-called Arminian ideas of works-based justification, Morimoto's saving disposition seems to take things a bit far. Edwards's treatise is ultimately about Reformed versus Arminian ideas, rather than Protestant versus Catholic. Moreover, if Edwards is seeking to eliminate antinomianism, a believing disposition that is not exercised in faith or not resulting in works would also not do the trick. In other words, Morimoto's point does not correspond precisely with Edwards's immediate stated intentions for the discourse or its historical circumstances. It is possible that Edwards is just being inconsistent and not sufficiently accomplishing the goals of his discourse. Yet there is something about attributing *realness* to the foundation of the *legal* that demands something like what Morimoto argues. Taking Edwards's statement together with his discovery after his conversion that the converted soul possesses all that God possesses, one has to admit that there is more to justification

---

75. *WJE* 14:333. To my knowledge, Edwards's comments here are not taken into consideration in any discussion.

than filling out divine paperwork. For this reason, I propose that there might be something of a both/and in this discussion, one that involves two important factors found in Edwards's writings, but unfortunately not brought together in the clearest form publicly: the incarnational analogy that gave his conversion meaning.

The Incarnational Analogy

As seen in the previous chapter, Edwards borrowed and modified the Spirit-Christology he found in the works of John Owen and used this as a model for his understanding of justification by faith and union with Christ. Owen understood the Spirit as the sanctifying agent of Christ. More than that, he is the bond between both the human and divine natures of Christ, so as to have one person. Christ the human could simultaneously have all that the divine possessed and yet remain entirely human. Edwards agrees with Owen, writing several "Miscellanies" directly connected to the incarnation while working up his draft of *Justification by Faith Alone*.[76] Following his understanding of consent and excellency, Edwards sees the Spirit, the agent in the incarnation, as the one that brings consent between two infinitely inequitable divine and human natures. Harmony of knowledge and will between both the divine and the human is made possible by the work of the Spirit. "The Spirit," he says "is the Sanctifier, for the Spirit is the very divine holiness" and Christ "received his first being into this world by the Spirit of holiness."[77] As the Spirit is what brings consent between the sinner and Christ, so also the Spirit brings consent between both the divine and human nature of Christ into one will:

> The man Jesus becomes one person by a communion of knowledge and will; but as in believers all divine knowledge is by the Spirit . . . 'tis by the Spirit that divine knowledge and consciousness is given to the man Jesus. And so, as 'tis by the Spirit of God that divine temper is given to men and angels, so I suppose 'tis by the Spirit of the Logos that the man Jesus hath the spirit and temper of the only begotten Son of God.[78]

---

76. See, for example, entries 487, 513, 624, 709, 738, 766, 767, 772, 781.
77. *WJE* 18:333, 334 ("Misc." 709).
78. *WJE* 13:530 ("Misc." 487).

"All that was divine in the man Christ Jesus is from the Spirit of God," writes Edwards in "Miscellanies" 766, "divine power, and divine knowledge, and divine will, and divine acts—and therefore, it must be that the divine Logos dwelt in him by the Spirit, or which is the same thing, was united to him by the Spirit."[79] The Spirit resides with the God-Human, uniting the two natures, acting so that they work together, without doing harm to the will of the second person of the Trinity. The parallels between the Spirit's work in the incarnation and the union of the Christian with Christ inform Edwards's controversial statement on what is "real" in the union.

While the influence of Owen on Edwards's understanding of the incarnation gets fairly little attention compared to other connections in his thought, the parallels in their views of justification are nearly unresearched in the literature. Stephen R. Holmes recognized the connection between Edwards and Owen on the issue of incarnation, but not the connection between incarnation and justification itself.[80] Likewise, in 2002, Amy Plantinga Pauw treated the similarities between Owen and Edwards on the incarnation, and rightly pointed to the fact that Edwards parallels what occurs in the incarnation to what occurs in justifying union. However, as it is outside the scope of her book, she does not explore the connection between the justification discourses of Edwards and Owen or the incarnational parallel all that far.[81]

In 2003, Robert W. Caldwell briefly examined the nature of the incarnation as a parallel for the bond of the Spirit, but also did not draw hard lines between Edwards and Owen in terms of the controversial statement on justification.[82] Similarly, in 2005, Kevin Woongsan Kang noted a few connections between the Christian's union with Christ and the incarnation of Christ in Edwards's thought.[83] Kang's argument demonstrates the connections between Edwards's understanding of union and Calvin's, especially on the point of the role of covenant theology, but his emphasis lands on the Reformed concept of a Covenant of Redemption as the "real" that is the foundation of the legal.[84] Kang's

---

79. *WJE* 18:413 ("Misc." 766).
80. Holmes, *God of Grace*, 136–38.
81. Pauw, "*Supreme Harmony of All,*" 146, n. 127.
82. Caldwell, "Holy Spirit as the Bond of Union," 91–128.
83. Kang, "Justified by Faith in Christ," 76.
84. This covenantal background is crucial for understanding justification for Edwards, but the underlying point is ultimately incarnational. The covenantal back-

point is important and helpful background to Edwards's understanding of union, but he stops short of demonstrating the full importance of Edwards's stronger incarnational parallel that is foundational for his view of justification.[85]

There is more to be said about the parallel between justification and the incarnation, and this begins first with justification's evil twin, original sin. The union of the person with Christ follows the pattern of the incarnation—the union of the divine and human natures—and therefore justification appears to go beyond a mere declaration. Likewise, the union the sinner has with Adam prior to justification, in which the sinner becomes guilty of Adam's sin in the garden, is also more than declarative.

THE FIRST AND SECOND ADAMS

What is real in the union between Christ and the Christian has a parallel in what is real in the union between Adam and his posterity in original sin. In Edwards's day, there were many potential views for a theologian to consider when it came to original sin, and no shortage of controversy to be found. In his *The Great Christian Doctrine of Original Sin Defended* (1758), Edwards's target is John Taylor (1694–1761), the son of a minister with a dissenter's background and a skilled Hebrew scholar. Two of Taylor's books, *A Paraphrase With Notes on the Epistle to the Romans* and *A Scripture-Doctrine of Original Sin,* are labeled by Edwards in his "Controversies" notebook and his *Original Sin Defended* as "Arminian," though Taylor did not fit the label in all its technicalities.[86]

Edwards had many reasons for taking an interest in Taylor, but likely at the forefront was the fact that the doctrine of original sin is essentially the doctrine of justification in reverse. Faith is juxtaposed against unbelief—Christ, the second Adam, against Adam himself—and union with Christ as the remedy for the consequences of the unity of humanity with Adam. In the long history of Christian theology, parallels

---

ground for Edwards's understanding of union is also briefly taken up in Bombaro's 2003 article, "Jonathan Edwards' Vision of Salvation" (63–64) and Waddington's "Jonathan Edwards's Doctrine of Justification" (363). I give more attention to Kang's argument in my PhD dissertation, "'Full of Wondrous and Glorious Things,'" 262–65.

85. He also relegates any connection between Owen and Edwards on justification to the bibliography (Kang, "Justified by Faith in Christ," 354).

86. *WJE* 3:68.

are often drawn between Christ and Adam.[87] As the Christian possesses all things through union with Christ, so also the sinner possesses all that is Adam's through union. There is a real union, solidarity, or presence of all humanity in Adam.

John Taylor ascribes guilt to the individual's actions only, rejecting the idea that anyone is guilty by Adam's sin or that all of humanity inherits a corrupt nature.

> A Representative the Guilt of whose Conduct shall be imputed to us, and whose Sins shall corrupt and debauch our Nature, is one of the greatest Absurdities in all the System of *corrupt Religion* ... But that any Man, without my Knowledge or Consent, should so represent me, that when he is guilty I am to be reputed guilty, and when he transgresses I shall be accountable and punishable for his Transgression, and thereby subjected to the Wrath and Curse of God; nay further, that his Wickedness shall give me a *sinful Nature,* and all this before I am born, and consequently while I am in no Capacity of knowing, helping or hindering what he doth; surely any one, who *dares* use his Understanding, must clearly see this unreasonable, and altogether inconsistent with the Truth and Goodness of God.[88]

Taylor interprets Rom 3:23 ("For all have sinned, and come short of the glory of God") as meaning "that Men of all Nations had corrupted themselves" through individual wickedness.[89] Adam's sin did bring physical death, says Taylor, but not original guilt.[90] Adam was able to sin without a sinful nature, making it unnecessary for his posterity to have inherited a sinful nature in order to sin.[91] Humans are free to will as they so desire; if they are wicked, they will be punished, however for their own actions, not Adam's.[92] Taylor also rejects the notion that Adam and his posterity are one.

Edwards attempts to formulate a position that takes seriously the objections of Taylor while being faithful to the Reformed Protestant emphasis on the guilt and consequences of Adam's first sin. He argues for

---

87. WJE 3:102–03; Weir, *Origins of the Federal Theology,* 3–4.
88. Taylor, *Scripture-Doctrine of Original Sin,* 109.
89. Ibid., 96.
90. Ibid., 99.
91. Ibid., 232.
92. Ibid., 232, 233, 234.

the imputation of Adam's sin upon the posterity, but he does not argue for an imputation that is merely representative or genetic. To paraphrase his statement from *Justification by Faith alone*, what is real in the union between Adam and his people is the foundation of what is legal; that is, it is something really in them, and between them, uniting them, that is the ground of the suitableness of their being accounted as one by the judge.[93] In *Original Sin* he insists that the choice to sin is both Adam's and all of humanity's. The type of oneness that human beings experience in Adam means that they possess all that he possessed. As Edwards writes:

> ... both guilt, or exposedness to punishment, and also depravity of heart, came upon Adam's posterity just as they came upon him, as much as if he and they had all coexisted, like a tree with many branches; allowing only for the difference necessarily resulting from the place Adam stood in, as head or root of the whole, and being first and most immediately dealt with, and most immediately acting and suffering.[94]

The person is not guilty simply for the sin of Adam; rather, all human beings consented to Adam's sin as all branches in a tree consent to the actions of the root.

This would make Taylor indignant. How could anyone be guilty of something he or she did not do personally? Does Edwards really not see that he has a different body, mind, and soul from Adam?

The first layer of Edwards's argument is that of *divine constitution*. In his large work on Edwards, John Gerstner argues for the union of Adam and his posterity by divine constitution; that is, by the mind and will of God, human beings are constituted as one with Adam, and this is the foundation for their unity and the reason for their guilt. "The guilt of Adam's posterity for Adam's initial transgression is not because it was imputed to them by virtue of their being represented in Adam," explains Gerstner, "but by virtue of their constituted identity with Adam."[95] The divine will is responsible for it all.

Gerstner's explanation is certainly behind Edwards's argument, but there is more to it. God's law, as Edwards sees it, is that though Adam and his posterity are separate beings physically—each having their own

---

93. Edwards later does refer to this union as a "real union" in *Original Sin* (*WJE* 3:406).

94. *WJE* 3:389.

95. Gerstner, *Rational Biblical Theology of Jonathan Edwards*, 324.

brain, arms, legs, torso, etc.—they are understood by the established laws of the universe to be one person. For Edwards, this principle is exemplified by a person's material structure throughout the human life span:

> . . . the body of a man at forty years of age, is one with the infant body which first came into the world, from whence it grew; though now constituted of different substance, and the greater part of the substance probably changed scores (if not hundreds) of times; and though it be now in so many respects exceeding diverse, yet God, according to the course of nature, which he has been pleased to establish, has caused, that in a certain method it should communicate with that infantile body, in the same life, the same senses, the same features, and many the same qualities, and in union with the same soul; and so, with regard to these purposes, 'tis dealt with by him as one body.[96]

If adults do not have the exact same body as their infant selves, yet they remain one person, so also one does not need to have the exact same body and mind as Adam to be one with him. The disposition for cancer in the person at birth, for example, still belongs, or is possessed by, the same individual as an adult of fifty-five, even if that adult does not share a single cell in common with his or her infant self.

As Edwards sees it, Taylor's premise is based on a false understanding of "*sameness* or *oneness*."[97] Edwards imagines the entire mass of humanity, coexisting and grossly connected physically, like the root to its branches. Humanity would "constitute as it were *one* complex person, or *one* moral whole" so that all acts of the root (Adam) would affect the remaining tree of humanity: "all jointly participating, and all concurring, as *one whole*, in the disposition and action of the head."[98] The question naturally arises: if we are one with Adam, if we were truly there, present, and consenting, why do we not remember it? "But 'tis evident," argues Edwards, "that the communication or continuance of the same consciousness and memory to any subject, through successive parts of duration, depends wholly on a divine establishment."[99] It is entirely up

---

96. *WJE* 3:398.

97. *WJE* 3:397; see also Helm, *Faith and Understanding*, 152–76. For an analysis of the metaphysics of original sin, see Crisp, *Jonathan Edwards and the Metaphysics of Sin*. Crisp is heavy on philosophy but light on history.

98. *WJE* 3:391 n. 1.

99. *WJE* 3:398.

to the will of God to pass on the memory of Adam's sin to his posterity, something that God has chosen not to establish as a law of nature.[100] According to Edwards's concept of oneness, human beings are sinners because they truly consented to Adam's sin as one person (mediate imputation) *and* because they are his posterity (immediate imputation).[101]

Edwards's doctrine of original sin, then, is justification's negative image. In fact, there is a parallel expression to his controversial statement in *Justification by Faith Alone* that appears in *Original Sin*. Adam's sin becomes humanity's, writes Edwards,

> by virtue of a real union between the root and branches of the world of mankind . . . and by virtue of the full consent of the hearts of Adam's posterity to that first apostacy. And therefore the sin of the apostacy is not theirs merely because God *imputes* it to them; but it is *truly* and *properly* theirs, and on that ground, God imputes it to them.[102]

One cannot but hear in these words the echo of his statement that "what is real in the union between Christ and his people, is the foundation of what is legal; that is, it is something really in them, and between them, uniting them, that is the ground of the suitableness of their being accounted as one by the Judge."[103] Edwards writes in his "Miscellanies" that "union with Christ, or a being in Christ, is the foundation of all communion with him."[104] Adam's posterity is united to him because biologically, even if they do not share a single atom together, they are of the same natural human tree; they are in communion with him. This is the natural law that God established in the universe. They are guilty of his sin because they, like branches to the root of the tree, were present biologically, consenting to his sin, even if they cannot remember it.

As seen previously, Edwards's incarnational theology bears a similar pattern, but with the second Adam, Christ. In the first Adam, the

---

100. *WJE* 3:399.

101. Edwards's citation of Johann Friedrich Stapfer—in which he appears to approve of Stapfer's use of both mediate and immediate imputation terminology—seems to confirm this point (*WJE* 3:391 n. 1). See Stapfer, *Institutiones Theologiæ Polemicæ Universæ Ordine Scientifico Dispositæ* for Edwards's source. For a theological analysis of Edwards's position see Otto, "Solidarity of Mankind," 205–21; Weddle, "Jonathan Edwards on Men and Trees," 155–75.

102. *WJE* 3:408.

103. *WJE* 19:158.

104. *WJE* 18:247.

bond of union is found in the natural relationship that God maintains by a law. In Christ, the bond of union between him and the Christian requires two things: first, a shared human nature, and second, a spiritual relationship in the law of faith, that is, a consent to Christ's work (the opposite of consent to Adam's sin). In his discourse on justification, Edwards argues that Christians are united as "members of the body with the head," and therefore they are "partaking of the life of the head. . . ."[105] The members must also consent to the head for them to be one, and faith "is that qualification in any person, that renders it meet in the sight of God that he [the sinner] should be looked upon as having Christ's satisfaction and righteousness belonging to him, viz. because it is that *in* him, which, on his part, makes up this union between him and Christ."[106] God establishes faith as that law by which he constitutes two persons as the same, the redeemed soul and Christ.

Faith, however, requires grace. The Holy Spirit is that grace that resides in the soul, making faith or consent possible. Much the same, in the incarnation, the human nature of Christ possesses all that the divine has, and the divine all that the human has, but by the bond of the Spirit who manages the communication of these attributes so as to preserve the distinct natures and make one person. The two natures are consenting in this relationship. In conversion, the Christian possesses all that Christ has (righteousness) and Christ possesses all that the sinner has (unrighteousness), and by the Spirit's work they maintain their proper positions, Christ as redeemer and Christian as redeemed, but as one body. "The union of the members with the head is the foundation of their communicating or partaking with the head," writes Edwards, "and so the union of the branch with the vine is the foundation of all communion it has with the vine, of all partaking of any degree of its sap or life or influence."[107] As he argues elsewhere, "believers are united to Christ, and in a sense are partakers of his nature, in that they are partakers of his Spirit . . . they are said to be partakers of the divine nature. . . ." As far as God is concerned, Christ's people are "as parts of him."[108] The Christian

---

105. *WJE* 19:156.
106. *WJE* 19:156.
107. *WJE* 18:247.
108. *WJE* 14:403.

has a "spiritual excellency and joy by a kind of participation of God" and God "put his own beauty, i.e., his beautiful likeness, upon their souls."[109]

Edwards formulated his Spirit-Christology and view of Christ's incarnation based on John Owen's work on the Holy Spirit, and he likely made a similar use of Owen's *The Doctrine of Justification by Faith Through the Righteousness of Christ, Explained, Confirmed, & Vindicated* (which Edwards lists in his "Catalogue of Reading" in 1724) when writing his own discourse on *Justification by Faith Alone*.[110] Not only does his controversial phrase on what is real behind the Christian's union with Christ have a parallel in his work on original sin, but it also appears to have some connection to a similar passage in Owen's work on justification. "This [mystical union] then," writes Owen, "I say is the *Foundation of the Imputation* [i.e., the legal] of the sins of the Church unto Christ, namely, that he and it are one Person."[111] One cannot mistake the linguistic and logical similarities between this conclusion of Owen's and Edwards's words that "what is real in the union between Christ and his people, is the foundation of what is legal; that is, it is something really in them, and between them, uniting them."[112]

As with Edwards, Owen understands the union between the Christian and Christ to be made possible by Christ's "*Assumption* of our nature" (the incarnation) and the power of the Holy Spirit.[113] "The principle Foundation hereof is," says Owen, "that *Christ and the Church*, in this Design, were one *mystical Person*, which state they do actually coalesce in, through the *uniting Efficacy* of the Holy Spirit." Christ, continues Owen, "is the Head, and Believers are the members of that one Person."[114] Also like Edwards, Owen sees this mystical union between Christ and the Christian as intimate as that of the "Union of the *Head and Members*" or the "*Vine and its Branches*."[115] Clearly, Edwards's *Justification by Faith Alone* discourse reflects the type of mystical union that is found in Owen's incarnational theology.

---

109. *WJE* 17:208.

110. "Catalogue of Reading," 30. Thomas Schafer dates the entry around June–August 1724 (*WJE* 13:95).

111. Owen, *Doctrine of Justification by Faith*, 249–50.

112. *WJE* 19:158.

113. Owen, *Doctrine of Justification by Faith*, 251.

114. Ibid., 246.

115. Ibid., 251.

Given this incarnational basis, the paradox that leads Morimoto to read Edwards as saying that justification includes something inherent to the person, and others to argue that he removes any possession of righteousness from the person, is Chalcedonian in nature. In one sense, there had to be a communication of attributes between the human and divine natures of Christ, but the natures had to remain distinct and without confusion. The human nature could not remain human if it took on the divine, and vice versa. Nevertheless, the human nature is one person with the divine, and therefore could be said to possess all that the divine possesses under the guidance of the Spirit, the one who maintains the integrity of the two natures.

Similarly, the person united to Christ must remain a pauper, incapable of bringing anything to the table of justification. If this does not happen, the person cannot be said to be in need of Christ's work. However, in union with Christ, the person possesses all that the God-Human possesses. One cannot participate in the divine nature and possess all things and not, in some sense, also possess the righteousness that saved that person originally. The redeemed person is essentially, in the language of Chalcedon, without confusion between sinner and savior and without division between sinner and savior. Like the incarnation, the integrity between the sinner and the savior is made possible by the Holy Spirit, a mediator of divine participation and the maintainer of that integrity. For example, in "Miscellanies" 736, Edwards defers to his reading of the ancient church theologian, John Chrysostom, noting that "the whole family in heaven, and on earth . . . are named of Christ . . . the eternal head of the whole family . . . all having one heavenly necessary bond of union . . . ," and it is "by the Spirit" that Christ's "light is continually communicated to that blessed assembly."[116]

It is no wonder, then, that so much debate has occurred over Edwards's intentions. If one takes into consideration his use of the incarnation and his incorporation of parallels in conversion, however, the supposed contradiction makes sense. Edwards is attempting to unite heaven and earth, a paradox that does not allow for easy explanations. Even he occasionally appears to stumble over his own choice of words

---

116. *WJE* 18:363. Like his exposure to most of the church fathers, Edwards reads Chrysostom secondhand through Hurrion's *Knowledge of Christ Glorified*, where Chrysostom is quoted at length (196–98).

and fine lines. For example, as he writes in his sermon, "None Are Saved by Their Own Righteousness":

> There is a two-fold righteousness that the saints have: an imputed righteousness, and 'tis this only that avails anything to justification; and an inherent righteousness, that is, that holiness and grace which is in the hearts and lives of the saints. This is Christ's righteousness as well as imputed righteousness: imputed righteousness is Christ's righteousness accepted for them, inherent holiness is Christ's righteousness communicated to them. They derive their holiness from Christ as the fountain of it. He gives it by his Spirit, so that 'tis Christ's holiness communicated, 'tis the light of the sun reflected. Now God takes delight in the saints for both of these: both for Christ's righteousness imputed and for Christ's holiness communicated, though 'tis the former only that avails anything to justification.[117]

Edwards is able to have his cake and eat it too, even if precision is sacrificed in the process. The real that is the foundation of the legal is truly real because it is modeled after the incarnation itself. If Christ could remain human and yet possess the divine, so also the Christian can remain a pauper, having nothing, yet possess all things in divine participation.

Closure

As a young man, Jonathan Edwards experienced a surprising conversion that allowed him to see God in everything. The crisis that came from that transformation and his cultural barriers drove him to seek answers. He found that in saving faith one is united to Christ in a way that one possesses all that the divine being possesses. The Christian participates in the divine being, finding answers and treasures beyond anyone's imagination. Over the years Edwards honed that thinking. In the Trinity, the Father and the Son are united by the Holy Spirit to make *one God*, that is, three persons and one nature. In the incarnation, Christ's divinity and humanity are united by the bond of the Spirit to make *one person* with two natures. On earth, however, human beings are trapped in a perilous unity with their first parent, Adam, making *one fallen humanity*. The Spirit is infused into their souls, bringing faith and uniting the person with Christ—much like the incarnation—and these persons, united with Christ (and to one another), make *one body*. The union with

---

117. *WJE* 14:340–41.

Adam is broken, and the union with Christ is forged. The Christian possesses all that Christ possesses, and Christ possesses all that belongs to the Christian.

Like his ancient fathers, Edwards believed that participation in the divine being was necessary to the explanation of his conversion. His way of coming to that conclusion may not be a direct route from, say, Origen or the Cappadocians, but the result is much the same. His spirituality is vibrant and full of divine energy, a process of becoming as God intended, that is, to reflect the divine excellency. As the next part of this book will show, Edwards also follows his ancient ancestors in understanding that this divine union and participation leads to a view of Scripture as possessing beautiful layers. By divine participation, the Christian has the privilege of diving into the depths of that divine ocean and discovering treasure beyond this world.

PART THREE

Jonathan Edwards's Spiritual Reading of the Sacred Text

6

Unlocking the Divine Treasure Chest

> . . . Scripture often includes various distinct things in its sense. It is becoming of him who is infinite in understanding and has everything in full and perfect view at once . . . to adapt his words to many things, and so to speak infinitely more comprehensively than others. . . .
>
> —Jonathan Edwards, "Miscellanies" 851[1]

> . . . the knowledge of divine things that the human nature had was by the Spirit of God, by his inspiration or revelation: for he taught and did the business of the great prophet of God by the Spirit.
>
> —Jonathan Edwards, "Miscellanies" 766[2]

Jonathan Edwards was not only obsessed with his own conversion, but was also acutely interested in the experiences of others. During the Great Awakening, conversions were as plentiful as dandelions throughout the colonies and Edwards's popularity soared. One such experience happened in his own household. In 1742, he invited the young and newly ordained Samuel Buell to fill his pulpit while he was away touring New England. Sarah Edwards later described the effects of Buell's preaching as "Heavenly Elysium."[3]

Sarah's spiritual dilemma occurred the day after Jonathan suggested in a conversation that she "failed in some measure in point of prudence." Such a criticism from her husband, which he no doubt saw as

---

1. *WJE* 20:80 ("Misc." 851).
2. *WJE* 18:413.
3. Dwight, *Life*, 178.

his obligation to her as her husband and pastor, seemed to "bereave" her of the "quietness and calm" of her mind.[4] When she heard that Buell was coming to town to preach, she feared the young upstart would outshine her husband—something of which Edwards's New England enemies may have loved to take advantage. However, under his preaching, she soon abandoned that fear; more importantly, she welcomed his success, as it served to transform her own spirituality.

So moved under Buell's preaching, Sarah was "at once filled with such intense admiration of the wonderful condescension and grace of God, in returning again to Northampton" that she lost her "bodily strength."[5] Faintings were not unusual in New England revivals. Her descriptions of her experience of personal revival during this time were nothing short of mystical. She writes in her personal account: "It appeared to me, that the angels in heaven sung praises, for such wonderful, free and sovereign grace, and my heart was lifted up in adoration and praise. I continued to have clear views of the future world, of eternal happiness and misery, and my heart full of love to the souls of men."[6] She experienced many faintings and spontaneous praisings during her rapturous moments. At one point, she felt that her "soul was drawn so powerfully towards Christ and heaven, that . . . [she] leaped unconsciously" from her chair.[7] What occurred carries with it a scent reminiscent of the incense of the Eastern mystics, which she described as "a ravishing sense of the unspeakable joys of the upper world."

Edwards, upon his return, was as impressed as a New England minister could be. He published a record of her experience but removed all indications of gender or age (protecting her from criticism and making it applicable for anyone reading). Sarah was not alone, as a greater revival caught the souls of others in her church. Children, for example, were "greatly affected," and they filled the rooms with "cries" and continued to wail through the streets on their way home from the meetinghouse. In some incidences, Edwards recognized what he saw as merely "childish affections," something he knew well from his own youthful search for conversion, but others appeared to him to be genuine.[8] Within sev-

4. Ibid., 172.
5. Ibid., 176.
6. Ibid.
7. Ibid., 177.
8. *WJE* 16:118.

eral weeks, the town was transformed.⁹ Many were in a state of salvific bliss as never before in their lives, some "lying in a sort of trance" and "remaining for perhaps a whole twenty-four hours motionless," even experiencing visions of heaven.¹⁰ One cannot help hearing similar spiritual experiences in Philo of Alexandria's works. His own experience "of Divine possession" pushed him into a "corybantic frenzy" where he obtained "an enjoyment of light" and "keenest vision."¹¹

Sarah was enraptured into a heavenly paradise much like Edwards's own conversion experience, which led him to read Scripture with a new perspective. When one approaches the biblical text with one's mind lifted up by the Spirit of God through one's union with Christ, as Edwards came to see it, the biblical interpreter becomes like Paul, soaring into the third heaven to gaze upon its beauty.

Biblical interpretation becomes divine participation in practice. This is possible, as Edwards sees it, not only because the Christian's mind is united to and participating in the divine being, but also because Scripture too follows an incarnational model. Scripture is human in its general, plain, literal, linguistic, and historical sense. It is human in its limitations of language and ability to bring the infinite into the finite world of the human authors. It is also divine in that it is God's book—Christ's revelation—moderated and written by the mind of the Spirit. In this form, there is a spiritual sense that transcends the literal and a love for that sense that can be enjoyed only by the redeemed. Scripture is incarnational, therefore, because the minds of human authors and the divine mind are united by the Spirit to form the paradox of one book.

The Human and Literal Side of Biblical Interpretation

On October 19, 1757, during his Stockbridge years, Edwards responded to an invitation from the Trustees of the College of New Jersey (to be known later as Princeton) to become the next President. His letter is full of excuses as to why he felt his gifts lay elsewhere, but his eventual acceptance of the position has driven scholars to question just how sincere Edwards's excuses were. The letter also provides something else of value: a short look at his research interests and methodology for

---

9. *WJE* 16:120.
10. *WJE* 16:120.
11. Philo, *Migration of Abraham*, 32–35.

studying Scripture. "My method of study, from my first beginning the work of ministry," writes Edwards, "has been very much by writing," which is apparent by the large collection of notebooks that make up the Edwards collection at Yale University. He set out to "improve every important hint" and pursue clues "when anything in reading, meditation or conversation" came to mind. "Thus penning what appeared to me my best thoughts, on innumerable subjects for my own benefit," continues Edwards. "The longer I prosecuted my studies in this method, the more habitual it became, and the more pleasant and profitable I found it."[12] His many notebooks remain a memorial to this methodology and to the organizing machine that was his brain, which managed to pull various entries from these notes together into sermons and books. He even provided his own handwritten indices and cross-references in each volume.

Most of the literature on Edwards's approach to biblical interpretation focuses on his use of typology or the spiritual sense. However, not all of Edwards's engagement with Scripture escaped the mundane, and his notebooks demonstrate that he explored it on many levels, often mimicking the commentary tradition, engaging the literal reading of the biblical text and its theological implications. His Yale training and reading taught him to nuance his interpretative method.

Some of his earliest influences were found in his reading of preaching manuals. One such manual was *The Preacher*, one of many books by the Reformed Anglican John Edwards that Jonathan Edwards found useful (and not just because of the similarities of their names) and included in his "Catalogue of Reading."[13] A manual concerned largely with the nurturing office of the pastor, *The Preacher* also encourages the exegete to know the biblical languages and to engage the text using "Sacred Criticism," that is, judging the "Original Copies," showing skill in etymology, dialects, phrases, chronology, context, etc. A proper exposition of the text, this author says, understands that there are tropes, figures of speech, and metaphors in the text.[14] One should consistently respect genre, such as poetry and proverbs. The evangelical preacher is to consistently return to biblical "Food and Sustenance" for the sake of the

---

12. *WJE* 16:726.

13. *WJE* 10:16. See *WJE* 10 for another look at John Edwards. Kimnach's contribution to the Yale series contains the best examination of the Edwardsian sermon to date. Edwards, "Catalogue of Books," entry 200 (see also 129, 132).

14. John Edwards, *Preacher*, 253.

listener's soul.[15] The preacher should teach the foundational doctrines of "Election," "Justification," and "Forgiveness of Sins."[16] True "Evangelical Preaching" focuses on important theological topics such as regeneration, the "Necessity of being *Supernaturally Enlightened*," and the doctrine of "*Justification by Faith alone*."[17] It is clear from his theological themes and principles that the two Edwardses had much in common.

But John Edwards was far from being the only influence on "our" Edwards. The Anglican emphasis on application and finding the moral meaning of a text, for example, came also from Jonathan Edwards's reading of Latitudinarians like Archbishop John Tillotson. For example, Edwards's New York sermon on 1 John 5:3 ("For this is the love of God, that we keep his commandments: and his commandments are not grievous"), titled "True Love to God," reflects the influence of Tillotson, whose morally driven sermon on the same passage, though not identical, carries more than a few similarities to Edwards's.[18]

Other important manuals for the biblical scholar in New England, such as John Wilkins' *Ecclesiastes, or A Discourse Concerning the Gift of Preaching*, would have told him how to engage the text in rather thorough ways.[19] The student who read Wilkins would discover that the exposition of Scripture and preaching are ultimately both a science and an art used for the edification of the church. Preaching, according to Wilkins, follows "Rules and Canons," requiring a knowledge of the languages, sciences, and divinity, with the goal of having a "right *understanding* of sound doctrine; an ability to propound, confirm, and apply it unto the *edification of others*."[20]

Wilkins reminds the student that there are various types of texts: historical, literal, typological, and allegorical. "*Allegoricall interpretations* may lawfully be used also," he writes, "when there is no such naturall reference, but merely a fitnesse by way of similitude to illustrate any doc-

---

15. Ibid., 17.

16. Ibid., 121.

17. Ibid., 43.

18. Tillotson, *Works*, 70–79. Edwards and Tillotson argue that love makes the difficulty of the Christian life bearable, as it did when Jacob worked several years for Rachel, which felt only as a few days due to his love for her.

19. For another examination of these manuals in sermon structure see Wilson H. Kimnach's introduction in *WJE* 10:16–21, 27–36.

20. Wilkins, *Ecclesiastes*, 1, 2.

trine." Yet, even with the allegorical, he warns that it is to be used "*sparingly* and *soberly*." The solid exegete, he says, will consider important "words and phrases" that harbor certain ambiguity but are "*Tropes* and *figures*," but he warns the student of Scripture about going overboard and roaming too far away from the literal meaning.[21] The minister is to look for anything that could offer some form of "instruction."[22] Wilkins's manual reflected the wider Puritan culture, summarizing in one volume an existing post-Reformation tradition and its complex approach to the Bible. Edwards's examination of the biblical text takes all of these concepts into consideration, appearing often in his intricate system of now well-documented notebooks and sermons.

The "Miscellanies" notes—where Edwards followed every lead, documented every thought, pondered every theological and philosophical possibility—make up the lion's share of his notes. Some of these entries are closely related and represent something on his mind for a period of time, while others appear in the midst of the manuscript, as if it was the child of a moment of inspiration. Recognizing the need to organize these thoughts, he eventually developed indices for some of the notebooks, and cross-referenced each numbered entry throughout with others on the same subject. This process made sermon preparation easier, allowing him to easily locate entries on the same subject matter.

While Edwards finds himself moving from one arresting theological or philosophical point of interest to another in his "Miscellanies," which are primarily organized by subject, other notebooks look more like the biblical commentary tradition that rose out of the Reformation (see chapters 1–2), focusing foremost on specific passages of Scripture. His "Notes on Scripture" and "Notes on the Apocalypse" are some of the earliest examples of this approach infiltrating his thinking. In each of these he engages in the examination and exegesis of specific biblical passages, breaking down their various parts and noting interesting commentary offered by other theologians and ministers whose works were at his disposal. These notebooks remained important to him throughout his life and resemble another complex set of note keeping, now called his "Blank Bible": an interleaved Bible alongside which Edwards kept copious notes on biblical passages. The exegetical tradition of his day can be recognized within these entries.

21. Ibid., 9, 10, 12.
22. Ibid.

The "Blank Bible" is organized largely by Scripture passage and, as a result, follows the order of biblical books by chapter and verse. It demonstrates the influence of the commentary tradition while remaining largely a notebook. Not every biblical passage receives a comment or is given equal exegetical attention. At times, Edwards engages in lengthy discussion of a verse or focuses on a single phrase; at other times he simply references another of his notebooks where he handled the text previously or a commentary that held something noteworthy on the passage. In the commentary references, it is not uncommon to find mentions of Puritan forerunners like Matthew Poole or Matthew Henry; contemporary scholars, like Philip Doddridge (1702–1751) and John Locke, also feature heavily throughout the notebook.[23]

One should not, however, see Edwards as a commentator of today's standards. He does not read the text as literature; it is, rather, a resource for right living, finding Christ, and building an armory for defending his theological positions. For example, while showing an appreciation of the poetic nature of Psalms, he is not fascinated by its features as literature. He is more interested in reading between the lines and looking for a christological message intended by the Spirit. However, while Edwards mines the text for his own theological inquiry, that does not mean that he entirely ignores the specific details of its context, history, and structure.

As many scholars have noted, his reading is strong on history and geography, and this comes out in his examination of the biblical text. He very much trusts the literal reading of the text. For example, while being struck by the imagery of Ps 18:7–15, in which God is said to protect David through thunder, lightning, and hailstones, Edwards is convinced that the reader should consider the historical backstory that informs the text. "The things here spoken of," writes Edwards, "God probably had at some time or times literally accomplished for David and against his enemies."[24] The creation account in Gen 1 or the great deluge from the days of Noah both are also real, literal, historical events for Edwards. He even spends time in the religions and myths of other peoples, comparing them with Scripture and hoping to prove the historicity of the biblical text. The fables of Saturn, for example, are believed by Edwards to be taken from the story of Noah.[25]

---

23. *WJE* 24:1.60, 67.
24. *WJE* 24:1.484.
25. *WJE* 24:1.127.

In the "Blank Bible" he also hones in on specific phrases, historical points, or typological references. In the case of the first, he finds certain Hebrew and Greek words or idioms to be important and occasionally delves into translation issues and, as he does in Ps 16:9, word studies.[26] How well Edwards understood biblical languages, particularly Hebrew, has been a matter of discussion. In the aforementioned letter to the Trustees of Princeton, written near the end of his life, he remarks that should he take on the proposed role as President, his only interest in teaching languages would be in Hebrew, so that he could "improve" himself, "by instructing others."[27] Hebrew was part of his training at Yale, but not nearly as much as Greek and Latin, which his father began with him before sending the young Edwards off to school. There is no doubt that he understood and read Hebrew, but this is the lesser of his biblical languages; often, when discussing Hebrew terms and phrases in his "Blank Bible," his notes are followed quickly with a reference to a lexicon, commentary, or book he was reading at the time. While demonstrating that he clearly knows Hebrew, Edwards seems more dependent on his tools than he does for his work in Greek or Latin, both of which he gives significant attention to in his notes.

There is another side to the literal reading of the text, however, that Edwards engages often—perhaps more than any other aspect of biblical interpretation—and that is the literal meaning intended by the Holy Spirit (as he would call it). Edwards enthusiastically engages in a post-Reformation tradition of seeking the mind of God in the text, which entails reading the Bible for the typological or spiritual messages. He appears to enjoy the solicitation of multiple textual meanings most. When writing on Dan 5:25, Edwards notes Daniel's use of multilayered interpretation and concludes: "That the words of God, especially the words of prophecy, may well be supposed sometimes to have several senses."[28] After noting the possibility of multiple senses in the text, he refers to his notes on Hos 11:1, a passage in which God is said to call Israel out of Egypt. In the Gospel of Matthew, this text is applied to Christ (Matt 2:15), as Joseph took Mary and the infant Jesus to Egypt to flee the possible wrath of Herod. How could two radically different takes on this passage be justified? Did the passage apply to Israel or did it apply to

26. *WJE* 24:1.482.
27. *WJE* 16:729.
28. *WJE* 24:1.764.

Christ? Edwards notes the difficulty, arguing that Christ is sometimes called Israel; "the Holy Ghost has an eye to many things, and has so contrived his words that the same expression shall be adapted to many things at the same time."[29] While there are many potential meanings to be found in a passage, these are not arbitrarily determined by the reader. In fact, as he sees it, they are intended by the Spirit as the divine author and are essentially another type of literal meaning.

Those who are regenerated by the Spirit, as Edwards sees it, are entirely justified in looking for that special meaning. The Christian is able to enjoy the beauty of this higher level of meaning because of his or her connection to the Spirit. The transformation of the soul by the Holy Spirit and union with the divine enable the interpreter to, as Edwards might explain it, read the Bible from the vantage point of heaven itself.

The Spiritual Sense(s) and Scripture's Layers

While the spiritual sense in Edwards's interpretation often has been commented on, its connection to the incarnation in his theological imagination still begs to be explored.[30] The spiritual sense is strongly related to Edwards's incarnational analogy, which he applies to both the converted reader and the biblical revelation. Like his ancient Christian counterparts, he thinks like a Christian Platonist and understands the incarnational bridge between heaven and earth as essential for a spiritual reading of the Bible. When converted, Edwards claimed to see Scripture differently—that is, spiritually—and this is only possible because the earthly and the heavenly are bridged by the *Logos*. However, while Edwards shares the ideas of his ancient theological ancestors, drawing straight lines to specific thinkers is not an easy task.

Through secondary sources, Edwards was able to mine the ancient Christian tradition and the Greek classics. As he wrote to the Trustees of the College of New Jersey, he was not as well versed in the Greek classics, and his training was primarily in the New Testament. Secondary

---

29. *WJE* 24:1.787.

30. No one has written as much on Edwards and the Bible's spiritual meanings as Stephen J. Stein has over the life of the Edwards project at Yale. The work of this chapter is not to simply reproduce what he has done. For a good sampling of Stein's work, see *WJE* 24 (the "Blank Bible" in two volumes) and *WJE* 15 (*Notes on Scripture*), along with his articles "Like Apples of God in Pictures of Silver," 324–37; "Quest for the Spiritual Sense," 99–113; and "Symbols of Spiritual Truth," 263–71.

sources provided the links to the world of Greek philosophers and even the church fathers. Their names appear in his notes, his "Catalogue" shows an interest in obtaining copies of them, and his theological conclusions are clearly influenced in various ways by the early Christian fathers. Through his work at Yale, he had easier access to important secondary sources, which helped open a window into the ancient world. For example, in appealing to Origen's take on Plato in his notes on Gen 3:24 in the "Blank Bible," Edwards is getting his information primarily from Theophilus Gale's *Court of the Gentiles*. In his later years, Edwards's notes were filled with names like Plato, Philo, or Justin Martyr, thanks to volumes like Ralph Cudworth's (1617–1688) ambitious *The True Intellectual System of the Universe* (1678).

Most scholars recognize that Edwards read Cudworth and other Cambridge Platonists later in life and that this is reflected in his "Miscellanies." Douglas A. Sweeney remarks, "he picked and chose from their works selectively, never engaging them head on."[31] For example, an entry in "The Mind" has an excerpt from Cudworth's *True Intellectual System* describing Plato's cave allegory, though this excerpt was likely a later addition to the notebook, despite the early creation of the notebook itself.[32] It is worth noting, however, that despite obtaining Cudworth's full *Intellectual System* late in life, the Dummer collection contributed to Yale in Edwards's student years did include Thomas Wise's abridged edition of Cudworth's *Intellectual System*, and Edwards could have been exposed to Cudworth in his early twenties.[33] Wise's abridged edition of Cudworth's book also had significant style changes, which resulted in the removal of the cave allegory section, solidifying the conclusion that the mention of Plato's allegory is a later addition to "The Mind."[34] Despite this, plenty of references to Plato's idealism remain in the abridged edition, and Edwards could have easily picked up on this early in life. His literary interests provide plenty of opportunity for him to engage the ideas that seem to pervade his works.

31. *WJE* 23:22.
32. *WJE* 6:359.
33. On its inclusion in the Dummer collections, see Bryant and Patterson, "List of Books Sent by Jeremiah Dummer," 467.
34. Cudworth and Wise, *Abridgement of Dr. Cudworth's True Intellectual System of the Universe*, "Intro": 12, 1:5. For more on the relationship between Edwards and the Cambridge Platonists see Watts's "Jonathan Edwards and the Cambridge Platonists"; Howe, "Cambridge Platonists of Old England," 87–119.

General post-Reformation works of divinity and commentary also provided Edwards a window into the Christian tradition and a model for theological development. For example, Philip Doddridge's *Family Expositor* commentary on Scripture is frequently appealed to in Edwards's "Blank Bible" and is definitely a source for ancient Christian ideas and philosophers like Philo.[35] Edwards's use of John Edwards's *Theologia Reformata* also would have exposed him to several ideas from the classics and fathers, including Augustine and the general Augustinian tradition.[36] He found access to John Chrysostom through John Hurrion's *The Knowledge of Christ Glorified* (London, 1729).

These secondary sources provided a window into important ancient figures indirectly, as seen in his use of Didymus of Alexandria's Spirit-Christology; Edwards did not read Didymus directly, but had access to him through Owen's *Pneumatalogia*. It would not be hard for Edwards to find secondary sources that provide large quotations of primary works. Some connections, however, could simply be the result of engaging similar ideas rather than the effect of reading the original authors. As Paul Ramsey notes, "it is not necessary to go so far back as Gregory or to Eastern Orthodoxy. Original that he was, Edwards may, indeed, have invented his own theological kinship with Orthodox theology, created out of the same flowing together of biblical and Platonic themes."[37]

Despite the difficulty of pinpointing his exact readings of the fathers (or any authors, for that matter, since Edwards did not always footnote his sources), there are significant and unmistakable similarities (as well as nuanced differences) between Edwards's theology and the tradition in regards to the spiritual sense. As discussed in Part II, the spiritual sense of the person is an indispensible tool for reading the spiritual sense of the text. As Edwards explains in his *Religious Affections*, the Spirit of God influences the minds of the saints, adding a new inward perception.

---

35. For example, see *WJE* 24:2.1115; *WJE* 26:171 ("Catalogue of Books," entry 267).

36. *WJE* 24:142 (entry 129); *WJE* 24:154 (entry 195). For further discussion on the connection between the two Edwardses see my dissertation, "Full of Wondrous and Glorious Things," chapter 5. There is plenty of room for research into these kinds of sources for Edwards's thought. For example, Edwards's use of the natural ability and moral inability categories seems to have some significant connection to his reading of William Bates (Bates, *Harmony of the Divine Attributes*, 64–66), whose language is very similar.

37. *WJE* 8:729.

As seen in chapter 1, Origen and other church fathers argued for five spiritual senses by which the Christian can see divine light and find the spiritual reading of the biblical text. Edwards falls within this tradition to varying degrees. In his *Religious Affections* he speaks (like the fathers) of the use of the physical senses in Scripture to denote spiritual senses. The "work of the Spirit of God in regeneration is often in Scripture compared to the giving a new sense, giving eyes to see, and ears to hear, unstopping the ears of the deaf, and opening the eyes of them that were born blind, and turning from darkness unto light."[38] He, like the ancient fathers, is willing to describe the spiritual changes in the soul in terms of the five senses.

While thoroughly embracing this idea of spiritual senses that correspond to physical senses, Edwards nuances his thought in such a way that he best represents the Augustinian appropriation of this spiritual-sense tradition. Drawing straight lines from his work to the Augustinian tradition in this area has been a matter of discussion since, while his ideas are often very similar to Augustine in this case, his direct citation is rare. His "Catalogue of Reading" mentions the need to secure a copy of Augustine's *Confessions*, which contains Augustine's famous statement on the five senses (10.6), and in his notebook for *Religious Affections* he mentions Augustine as one to find and cite; however, he does not offer up direct statements of indebtedness, making the job of interested scholars difficult.[39]

For Augustine, while there are five spiritual senses, the emphasis falls on these senses holistically, meaning he speaks of them in the general terms of "spiritual understanding." As the brain takes the whole of our physical senses to provide a picture or understanding of the world, so also, the spiritual senses are tools for providing a total understanding of God. The Augustinian vocabulary then falls on the use of the understanding rather than individual senses. In his use of words like *taste*, smell, and sight in reference to spiritual things, in his *Religious Affections* Edwards mostly follows the Augustinian tradition of seeing the overall spiritual change as light shed upon the soul and therefore prefers the overarching singular category of *spiritual understanding*.[40] The "spiritual sense is not a new faculty of understanding," he writes, "but it is

---

38. *WJE* 2:206.
39. *WJE* 26:64.
40. *WJE* 2:47.

a new foundation laid in the nature of the soul, for a new kind of exercises of the same faculty of understanding." This nuance—whether one should speak of senses, plural, or group these into the category of spiritual understanding—is one of frequency. Origen, too, sees the result of the spiritual senses as their acting as one—that is, understanding and knowledge comes from the use of all the senses in perceiving—but his emphasis falls less on the total package of understanding than it does for Edwards and Augustine.

Whether we are discussing Origen, Augustine, or Edwards, these spiritual senses reveal something about Scripture in a way that was— prior to the soul being transformed—impossible to perceive. This brings out another slight difference between Edwards and the ancient fathers. Origen, for example, believed the Spirit of God vivifies the soul, creating spiritual eyes for seeing types and allegories in the biblical text. "Indeed, these passages not only refer to spirit, they *are* spirit," as Gordon Rudy explains, "and Origen does not neatly segregate them from the *sensus divinus* in the person."[41] One's ability to see the deeper meanings of the text comes not only from having a soul changed by the Spirit, according to Origen, but also through Christian maturity and growth in holiness.

Edwards agrees that they are inseparable, that is, that the spiritual senses are tied to the spiritual reading of the text, but this advantage does not so much result in seeing allegories as it does in being able to see the beauty of those allegories or typologies. Finding beauty and joy in the text is the greatest accomplishment of the spiritual senses, giving it more significance. Origen does not deny this point of view, and in fact argues for it as well; however, he also sees the spiritual senses as absolutely necessary for any knowledge of the allegorical. On this point, then, Edwards and Origen diverge. "Hence it appears," writes Edwards, "that the spiritual understanding of the Scripture, don't consist in opening to the mind the mystical meaning of the Scripture, in its parables, types and allegories; for this is only a doctrinal explication of the Scripture."[42] The tradition of looking for the spiritual sense appears to converge with the post-Reformation emphasis on the Bible as a manual for doctrine. Edwards reminds the reader that in 1 Cor 13:2 Paul insists that anyone that has all mysteries and knowledge without love has nothing. In other words, knowing the mystery in its propositional form (even the allegori-

41. Rudy, *Mystical Language of Sensation*, 28.
42. *WJE* 2:278.

cal) is not equal to loving it. The person without spiritual understanding may see allegories in the text, but not know allegories, types, or mysteries as they are in "holy beauty" or excellency. Loving the beauty of the type and allegory is part of understanding its deeper meaning and requires a changed heart; it is a spiritual experience of enjoying the presence of God in the text itself.

The Christian's converted mind has the edge in reading the Bible. "When the mind is enlightened spiritually and rightly to understand Scripture," writes Edwards, "it is enabled to see that in the Scripture, which before was not seen, by reason of blindness."[43] The person's "eyes of the mind" are opened, and he or she can see the "wonderful spiritual excellency of the glorious things contained in the true meaning of it."[44] Unregenerate human beings can see the propositional details, and some are even given, as Edwards is willing to entertain later in life, some form of inspiration. "Inspiration is not so high an honor and privilege of God's special favorites," he wrote in "Miscellanies" 1162. The great Greek philosophers or the prophet Balaam, as Edwards writes, were under "some degree" of inspiration, but they did not enjoy spiritual light.[45] Unlike those with converted eyes, the great philosophers or famous prophets cannot find the joy of divine beauty. He compares this to a person eating. One can know that food is good in a clinical way, that is, that it contains nutrients and is pleasurable, but only a "rectified palate" knows real quality when tasting it. Scripture is spiritual food, for Edwards, but only the rectified spiritual sense can taste its goodness.[46] This is essentially a deeper, but more emotional level or high, much as he experienced in his conversion.

When it came to his hunger for typology, Edwards was a glutton. After his conversion, Edwards concluded that the things of this world were mere shadows, lower beauties that reflected the heavenly and divine form. In his "Types of the Messiah" notebook, Edwards argues for the "typical world" and the "antitypical world," or that which represents the spiritual in this world and that which is the fulfillment. While Puritans tended to speak of typology as a product of Scripture, Edwards believed that types were to be found in both Scripture and the natural world. A

43. *WJE* 2:280.
44. *WJE* 2:281.
45. *WJE* 23:84; *WJE* 2:206, 207.
46. *WJE* 2:281.

type is a shadow, a "carnal" and "transitory part of the universe." It is "imperfect" but it represents "the moral, spiritual and intelligent world, or the City of God."[47] The same could be said for the literal and spiritual readings of Scripture. As he writes in his notebook "Types":

> I expect by very ridicule and contempt to be called a man of a very fruitful brain and copious fancy, but they are welcome to it. I am not ashamed to own that I believe that the whole universe, heaven and earth, air and seas, and the divine constitution and history of the holy Scriptures, be full of images of divine things, as full as language is of words . . .[48]

This goes back to the Platonism he shares with ancient Christians and his emphasis on lower and higher beauty. Types and allegories are lower beauties or shadows of the true beauty of heaven. However, without spiritual understanding that higher beauty or reality that emanates through nature or the text cannot be fully seen or loved for what it is. It is clear that Edwards took pleasure in types and allegories and attributed this pleasure to their beauty and his ability to see that beauty via his redemption. His "Blank Bible" and his notebooks like "Shadows of Divine Things" demonstrate this fascination or even obsession. While Edwards apparently believed that, propositionally speaking, types or allegories should be confirmed by the biblical text in order to avoid enthusiasm, as it was called, he nevertheless found himself engaging in large amounts of typological discourse in his notes and sermons.

While types and allegories were intended to teach doctrinally, as Edwards sees it, they are primarily to be found in Scripture for the purpose of pointing others to Christ. This is made abundantly clear not only in his typological notes but also his "Blank Bible," in which the Psalms are repeatedly understood within a christological framework. In Ps 8:5–9, for example, Edwards's King James reads, "For thou hast made him [humanity] a little lower than the angels," a passage that Edwards understands to imply humanity's role as vice-regent on earth. The crowning of humanity with glory and honor, as he sees it, is also a shadow of the future incarnation of Christ.[49] In a similar vein, he writes in his "Types of the Messiah" notes that the burning bush encountered by Moses is

---

47. *WJE* 11:191.
48. *WJE* 11:152.
49. *WJE* 24.1.478.

also a type of Christ's incarnation.⁵⁰ He finds Christ everywhere. Even the ascension of the ark upon the hill in Bashan in Ps 68:16, as Edwards reads it, "is a type of heaven, and the ark's ascending into it is a type of Christ's ascension into heaven."⁵¹ His reading is not without justification, however, as there is a theological precedent from within the tradition; Paul quotes this passage in reference to Christ's ascension in Eph 4:8. For Edwards, the very reading of Scripture typologically is understood as the method preferred by the New Testament writers themselves, where these types or shadows are fulfilled in the work of Christ.

Similar appeals to typology can be found in his comments on the Song of Solomon. Edwards is uncomfortable with the lover's invitation in 1:4 to the others to love the king, and argues that there must be a better reading than understanding the text as a human love song. "'Tis the nature of earthly love to dislike a rival, and to be averse to plurality," he writes, but, "she speaks of virgins' [sic] loving her loved, and having enjoyed his love, with manifest approbation and delight." Rather than understanding this as some form of call for other women to embrace her beloved, even poetically, he argues for a different, typological interpretation. The "virgins are the saints, who are spiritual virgins" and "this song is intended as a song of love between Christ and the church, or the assembly of saints."⁵² Later, the lover says to the beloved, "I am black." Edwards sees this as referring to her outward "meanness, obscurity, and affliction." His interpretation comes back to the church once again: "This meanness and affliction is in great measure owing to the contempt and hard usage of false churches and false professors, which appears very much in their keeping them under and in a state of servitude to serve their temporal interests, and to maintain their worship."⁵³ He concludes that this song is about Christ and the saints. As a result, he naturally interprets the text in a mystical or allegorical form that allows him to apply a gospel reading rather than accept its overall erotic nature.

Christ, for Edwards, is the bridge between heaven and earth, and the incarnation is central to everything and to all typology; and so it makes sense that Scripture would often refer to Christ typologically. This comes out in his reading of Ps 144:5: "Bow thy heavens, O Lord, and

---

50. *WJE* 11:238.
51. *WJE* 24.1.505.
52. *WJE* 24.1.609, 610.
53. *WJE* 24.1.610.

come down." This call for God to appear like a theophany is believed by Edwards to have its ultimate fulfillment in Christ's first and second comings. "This was never so remarkably fulfilled as in the incarnation of Jesus Christ, when heaven and earth were as it were brought together. Heaven itself was as it were made to bow that it might be united to the earth." Early on, Edwards speculated on the reasons for an incarnated Christ. The *Logos*, he points out in "Miscellanies" 81, became incarnate to have communion with humanity, to reveal God without fear, and to "bring God near to us."[54]

Christ as *Logos* is necessary for bridging the heavenly with its earthly type. Later in life, his discussion of the *Logos* took an interest in the various appropriations or types of the idea in the classic philosophers and myths. For example, in reading Andrew Michael Ramsay's (1689–1743) *Philosophical Principles of Natural and Revealed Religion*, Edwards looked for imitations of the Trinity among ancient Jews, noting Philo's description of the *Logos* as the eternal Son of God and the creator.[55] In his reading of Ralph Cudworth, he copied a significant section in which Cudworth shows the similarities between Platonic ideas of the *Logos* and the early fathers' perception as found in Clement of Alexandria and Origen.[56] In "Miscellanies" 1355, a large portion of text copied from Ramsay is apparently noted by Edwards for the purpose of showing other ancients in agreement with Christian ideas of God, particularly noting Justin Martyr's appeal to the Greek philosophers as being inspired by God when writing about the *Logos*. He even compares the words of these philosophers with Scripture itself.[57] Christ brings heaven and earth together, allowing the eternal to show through nature in general, in scriptural types specifically, and even in the pagan philosophers.

Why is Scripture, however, so much greater than nature's revelation and so far superior to the world's religions? According to Edwards, Scripture is the fullest expression of the divine truth, the complete unveiling of eternity in time. Nature does not have the specifics, and other religions, as admirable as their attempts may be, are flawed copies of the truth, as he sees it. More specifically, the words of philosophers are

54. *WJE* 13:248 ("Misc." 81).
55. *WJE* 23:191 ("Misc." 1256).
56. *WJE* 23:675–76 ("Misc." 1359).
57. *WJE* 23:560 ("Misc." 1355).

"conversant" on divine things, but when compared to Scripture they are "dirt and dung."[58] The Word of God, however, is "full of wondrous and glorious things" because it is "a cabinet of most precious jewels" that like Christ, the Word, is sent by God "from heaven down to man."[59] Scripture is another incarnation.

Scripture as Incarnation

As seen before, Edwards's Spirit-Christology is the backdrop for his understanding of the incarnation of Christ and the union of the Christian to Christ. The latter follows the analogy of the incarnation itself and entails another sort of incarnation. The first significant entry in the "Miscellanies" that handles this discussion (entry 487) briefly argues for an incarnational parallel; in the incarnation, the Spirit takes the divine *Logos* and the human nature and forms one person, and the Spirit takes this God-Human person and the Church and unites them together forming one body. In this entry, Edwards sees the humanity of Christ as finite and whose communion with the divine easily could be overwhelmed if not for the Spirit—after all, human minds can handle only so much knowledge. As a solution to this problem, Edwards notes that all knowledge possessed by the God-Human, as a single person of two natures, is maintained by the Holy Spirit. The will and knowledge of Christ, limited and infinite, come together in one person by the work of the Holy Spirit, who maintains the integrity of the two natures, which would otherwise not be able to act as one person.

Christians, likewise, as finite and fallen beings, can also handle only so much divine knowledge. They participate in the divine and have a right to all knowledge after conversion, but do not have the ability to assimilate it perfectly or entirely, especially while still in a sinful condition. The Spirit, as the bond of this union, maintains the integrity of the infinite and finite by facilitating this knowledge according to human limitations, even that of Scripture's human authors.

Within his incarnational discussion in "Miscellanies" 487, there is another comparison or analogy to the incarnation, but this time to Scripture, and it is briefly mentioned. "The man Jesus becomes one person by a communion of knowledge and will," writes Edwards, "but

---

58. *WJE* 14:252.
59. *WJE* 19:46.

as in believers all divine knowledge is by the Spirit—'tis by the Spirit that the knowledge of inspiration and prophecy is given, and 'tis by the Holy Ghost that the spiritual knowledge of all believers is given. . . ."[60] Taking note of the line, "'tis by the Spirit that the knowledge of inspiration and prophecy is given," it is clear that Scripture, the other Word of God, is incarnational. The Spirit enables communication between God and humanity. This is because Scripture, like Christ, is also both divine and human. The concept of *finitum non capax infiniti* applies to Scripture as well.

Scripture possesses both a divine and human "nature," for lack of a better word. It is God's infinitely complicated communication made assessable, or as Edwards writes, spoken "after the manner of men."[61] What is revealed in Scripture, as "Miscellanies" 487 would indicate in its context, is limited by what the Spirit would allow. This has many important implications, but is an underused and underdeveloped aspect of Edwards's theological conclusions.

Edwards is able to find room for God's accommodation of his divine message to the limits of human nature. Edwards's statement in "Miscellanies" 487 is brief, but in the context, the communication of divine knowledge in the inspiration of Scripture is being compared to that of the communication of knowledge to the mind of Christ. Edwards took seriously that for Christ to have divine and human natures, the human nature must include a mind. During the early christological controversies, the orthodox insisted—contrary to some—that Christ had to have a human mind. This disagreement led to Gregory Nazianzus's sarcastic quip: "If anyone has put his trust in Him as man without a human mind, he is really bereft of mind, and quite unworthy of salvation."[62] Edwards agrees with Gregory on the issue of Christ's mind, and he believes that the human mind of Christ is limited by the boundaries of its nature.

John Owen again enters this discussion. As noted in the fourth chapter, Owen responded to the Socinian question that if Christ was fully God, how is it that he grew in wisdom and stature (Luke 2:40)? Owen's response was to implement his Spirit-Christology. Christ is both divine and human, and the human side comes with its limitations. In order for Christ to be truly and fully human, the divine and human na-

---

60. *WJE* 13:530.
61. *WJE* 19:47.
62. Gregory Nazianzus, "Letter to Cledonius" (*NPNF* 7:440).

tures must maintain their integrity, including that limitation of human knowledge. What Christ did know and was supposed to know for the purposes of his ministry was given to him by the Holy Spirit, who was responsible for the communion of attributes between natures.

Amy Plantinga Pauw sees two distinctions between Owen and Edwards on the incarnation and the role of the Spirit. The first of these (as seen previously) is that Owen takes the more traditional view that the *Logos* immediately brought the anhypostatic nature into hypostatic union, while Edwards understands the uniting of the *Logos* with the human nature as the product of the Holy Spirit from the beginning. That Edwards understands the Spirit as having the primary, immediate role in this aspect of the incarnation seems clear.[63] This leads to a second distinction: for Owen, as Pauw notes, the uniting is done by the Son, but the "historical unfolding of Christ's life in ever increasing union with God was the work of the Holy Spirit."[64] Two agents were involved, for Owen, and the work of the Spirit was directed at Christ's growth in grace and wisdom according to the capacity of his faculties. In contrast, Pauw believes that Edwards finds the human nature of Christ as having "no need for growth in wisdom or stature (Luke 2:40)." She adds that the Spirit, according to Edwards, "protected the incarnate Christ from the limitations of human ignorance."[65] This second distinction may overstate the case.

Edwards does not appear to exempt Christ from the limitations of human mental capacities. In "Miscellanies" 1358, he wonders who upheld the world "while Christ was in his humbled state?"

> and while an infant, when he had less knowledge than afterwards, when it is said that he increased in wisdom and stature, and [had] far less strength than he had afterwards? when we are told that he was wearied with his journey, wearied and his strength in a measure spent only with the governing the motions of his own body? Who upheld and governed the world at that time?[66]

---

63. Hastings, "'Honouring the Spirit,'" 279–99. Compare *WJE* 18:335 with *WJE* 18:414. Also helpful on this subject is Kapic, "The Son's Assumption of a Human Nature," 154–66. See also "Miscellanies" 487, 709, 767.

64. Pauw, *"Supreme Harmony of All,"* 147.

65. Ibid., 147, 148.

66. *WJE* 23:609. Paul Ramsey notes this passage in his Appendix "Heaven is a Progressive State" to *WJE* volume 3 (3:734), in which he writes that "Edwards rejected the age-old kenotic theology that came to flourish later, in the nineteenth century."

Christ appears to be subject to change, according to Edwards. Similarly, in 1738, when addressing the question of whether Christ is the same, yesterday, today, and forever (as Hebrews 13:8 indicates), Edwards affirms the impeccability of Christ, but denies that his human nature was unchangeable. Christ's human nature, he concludes, went through "many changes" both in body and mind, and in wisdom and stature.[67] Edwards finds that Christ's knowledge is sometimes limited. For example, John 17:5 (KJV) reads, "And now, O Father, glorify thou me with thine own self with the glory which I had with thee before the world was." In this passage, Christ has an idea of the kind of glory he possessed "before the world was." In "Miscellanies" 205 Edwards asks the question: could Christ, as the God-man, have the same understanding of that glory that—as infinite as it would have to be—he had "before the world was"? He concludes: "The man Christ Jesus, being the same person with the eternal Son of God, has a reminiscence or consciousness of what appertained to the eternal Logos," but "when he remembered those things, he could not remember [them] as they were in the infinite mind, for the idea of the Creator cannot be communicated to the creature as it is in God...."[68]

More than mere limitation, lack of knowledge also appears to be part of the God-Human package. For example, in Matt 24:36 and Mark 13:32, Christ admits ignorance of the day and hour of his return. This piece of factual information is understood to be withheld from Christ, according to Edwards, but only according to his human nature.[69] All knowledge of the divine that the human nature had, according to Edwards, was by the Spirit's "inspiration and revelation" to the mind of the human nature.[70] This has significant implications for his understanding of Scripture as revelation inspired by the Spirit. As Christ had

---

Edwards's Spirit-Christology allows for limitations on behalf of the human nature of Christ, which includes limits on omniscience. Christ as an infant does lack knowledge, but this is not so much a giving up of knowledge in his divine nature as it is about the communication of attributes by the Spirit. Edwards appears to reject the idea that Christ gave up the upholding of the universe as an infant, but not the possibility that, as to his human nature, his knowledge is limited.

67. Edwards, "I Cor. 13:1–10(b)" in *WJE Series II* 53:5–6.
68. *WJE* 13:340, 341.
69. *WJE* 23:634–35.
70. *WJE* 18:413 ("Misc." 766).

limitations on his human side, so do the human authors and the sacred text they produced.

The limitations of Christ's human nature as contrasted with the divine, particularly as discussed by both Owen and Edwards, may appear to some theologians to strike too hard a line between the two. In Chalcedonian terms, it may appear that Edwards and Owen are dancing with a Nestorian position. On the contrary, both theologians do appear to borrow from those who are, in fact, considered the fathers of orthodoxy (e.g., Nazianzus, Didymus, and Augustine), and in the case of Owen, with the specific goal of defeating the non-orthodox position of Socinianism. Neither appear to perceive Christ as other than a single person, and for both it appears that whether knowledge is human or divine, the point is ultimately about a logical category for understanding the single divine-human being. Nevertheless, the temptation may be for the theologian to tie Edwards or Owen to the metaphorical chair and to interrogate them on the question, but the historical solution is to simply recognize that they do not appear to address it beyond what is written.

When writing on the mysteries of the Christian religion, Edwards clearly finds room for God's accommodation to human limitations. If the "indisputable truths" of eighteenth-century philosophy were "revealed from heaven to be truths in past ages," writes Edwards, "they would be looked upon as mysterious and difficult, and would have seemed as impossible as the most mysterious Christian doctrines do now."[71] Divine revelation is often "beyond our understanding," he argues, and "I believe that even now, if there should come a revelation from heaven of what is the very truth in these matters, without deviating at all to accommodate it to our received notions and principles, there would be many things in it that would seem to be absurd and contradictious."[72] In the case of divine revelation, however, God "considers the weakness of our sight." God refuses to depart from the truth itself, but "I believe," says Edwards, that "he accommodates himself to our way of understanding in his manner of expressing and representing things, as we are wont to do when we are teaching little children."[73]

The limited nature of Scripture plays out in doctrinal matters as well. Some divinely revealed doctrines are too difficult for human beings to

71. *WJE* 18:119.
72. *WJE* 18:119.
73. *WJE* 18:119.

accept right away. As a result, God finds avoiding the discussion acceptable. When preaching on the "Perpetuity and Change of the Sabbath," a sermon birthed in large part from "Miscellanies" 160, Edwards considers the problem of the Christian Sabbath. The New Testament's lack of plain speaking on the subject posed a problem for post-Reformation insistence that Sunday was the new Sabbath. For Edwards, this was less a problem because of his understanding of divine inspiration. Though "nothing more plainly" was said about the Lord's Day before the book of Revelation, this was "not an obstacle" for Edwards:

> In all probability it was purposely avoided by the Holy Spirit in the first settling of Christian churches in the world, both amongst heathen and Jews, but especially for the sake of the Jews out of tenderness to the Jewish Christians . . . God had made so much of it, so solemnly, frequently, and carefully commanded it, and often so dreadfully punished the breach of it, that there was more color [i.e., justification] for their retaining their custom.[74]

Edwards's God had pushed the Sabbath for so long that he could not bring himself to break the news to them just yet. Similarly, says Edwards, Christ had many things to say, but held back for the sake of those who could not handle the truth. He revealed what he could but gradually or "as they could bear." Likewise, even the apostles, according to Edwards, were gracious, "careful and tender" to those to whom they ministered.[75]

It is at this point in the sermon that one might be able to hear Edwards pause and take a deep breath before taking his thoughts one step further. In the sermon he tells his congregation: "But I will say this, that it was very possible that the apostles themselves *at first* [emphasis mine] might not have had this change of the day of the Sabbath fully revealed to them." He carefully adds the words "at first" in this sermon, which he leaves out in his private notes, perhaps to make sure it was clear to his congregation that the apostles could have discovered that fuller meaning later.[76] To continue to press the ignorance of the biblical writers was a dangerous thing to do in eighteenth-century New England. Instead, he tells them that some things had to wait until the church was firmly established, but how long he understands this establishment to take was left open-ended.

74. *WJE* 17:241.
75. *WJE* 17:241.
76. *WJE* 17:242; *WJE* 13:317 ("Misc." 160).

Edwards expresses a similar thought on the limitations of the authors of Scripture in another early "Miscellanies." In a note on Scripture, he writes that "God had a design and meaning which the penmen never thought of"; God did, however, leave clues in the text that prompt the reader to look for more, better, and fuller truth. This happens "frequently," according to Edwards, particularly when the biblical writer's choice of words is not "agreeable to strict philosophical verity" and when God "condescended to their manner of speaking and thinking...."[77] Humans are limited in so many areas, including their capacity for knowing, their ability to change quickly without being traumatized, and the boundaries drawn within their historical and cultural contexts. Edwards appears to understand that this duality in Scripture, a divine message that is, in some sense, circumscribed by human limitations, is a parallel to the incarnation of Christ.

As Origen and the Cappadocian fathers phrased it, God spoke like a parent to a child, or used "baby talk."[78] The *Logos*, writes Edwards, "came down from his infinite perfection, and accommodated himself to our nature and manner by being made man, as he was in the person of Jesus Christ."[79] Edwards would have recognized himself, to some extent, in the words of Cambridge Platonist John Smith, who wrote: "*Divine Truth* becomes many times in Scripture *incarnate*, debasing itself to assume our rude conceptions, that so it might converse more freely with us . . ." Scripture is not, as Smith says, written in the "language of *Eternity*"; rather, it wears "our mantles," learns "our language," and conforms "itself as it were to our dress and fashions."[80]

There are interesting conclusions that Edwards could have drawn had he carried this incarnational view of Scripture further. For example, despite Edwards's great interest in the newest science, which included a hefty dose of Newton, in his sermon "God's All-Sufficiency for the Supply of Our Wants," he clearly espouses a Ptolemaic view of the universe, referring to God as "forming and fixing those vast globes over our heads."[81] Kenneth P. Minkema notes this feature of the sermon and

77. *WJE* 13:348 ("Misc." 229).

78. Origen, *Against Celsus*, 4.71. For a discussion on early Christian accommodationism see Sparks, "Sun Also Rises," 112–32.

79. *WJE* 18:410 ("Misc." 763).

80. Smith, *Select Discourses*, 171, 172. Smith's *Discourses* appear in Edwards's "Catalogue" (*WJE* 26:281–82).

81. *WJE* 14:475.

its inconsistency with Edwards's use of the new science of the day. He notes that in Edwards's day Copernicus was not yet universally accepted; for example, Samuel Sewall found Cotton Mather's preaching favorably about it in 1714 in Boston as coming at a bad time. "If the (relatively) cosmopolitan community of Boston had trouble accepting Copernicus," writes Minkema, "then it is possible that Northampton too would object to hearing his view from their pulpit."[82] But if Scripture is incarnational, maintaining this outdated science was unnecessary; Edwards's incarnational view could certainly have opened the door for him to move on to a Copernican perspective. It would have provided a better means for dealing with early-modern critics of the Bible as well.

If Edwards had pressed this perspective further, his position could have set up future evangelicals with a means for handling and interpreting the challenges of the next two and a half centuries. Deists of his day challenged the supernatural elements of Scripture, labeling them as antiquated and superstitious. They challenged biblical history when it did not come with the body of historical knowledge in their day. The challenge for Edwards was mostly sustaining the reasonableness of the supernatural and demonstrating—using the assumed premise of *prisca theologia*—that other religions pulled their ideas and history from Scripture. However, in the subsequent centuries, discoveries of other ancient manuscripts, law codes, and creation accounts, along with scientific discoveries of evolution and the expansion of the universe, have offered an enormous challenge to those theological descendents who persist with an inerrant Scripture. Early in the twentieth century, the tactic taken by evangelicals of the fundamentalist persuasion was to deny the validity of these discoveries. Today, more evangelicals refuse to ignore the challenges and have moved to create their own understanding of Scripture as incarnational, often landing in hot water for it.[83] The seeds of this idea are present in Edwards's robust incarnational theology of Scripture.

The Divine Treasure

Edwards offers a full and vibrant perspective on Scripture. One should not conclude, however, that Edwards fully developed this incarnational

---

82. *WJE* 14:475 n. 4.
83. For an example of this, see Enns, *Inspiration and Incarnation* (2005).

approach to Scripture. This incarnational theme appears on occasion, but he does not follow it up with a major treatise on the subject. As a product of his time, he is concerned with confirming Scripture's infallibility and less inclined to readily accept any validity challenges of his day. For example, Moses, according to Edwards, is definitely the author of the Torah. He does accept that other editors could have changed some minor details to update the book; names of places could have been updated "by a later hand" for a new generation, and Moses probably did not record his own death.[84] However, he is concerned primarily with defending the text as is. His use of the incarnational analogy is primarily for discussion of doctrinal issues and for understanding the place of typology, that is, that the human writers did not always know the second layer of types that were intended in their renderings of history, poetry, and prophecy.

Though Edwards's later years were often focused on arguing with Deists and verifying biblical historical data and theological ideas, his reading of the biblical text was primarily driven by his hope of experiencing Christ. For him, reading Scripture is a spiritual event first and foremost. The converted human soul that is united to Christ can see the beauty of heavenly things in nature and in Scripture, because both that person and Scripture are part of both worlds, after an incarnational analogy. The Spirit unites the divine and human natures into one person; the church and Christ into one body; and the biblical text's human and divine messages into one Scripture. Scripture is a divine treasure chest, and for the transformed soul who reads it or hears it preached, it brings a "Heavenly Elysium" or, as Edwards describes elsewhere, "a surprising and amazing joy."

---

84. *WJE* 15:467 (Entry 416).

7

The Lasting Voice of Edwards

> This new nature is from God, and is something of God; and therefore it tends to God again, and is contented with nothing short of God, and a perfect conformity to him.
>
> —Jonathan Edwards, "Striving after Perfection," 1737[1]

> In having the Spirit, we have communion with Christ in his life, for to have the Spirit dwelling in us is life. The Spirit is the beauty and joy of the divine nature, and therefore must be the highest perfection and happiness of ours....
>
> —Jonathan Edwards, "Blank Bible" on Romans 8:1–4[2]

ON MARCH 22, 1758, the fifty-four-year-old Jonathan Edwards died from a smallpox inoculation gone awry. He had received the vaccination a month earlier; being an optimist when it came to many scientific advances, he was eager to set an example by having his family inoculated.[3] The threat of smallpox was a fact of life in the colonies. In 1752, he had encouraged the Reverend Aaron Burr to find a "skillful, prudent physician" to get the inoculation.[4] A year later, on April 1, 1753, when it appeared that Edwards's fourteen-year-old son, Timothy, might have smallpox, Edwards encouraged Timothy to seek a greater cure, one that works to "save from eternal misery, and to bestow eternal life."[5]

---

1. *WJE* 19:691.
2. *WJE* 24:2.1011.
3. Marsden, *Jonathan Edwards*, 493; *WJE* 16:738.
4. *WJE* 16:478.
5. *WJE* 16, 579.

"In God's favor is life," he tells Timothy, "and his lovingkindness is better than life." Nothing avails before God, whether they be "desires, and pains, and prayers," unless "you have savingly believed in Christ."[6] More than a comforting "get well" letter, Edwards sends his son a conversion sermon, reminding him that in the end, only Christ matters.

Incidents like this theological response to this most serious of circumstances—circumstances that foreshadow how he himself will die a few years later—demonstrate how foundational conversionism and biblicism were for him. David Bebbington understands these marks of early evangelicalism as coming out of Edwards's Enlightenment context. There is no doubt, as many of Edwards's sources (such as Locke) indicate, that he is speaking from and to that context, at least in part. It would be unrealistic, however, to demand that Edwards cozily fit into one era or another perfectly. Such an attempt misses the complexity of influences (parental, pastoral, and academic), including those conversation partners he discovered in books.

These multilayered influences make the labeling of Edwards difficult. Through which lens do we view him first? He could be a Connecticut Valley Yankee in a Cappadocian court, or a Reformed court, or a Thomistic court. His ability to evade classification has left us with a diversity of portraits to consider over the last century.

Finding Edwards's Voice

From Peter Gay calling Edwards the "last medieval American," the producer of "pathetic" work, and Ola Winslow, who wrote that his "dogmatic system" is "outworn," a system that needed not to be amended but "demolished," to Michael J. McClymond, who finds in Edwards the powerful voice of Gregory Palamas, scholars have reached no final consensus on just who the man is.[7] The varying labels many have given to Edwards are partly the result of the confusion Perry Miller generated in his attempts to save Edwards from himself. The man Miller once praised for speaking "from an insight into science and psychology so much ahead of his time that our own can hardly be said to have caught up with him" also has been depicted as belonging to a generation brimming with archaic and outmoded systems of belief.[8] Miller, recognizing

---

6. *WJE* 16:579.
7. Gay, *Loss of Mastery*, 113; Winslow, *Jonathan Edwards*, 326.
8. Miller, *Jonathan Edwards*, xiii.

the difficulty of making a Calvinist palatable to modern scholars, tried to add a little sugar.

As Harry S. Stout notes in his "The Puritans and Edwards," scholars of a few generations ago, such as Vernon Parrington, were "lumping the Puritans and Edwards together as one continuous and repressive 'anachronism' retarding America's progress to enlightened liberalism."[9] While Perry Miller describes Edwards as a man out of his time, Parrington portrays him as leading a life of "futility," with "great powers baffled and wasted."[10] Poor Edwards appears to let the "theologian" triumph over the "philosopher." He is, according to Parrington, "the last and greatest of the royal line of Puritan mystics."[11] Miller's rehabilitation of Edwards came by striking hard differences between Edwards and his Puritan ancestors. In doing so, Miller said too much. Edwards is, as Stout writes, "even more a Puritan than Miller or his revisionists concede."[12]

What about Edwards the biblicist? What Miller did for Edwards, by distancing him from Puritans, he also did for the Puritans themselves by distancing them from their own reputation. George Marsden notes that Miller often minimizes the "unattractive aspects of Puritan religion." Among Marsden's list of Miller's modifications are "Puritan Biblicism" and "Calvinism." Miller's Puritan is satisfied with extrabiblical sources, and according to Marsden, Miller "seems to assume the Puritans were very seldom strictly guided by biblical precedents."[13] But the Puritans were the leading biblicists of their day. The label of biblicist in reference to Edwards or the Puritans appeared to be a problem for anyone hoping to see Edwards as standing above others in his day, being forward-thinking and inventive. Depending on what aspect of his thought one examines, he was forward-thinking for his day, but he is still a product of his time and tradition, and to miss this is to forfeit an historical appreciation of his work.

The "Edwards renaissance" of recent years, including Yale's impressive critical edition, offers a better understanding of Edwards and his

---

9. Stout, "Puritans and Edwards," 9.

10. Parrington, *Main Currents in American Thought*, 162.

11. Ibid., 56, 152.

12. Stout, "Puritans and Edwards," 157, 143; see also my "Future of Hope," 75–98, and "An Empty Threat," 69–92.

13. Marsden, "Perry Miller's Rehabilitation of the Puritans," 93, 94.

times, with a bit more openness to his biblicism.[14] Stephen Stein, in his introduction to the *Works* volume, *Notes on Scripture*, draws attention to this deficit, arguing that "early estimations overstated Edwards's scientific and philosophical precociousness and contributed to the masking of this aspect of his thought."[15] A "proper correction," he asserts, "calls for a more thorough examination of the biblical dimension of Edwards' study habits and his writings and a recognition of his selective appropriation of the work of others."[16] Scholars like Robert Brown have engaged Edwards's biblical work within the context of critical and pre-critical periods, particularly in reaction to Deist challenges. Brown's work gives Edwards's New England culture of the Bible serious consideration and awakens the reader to some of the lesser-known but more important and more contemporary sources of Edwards's found in his "Catalogue of Reading." Douglas A. Sweeney has also continued the discussion of Edwards and the Bible within a context of his pastoral work.[17] Both Brown and Sweeney firmly plant Edwards within the category of a biblicist.

What has been demonstrated in this book, however, is that understanding Edwards as a biblicist means getting to his view of conversion, which is founded on a divine participation or deification centered in the incarnation. His biblicism has a distinctly mystical side to it, one that transcends a plainer reading of the text and eagerly returns to a reading of Scripture that involves multiple layers and, in Edwards's experience, a spiritual flight to the highest of heavens. This element of his thought goes beyond his strict placement within—and only within—the Enlightenment world.

What has been demonstrated in the pages preceding is that Edwards has many influences, some of which he is aware of and acknowledges, but many of which he finds through secondary sources and shared philosophical foundations. Being a preacher, for example, his interest in the Bible is something he shares with his Puritan ancestors, but in

14. *The Works of Jonathan Edwards* produced by Yale University.

15. *WJE* 15:21–22.

16. *WJE* 15:22. Others have been less than happy with this interpretation of Edwards. In 2001, Bruce Kuklick, uninterested in Edwards's more Puritan sources, did an about-face on his previously enthusiastic view of Edwards (Kuklick, "Review Essay," 115).

17 Sweeney, *Jonathan Edwards and the Ministry of the Word*, 83–106. See also Sweeney, "'Longing for More and More of it'?" 26.

his case it is driven by a vibrant sense of divine participation that would find more resonance with ancient Christian theologians. Accepting this intellectual diversity, sometimes intensely Calvinist and other times more medieval or ancient, or even innovatively elusive, provides a better historical portrait.

His theological perspective was initially forged in the middle of a public and personal crisis. In his conversion, Edwards believed heaven and earth came together through an incarnational moment. Christ bridged heaven and earth in the incarnation by the work of the Spirit; and like Christ, the earthly Christian is united to the heavenly God by virtue of a union with Christ. Human beings participate in the divine being, and by their union with the divine, have access to all that Christ owns. Thus the Christian "really possess all things," insists Edwards:

> God three in one, all that he is, and all that he has, and all that he does, all that he has made or done—the whole universe, bodies and spirits, earth and heaven, angels, men and devil, sun moon [and] stars, land and sea, fish and fowls, all the silver and gold, kings and potentates as well as mean men—are as much the Christian's as the money in his pocket, the clothes he wears, or the house he dwells in, or the victuals he eats; yea more properly his, more advantageously, more *his*, than if he [could] command all those things mentioned to be just in all respects as he pleased at any time, by virtue of his union with Christ....[18]

The surprising joy that Edwards experienced in his conversion and that drove so much of his theological endeavors was, as he understood it, the participation with or becoming one with the divine being. God puts "his own beauty, i.e. his beautiful likeness, upon their souls."[19] Edwards's conversion offered a view of the highest beauty, the discovery of the divine treasure chest, where, within the biblical text, lay a glittering variety of mystical layers to explore. Edwards loves the Bible as a divine communication to humanity, but he loves it foremost for its participation in the heavenly world.

His form of biblicism, therefore, is centered on conversion; this is the incarnation of Christ in reverse. Christ became man, said Athanasius, so that we might become God. He came down to earth, as Edwards and the Greek fathers see it, so that we might enjoy heaven.

---

18. Bebbington, *Evangelicalism in Modern Britain*, 3; *WJE* 13:183, 184 ("Misc." ff.).
19. *WJE* 17:208.

"This nature, as 'tis from God, so it is a divine or godlike nature," says Edwards. "It is as it were a communication . . . of the holy nature of God. *2 Peter 1:4*, 'Whereby ye are made partakers of the divine nature.'"[20] This new nature belongs to the human, but without confusion or separation. In his language of "union" one might see Edwards as simply repeating the language of Calvin, but in fact he benefits more broadly from the diversity of the Christian tradition. If he is examined only within his immediate Reformed tradition, to the exclusion of these other demonstrable, varied streams of influence, significant points can be—and have been—lost. A more nuanced understanding of his thought recognizes his passionate embrace of a mystically centered theology that defies simple classification.

Divine Participation at the End of Creation

Towards the end of his life Edwards crafted his *Two Dissertations*, published posthumously. The first dissertation, *Concerning the End for Which God Created the World*, takes divine participation to its fullest level by including all of creation. God created the world for his own glory, says Edwards. This glory, as explored previously, is the communication of the Trinitarian essence *ad extra* to creation. "Thus it appears reasonable to suppose," writes Edwards, "that it was what God had respect to as an ultimate end of his creating the world, to communicate of his own infinite fullness of good [the disposition of God's being] . . . that there might be a glorious and abundant emanation of his infinite fullness of good *ad extra*. . . ."[21] God diffuses his own essence or disposition to creation like the root of a tree communicates sap to its branches and leaves, he notes. "We may suppose that *a disposition in God*," writes Edwards, "*as an original property of his nature, to an emanation of his own infinite fullness, was what excited him to create the world*. . . ."[22]

Edwards's idea of God communicating his nature to creation in this treatise is essentially a recapitulation of those conclusions he drew from his original conversion experience. As discovered in chapter 3, Edwards experienced a sweetness of the divine being, seeing God's essence in all of creation, and discovering that fullness internally. After his conver-

---

20. *WJE* 19:691.
21. *WJE* 8:433.
22. *WJE* 8:435.

sion, his "sense of divine things gradually increased, and became more and more lively, and had more of that inward sweetness." Nothing in nature appeared to his eyes as it once did, instead "there seemed to be, as it were, a calm, sweet cast, or appearance of divine glory, in almost everything. God's excellency, his wisdom, his purity, and love, seemed to appear in everything; in the sun, moon and stars; in the clouds, and blue sky; in the grass, flowers, trees; in the water, and all nature. . . ."[23] By the end of his life, Edwards had the vocabulary and theological proficiency to make mature sense of it for himself, and the language of *Concerning the End* is pulled from the lessons learned of those early years.

God's communication with his creation is more than simple information found in the Bible. God creates and emanates his nature and in doing so, he also communicates to his creatures "virtue and holiness." In this way, says Edwards, "the creature partakes of God's own moral excellency, which is properly the beauty of the divine nature."[24] Through the emanation of the "divine fullness," "divine knowledge" is communicated to the creature and put in "conformity to God." In a "participation of what is in God," the creature finds "happiness," a theme that filled Edwards's early notebooks. "What is communicated," writes Edwards, "is divine, or something of God: and each communication is of that nature, that the creature to whom it is made, is thereby conformed to God, and united to him."[25] Christ, in his mediatorial role, is "made king of angels and men; set at the head of the universe, having all power given him in heaven and earth, to that end that he may promote their happiness . . ."[26] The union the creature has to God is an eternal process, one in which the creature "will forever come nearer and nearer to that strictness and perfection of union which is between the Father and the Son."[27]

Participating in the divine being is unmistakably central to *Concerning the End*. The immensely personal nature of the union that comes from participation has (as seen in chapter 4) led some to wonder if Edwards is a monist.

> In the creature's knowing, esteeming, loving, rejoicing in, and praising God, the glory of God is both exhibited and acknowl-

23. *WJE* 16:793–94.
24. *WJE* 8:442.
25. *WJE* 8:441, 442.
26. *WJE* 8:506.
27. *WJE* 8:443.

edged; his fullness is received and returned. Here is both an *emanation* and *remanation*. The refulgence shines upon and into the creature, and is reflected back to the luminary. The beams of glory come from God, and are something of God, and are refunded back again to their original. So that the whole is *of* God, and *in* God, and *to* God; and God is the beginning, middle, and end in this affair.[28]

There is no doubt that this idea of participation in the divine being holds a lasting place in Edwards's thought. Even in 1738, as Edwards was publishing his justification discourse, his sermon series on charity (published posthumously with the title *Charity and Its Fruits*) was replete with this participatory language. "The love of God flows out towards Christ the Head, and through him to all his members," writes Edwards. This is like the light of the sun, he notes. The sun can shine by its own light, but the planets "shine by reflecting the light of the sun. And this light is reflected . . . back to the sun itself." The love of God is given and reflected back, or "emanated" and "remanated" back to him. Participation of the earthly in the heavenly is only possible through the headship of Christ, as Edwards sees it. With participation in mind, God creates the world, sends his son in the incarnation, and redeems the world. Edwards's books, notes, sermons, letters—all appear to engage the subject of divine participation in more than just a passing reference.[29]

Edwards's emphasis on the incarnation and divine participation makes his thought a Protestant candidate for continuing interests in ecumenical dialogue between Western and Eastern Christians. John Calvin, due to his emphasis on union with Christ, often has been mined for potential connections, but Edwards's gleaning from Platonism and his mystical view of conversion offers more points of contact, and yet remains relatively untapped.[30] The language of deification and the spiritual reading of Scripture found in the writings of ancient Christians (see chapter 1) clearly have a kindred spirit in the ideas of Edwards as explored throughout this book.

This brilliant colonial thinker could not escape the influences of his father and grandfather, but neither were they his only conversa-

---

28. *WJE* 8:531.

29. See, for example, his 1745 letter discussing divine participation in *WJE* 16:199.

30. See for example, Billings, "John Calvin," 200–18; and Habets, "Reforming Theōsis," 146–67.

tion partners. His New England context was full of Calvinists, but the libraries of the time provided an intersection where every sort of voice, ancient Christian and otherwise, could meet. Edwards was driven to these in developing a theological explanation for the unexpected nature of his conversion. While other thinkers of his day passed away quietly in the dusty archives of libraries across the world, his colorful weaving of backgrounds both ancient and early modern produced a depth and versatility that allows him to this day to be read in fresh ways by the lay person as well as the academic. The story of Jonathan Edwards's theological journey—of his seeking, finding, and participating with the divine being, and dreaming that one day all of creation would return to him and become part of him—began in his childhood three hundred years ago but continues to find a voice long after his death.

Bibliography

Primary Sources

Ames, William. *English Puritanisme, Containing the Maine Opinions of the Rigidest Sort of Those That Are Called Puritans in the Realme of England.* N.p., 1641.

———. *The Marrow of Theology.* Edited by John D. Eusden. Grand Rapids: Baker, 1968.

———. *Medulla SS. Theologiae, Ex Sacris Literis, Earumque Interpretibus, Extracta and Methodice Disposita Per.* London: Robertum Allotium, 1630.

Augustine. *The City of God.* Translated by Marcus Dods. New York: Modern Library, 1950.

———. *De Trinitate.* Vol. 5 of *The Works of Saint Augustine: A Translation for the 21st Century.* Edited and translated by Edmund Hill. New York: New City, 1991.

———. *Homilies on the Gospel of John; Homilies on the First Epistle of John; Soliloquies.* Vol. 7 of *A Select Library of the Nicene and Post-Nicene Fathers of the Christian Church.* Edited by Philip Schaff. New York: Christian Literature, 1888.

———. *On Genesis: A Refutation of the Manichees, Unfinished Literal Commentary on Genesis, The Literal Meaning of Genesis.* Vol. 1 of *The Works of Saint Augustine: A Translation for the 21st Century.* Edited by John E. Rotelle. Translated by Edmund Hill. New York: New City, 2002.

———. *Responses to Miscellaneous Questions: Part 1.* Vol. 12 of *The Works of Saint Augustine: A Translation for the 21st Century.* Edited by Boniface Ramsey and Raymond F. Canning. Translated by Boniface Ramsey. New York: New City, 2008.

———. *St. Augustine: Sermons for Christmas and Epiphany.* Edited by Thomas Comerford Lawler. New York: Paulist, 1952.

Bates, William. *The Harmony of the Divine Attributes, in the Contrivance and Accomplishment of Man's Redemption by the Lord Jesus Christ or Discourses Whererin is Shewed, How the Wisdom, Mercy, Justice, Holiness, Power, and Truth of God are glorified in that Great and Blessed Work.* London: Nathaniel Ranew and Jonathan Robinson, 1674.

Baxter, Richard. *An End of Doctrinal Controversies Which Have Lately Troubled the Churches by Reconciling Explication Without Much Disputing.* London: John Salusbury, 1691.

———. *The Practical Works of Richard Baxter: With a Preface, Giving Some Account of the Author and of this Edition of his Practical Works; An Essay on His Genius, Works, and Times; and A Portrait in Four Volumes.* Vol. 1. London: George Virtue, 1838.

Berkeley, George. *Alciphron, or the Minute Philosopher in Seven Dialogues, Containing an Apology for the Christian Religion, Against Those Who Are Called Free-Thinkers.* New Haven: Sidney's, 1803.

———. *A Treatise Concerning the Principles of Human Knowledge, Wherein the Chief Causes of Error and Difficulty in the Sciences, with the Grounds of Skepticism, Atheism, and Irreligion Are Inquired Into.* N.p., 1710.

Blount, Charles. *The Miscellaneous Works, 1695.* New York: Garland, 1979.

Calvin, John. *Commentarius in Epistolam Pauli ad Romanos.* Vol. 3 of *Opera Exegetica.* Edited by T. H. L. Parker and D. C. Parker. Geneva: Librairie Droz, 1999.

———. *The Epistles of Paul the Apostle to the Galatians, Ephesians, Philippians, and Colossians.* Vol. 11 of *Calvin's Commentaries.* Edited by David W. Torrance and T. F. Torrance. Translated by T. H. L. Parker. Grand Rapids: Eerdmans, 1965.

———. *The Epistle of Paul the Apostle to the Romans and to the Thessalonians.* Vol. 8 of *Calvin's Commentaries.* Translated by Ross Mackenzie. Edinburgh: Oliver and Boyd, 1961.

———. *Institutes of the Christian Religion in Two Volumes.* Edited by John T. McNeill. Translated by Ford Lewis Battles. Louisville: Westminster John Knox, 1960.

———. *Matthew, Mark, and Luke and the Epistles of James and Jude.* Vol. 3 of *Calvin's Commentaries.* Edited by David W. Torrance and T. F. Torrance. Grand Rapids: Eerdmans, 1972.

———. *The Second Epistle of Paul the Apostle to the Corinthians and the Epistles to Timothy, Titus, and Philemon.* Vol. 10 of *Calvin's Commentaries.* Edited by David W. Torrance and T. F. Torrance. Translated by T. A. Smail. Grand Rapids: Eerdmans, 1964.

Chauncy, Charles. *Enthusiasm Described and Caution'd Against: A Sermon Preach'd at the Old Brick Meeting-House in Boston, the Lord's Day after the Commencement, 1742.* Boston: S. Eliot Cornhill and J. Blanchard, 1742.

Chillingworth, William. *The Works of William Chillingworth in Three Volumes.* Vol. 2. Oxford: Oxford University Press, 1838.

Chrysostom, John. *The Fathers of the Church: Commentary on Saint John the Apostle and Evangelist: Homilies 1–47.* Translated by Sister Thomas Aquinas Groggin. New York: Catholic University of America Press, 2000.

———. *First Epistle of St. Paul the Apostle to the Corinthians. Homilies 1–24.* Part 1 of *A Library of Fathers of the Holy Catholic Church: Anterior to the Division of the East and West.* Oxford: John Henry Parker, 1842.

———. *The Gospel of Matthew: Part 1. Hom. I–XXV.* London: Walter Smith, 1885.

Chubb, Thomas. *A Collection of Tracts on Various Subjects.* London: n.p., 1730.

Cooper, Anthony Ashley. *Characteristics of Men, Manners, Opinions, and Times.* London: n.p., 1711.

———. *An Inquiry Concerning Virtue In Two Discourses.* London: A. Bell and S. Buckley, 1699.

Crellius, John. *Touching One God the Father Wherein Many Things Also Concerning the Nature of the Son of God and the Holy Spirit are Discoursed of.* Kofmoburg: n.p., 1665.

Cudworth, Ralph. "Sermon Preached Before the Honorable House of Commons." In *The Cambridge Platonists*, edited by Gerald R. Cragg, 369–407. New York: Oxford University Press, 1968.

———. *The True Intellectual System of the Universe, The First Part, Wherein, All the Reason and Philosophy of Atheism is Confuted; And Its Impossibility Demonstrated.* London: Richard Royston, 1678.

Culverwel, Nathanael. *An Elegant and Learned Discourse of the Light of Nature with Several Other Treatises: Viz. The Schisme, The Act of Oblivion, The Childes Returne, The Painting Soul, Mount Ebal, The White Stone, Spiritual Opticks, The Worth of Souls.* London: John Rothwell, 1652.

Davenport, John. *Another Essay for the Investigation of the Truth in Answer to Two Questions, I. The Subject of Baptism, II. The Consociation of Churches.* Cambridge: Marmaduke Johnson, 1663.

Didymus. *De Spiritu Sancto.* Vol. 39 In *Patrologiae Graecae, Cursus Completus.* Edited by Jacques Paul Minge. Paris: J. P. Minge, 1858.

Durham, James. *An Exposition of the Song of Solomon.* Carlisle, PA: Banner of Truth Trust, 1840.

Dwight, Sereno Edwards. *The Life of President Edwards.* New York: G. & C. & H. Carvill, 1830.

Edward, Lord Herbert of Cherbury. *De Veritate.* Translated by Meyrick H. Carré. Bristol: University of Bristol, 1937.

Edwards, John. *The Preacher: A Discourse Shewing, What Are the Particular Offices* and *Employments of Those of That Character in the Church, With a Free Censure of the Most Common Failings and Miscarriages of Persons in that Sacred Employment, to Which is Added, A Catalogue of Some Authors Who May Be Beneficial to Young Preachers and Students of Divinity.* Vol. 1. London: F. Robinson and J. Lawrence, 1705.

———. *Theologia Reformata, or The Body and Substance of the Christian Religion, Comprised in Distinct Discourses or Treatises upon The Apostle's Creed, The Lord's Prayer, and The Ten Commandments.* Vol. 1. London: John Lawrence, John Wyat, and Ranew Robinson, 1713.

Edwards, Jonathan. *Apocalyptic Writings.* Vol. 5 of *The Works of Jonathan Edwards.* Edited by Stephen J. Stein. New Haven: Yale University Press, 1977.

———. *The "Blank Bible."* Vol. 24 of *The Works of Jonathan Edward.* 2 Vols. Edited by Stephen J. Stein. New Haven: Yale University Press, 2006.

———. *Catalogue of Books.* Vol. 26 of *The Works of Jonathan Edwards.* Edited by Peter J. Thuesen. New Haven: Yale University Press, 2008.

———. *Ecclesiastical Writings.* Vol. 12 of *The Works of Jonathan Edwards.* Edited by David D. Hall. New Haven: Yale University Press, 1994.

———. "The Eternity of Hell Torments." In *Forty Sermons on Various Subjects.* Vol. 4 of *Works of President Edwards in Four Volumes.* New York: Leavitt and Allen, 1855.

———. *Ethical Writings.* Vol. 8 of *The Works of Jonathan Edwards.* Edited by Paul Ramsey. New Haven: Yale University Press, 1989.

———. *Five Discourses on Various Important Subjects, Nearly Concerning the Great Affair of the Soul's Eternal Salvation.* Boston: S. Kirkland and T. Green, 1738.

———. *Freedom of the Will.* Vol. 1 of *The Works of Jonathan Edwards.* Edited by Paul Ramsey. New Haven: Yale University Press, 1957.

———. *The Great Awakening.* Vol. 4 of *The Works of Jonathan Edwards.* Edited by C. C. Goen. New Haven: Yale University Press, 1972.

———. *Letters and Personal Writings.* Vol. 16 of *The Works of Jonathan Edwards.* Edited by George S. Claghorn. New Haven: Yale University Press, 1999.

———. *The "Miscellanies" (Entry Nos. a-z, aa-zz, 1–500)*. Vol. 13 of *The Works of Jonathan Edwards*. Edited by Thomas A. Schafer. New Haven: Yale University Press, 1994.

———. *The "Miscellanies" (Entry Nos. 501–832)*. Vol. 18 of *The Works of Jonathan Edwards*. Edited by Ava Chamberlain. New Haven: Yale University Press, 2000.

———. *The "Miscellanies" (Entry Nos. 833–1152)*. Vol. 20 of *The Works of Jonathan Edwards*. Edited by Amy Plantinga Pauw. New Haven: Yale University Press, 2002.

———. *The "Miscellanies" (Entry Nos. 1153–1360)*. Vol. 23 of *The Works of Jonathan Edwards*. Edited by Douglas A. Sweeney. New Haven: Yale University Press, 2004.

———. *Notes on Scripture*. Vol. 15 of *The Works of Jonathan Edwards*. Edited by Stephen J. Stein. New Haven: Yale University Press, 2000.

———. *Original Sin*. Vol. 3 of *The Works of Jonathan Edwards*. Edited by Clyde A. Holbrook. New Haven: Yale University Press, 1970.

———. *The Religious Affections*. Vol. 2 of *The Works of Jonathan Edwards*. Edited by John E. Smith. New Haven: Yale University Press, 1959.

———. *Scientific and Philosophical Writings*. Vol. 6 of *The Works of Jonathan Edwards*. Edited by Wallace E. Anderson. New Haven: Yale University Press, 1979.

———. *Sermons, Series II, 1738, and Undated, 1734–1738*. Vol. 53 of *The Works of Jonathan Edwards Online*. Jonathan Edwards Center: Yale University, 2008.

———. *Sermons and Discourses, 1720–1723*. Vol. 10 of *The Works of Jonathan Edwards*. Edited by Wilson H. Kimnach. New Haven: Yale University Press, 1989.

———. *Sermons and Discourses, 1723–1729*. Vol. 14 of *The Works of Jonathan Edwards*. Edited by Kenneth P. Minkema. New Haven: Yale University Press, 1997.

———. *Sermons and Discourses, 1730–1733*. Vol. 17 of *The Works of Jonathan Edwards*. Edited by Mark Valeri. New Haven: Yale University Press, 1999.

———. *Sermons and Discourses, 1734–1738*. Vol. 19 of *The Works of Jonathan Edwards*. Edited by M. X. Lesser. New Haven: Yale University Press, 2001.

———. *Sermons and Discourses, 1739–1742*. Vol. 22 of *The Works of Jonathan Edwards*. Edited by Harry S. Stout and Nathan O. Hatch, with Kyle P. Farley. New Haven: Yale University Press, 2003.

———. *Typological Writings*. Vol. 11 of *The Works of Jonathan Edwards*. Edited by Wallace E. Anderson. New Haven: Yale University Press, 1993.

———. *Writings on the Trinity, Grace, and Faith*. Vol. 21 of *The Works of Jonathan Edwards*. Edited by Sang Hyun Lee. New Haven: Yale University Press, 2002.

———. *The Works of Jonathan Edwards*. Vol. 1. Edited by Sereno E. Dwight and Edward Hickman. Carlisle, PA: Banner of Truth, 1979.

Edwards, Timothy. Select Unpublished Correspondence. The Claghorn Collection. Westminster Theological Seminary, Montgomery Library, Philadelphia, PA.

Fenner, Dudley. *The Artes of Logike and Retorike, Plainelie Set Foorth in the Englishe Tounge, Easie to Be Learned and Practised: Together with Examples for the Practice of the Same, for Methode in the Government of the Familie, Prescribed in the Word of God: And for the Whole in the Resolution or Opening of Certaine Partes of Scripture, According to the Same*. N.p., 1584.

Gregory (the Great). "Moralia in Job." In *History of Biblical Interpretation: A Reader*, edited by William Yarchin, 86–92. Peabody, MA: Hendrickson, 2004.

Gregory Nazianzus. *Cyril of Jerusalem, Gregory Nazianzus*. Vol. 7 of *Nicene and Post-Nicene Fathers, Second Series*. Edited by Philip Schaff and Henry Ware. Peabody, MA: Hendrickson, 1894.

Gregory (Nyssa). *The Life of Moses: Classics of Western Spirituality*. Edited by John Meyendorff, Abraham Malherbe, and Everett Ferguson. Mahweh, NJ: Paulist, 1978.

———. "Sermon on 1 Corinthians 15:28, [32–44]." In *Documents in Early Christian Thought*. Edited by Maurice F. Wiles and Mark Santer, 257–58. Translated by J. K. Downing. New York: Cambridge University Press, 1975.

Henry, Matthew. *Acts to Revelation*. Vol. 6 of *Matthew Henry's Commentary on the Whole Bible, Wherein Each Chapter is Summed Up in its Contents: The Sacred Text Inserted at Large in Distinct Paragraphs: Each Paragraph Reduced to its Proper Head: The Sense Given, and Largely Illustrated with Practical Remarks and Observations*. New York: Revell, 1970.

———. *Job to Song of Solomon*. Vol. 3 of *Matthew Henry's Commentary on the Whole Bible, Wherein Each Chapter is Summed Up in its Contents: The Sacred Text Inserted at Large in Distinct Paragraphs: Each Paragraph Reduced to its Proper Head: The Sense Given, and Largely Illustrated with Practical Remarks and Observations*. New York: Revell, 1970.

Heraclitus. *Fragments: A Text and Translation with a Commentary*. Translated by T. M. Robinson. Toronto: University of Toronto Press, 1987.

Hurrion, John. *The Knowledge of Christ Glorified*. London, 1729.

Locke, John. *An Essay Concerning Human Understanding*. Edited by Peter H. Nidditch. Oxford: Clarendon, 1975.

———. *A Letter To the Right Reverend Edward Lord Bishop of Worcester, Concerning Some Passages Relating to Mr. Locke's Essay of Human Understanding in a Late Discourse of his Lordships, in Vindication of the Trinity*. London: H. Clark, 1697.

———. *A Paraphrase and Notes on the Epistles of St. Paul to the Galatians, I & II Corinthians, Romans and Ephesians to Which is Prefixed An Essay for the Understanding of St. Paul's Epistles, by Consulting St. Paul Himself*. London: A. Miller, 1763.

———. *The Reasonableness of Christianity As Delivered in the Scriptures*. London: Awnsham and John Churchil, 1695.

Malebranche, Nicolas. *Search After Truth or a Treatise of the Nature of the Human Mind and of Its management for avoiding Error in the Sciences*. 2 Vols. London: I. Dunton, 1694.

Mather, Cotton. *Manuductio ad Ministerium: Directions for a Candidate of the Ministry*. New York: Columbia University Press, 1938.

Mather, Increase. *The First Principles of New-England Concerning the Subject of Baptisme and Communion of Churches*. Cambridge: Samuel Green, 1675.

———. *The Order of the Gospel Professed and Practised by the Churches of Christ in New England, Justified, by the Scripture, and by the Writings of Many Learned Men, both Ancient and Modern Divines; In Answer to Several Questions, Relating to Church Discipline*. Boston: Nicholas Buttolph, 1700.

Mather, Richard. *A Defense of the Answer and Arguments of the Synod Met at Boston in the Year 1662*. Cambridge: Hezekiah Usher, 1664.

Mather, Samuel. *The Figures or Types of the Old Testament by Which Christ and Heavenly Things of the Gospel Were Preached and Shadowed to the People of God of Old; Explained and Improved in Sundry Sermons*. Dublin: H. Sawbridge, 1685.

More, Henry. *A Collection of Several Philosophical Writings*. Vol. 1. London: n.p., 1662. Reprint, New York: Garland, 1978.

Newton, Isaac. *The Principia*. Translated by Andrew Motte. Amherst, NY: Prometheus, 1995.
Nieuwenty, Bernard. *The Religious Philosopher, or the Right Use of Contemplating the Works of the Creator*. London: n.p., 1745.
Origen. *Commentary on John*. Vol. 9 of *The Ante-Nicene Fathers: Translations of the Fathers Down to A.D. 325*. Edited by Allan Menzies. New York: Scribner's, 1912.
———. *Contra Celsum*. Translated by Henry Chadwick. New York: Cambridge University Press, 1953.
———. *On First Principles*. Translated by G. W. Butterworth. Gloucester, MA: Peter Smith, 1973.
Owen, John. *The Doctrine of Justification by Faith Through the Imputation of the Righteousness of Christ, Explained, Confirmed, and Vindicated*. London: R. Boulter, 1677.
———. *Exercitations on the Epistle to the Hebrews*. London: Nathaniel Ponder, 1676.
———. *The Holy Spirit*. Vol. 3 of *The Works of John Owen*. Edited by William H. Goold. Carlisle, PA: Banner of Truth, 2000.
———. *True and False Religion*. Vol. 14 of *The Works of John Owen*. Edited by William H. Goold. Carlisle, PA: Banner of Truth, 1965.
Palamas, Gregory. *The Triads*. Edited by John Meyendorff. Translated by Nicholas Gendle Mahwah, NJ: Paulist, 1983.
Patrick, Simon. *A Brief Account of the New Sect of Latitude-Men, Together with Some Reflection upon the New Philosophy*. London: n.p., 1662.
Perkins, William. *A Golden Chaine or the Description of Theologie, Containing the Order of the Causes of Salvation and Damnation, According to God's Word*. London: Edward Alde, 1592.
Philo. *Allegorical Interpretation*. Vol. 1 of *Loeb Classical Library*. Edited by F.H. Colson and G. H. Whitaker. Cambridge: Harvard University Press, 1962.
———. *The Migration of Abraham*. Vol. 4 of *Loeb Classical Library*. Edited by F. H Colson and G. H. Whitaker. Cambridge: Harvard University Press, 1958.
———. *On Abraham*. Vol. 6 of *Loeb Classical Library*. Edited by F. H. Colson. Cambridge: Harvard University Press, 1959.
———. *One the Confusion of Tongues*. Vol. 4 of *Loeb Classical Library*. Edited by F. H. Colson and G. H. Whitaker. Cambridge: Harvard University Press, 1958.
Poole, Matthew. *Annotations Upon the Holy Bible*. Vol. 1. London: John Richardson, 1683.
———. *Annotations Upon the Holy Bible*. Vol. 2. London: Thomas Parkhurst, 1685.
Ramus, Peter. *The Logike of the Moste Excellent Philosopher P. Ramus Martyri*. Translated by Roland MacIlmaine. Northridge, CA: San Fernando Valley State College, 1969.
———. *P. Rami. Dialecticae Libri Duo*. Cambridge: n.p., 1584.
Shepard, Thomas. *The Parable of the Ten Virgins*. London: n.p., 1695.
Smith, John. *Select Discourses*. London: F. Flesher and W. Morden, 1660.
Spinoza, Benedictus de. *A Theologico-Political Treatise and A Political Treatise*. Vol. 1 of *The Chief Works of Benedict de Spinoza*. Translated by R. H. M. Elwes. New York: Dover, 1951.
Stapfer, Johann Friedrich. *Institutiones Theologiæ Polemicæ Universæ Ordine Scientifico Dispositæ*. 5 Vols. Tiguri: Apud Heideggerum & Socios, 1743–47.

Stebbing, Henry. *A Treatise Concerning the Operations of the Holy Spirit: Being the Substance of the Late Reverend and Learned Dr. William Clagett's Discourse upon that Subject.* London: n.p., 1719.

Stillingfleet, Edward. *Irenicum, A Weapon-Salve for the Churches Wounds.* London: Henry Mortlock, 1662.

Stoddard, Solomon. *The Doctrine of the Instituted Churches Explained and Proved from the Word of God.* London: Ralph Smith, 1700.

———. *A Guide to Christ or, the Way of Directing Souls that are under the Work of Conversion.* Morgan, PA: Soli Deo Gloria, 1993.

———. *The Safety of Appearing at the Day of Judgement, in the Righteousness of Christ.* Boston: Samuel Phillips, 1687.

———. *A Treatise Concerning the Nature of Saving Conversion.* Boston: n.p., 1719. Reprint, Morgan, PA: Soli Deo Gloria, 1999.

Taylor, John. *A Paraphrase with Notes on the Epistle to the Romans.* London: J. Waugh and W. Fenner, 1754.

———. *The Scripture-Doctrine of Original Sin Proposed to Free and Candid Examination.* London: W. Fenner, 1741.

Tillotson, John. *The Rule of Faith or an Answer to the Treatise of Mr. I.S. Entituled Surefooting.* London: A. Maxwell, 1666.

———. *The Works of the Most Reverend Dr. John Tillotson, Late Lord Archbishop of Canterbury, Containing Fifty Four Sermons and Discourses, on Several Occasions, Together with The Rule of Faith.* London: n.p., 1696.

Toland, John. *Christianity Not Mysterious: or, A Treatise Shewing, That there is nothing in the Gospel Contrary to Reason, Nor Above it: And that No Christian Doctrine Can Properly Be Call'd A Mystery.* London: Sam Buckley, 1696.

Turretin, Francis. *Eleventh Through Seventeenth Topics.* Vol. 2 of *Institutes of Elenctic Theology.* Edited by James T. Dennison Jr. Translated by George Musgrave Giger. Philipsburg, NJ: P&R, 1994.

Van Mastricht, Peter. *Novitatum Cartesianarum Gangraena, Nobiliores Plerasque Corporis Theologici Partes Arrodens et Excedens, Seu Theologia Cartesiana Detecta.* Amsterdam: n.p., 1677.

———. *Theoretico-Practica Theologia, Quâ, Per Singula Capita Theologica, Pars Exegetica, Dogmatica, Elenchtica, and Practica, Perpetua Successione Conjugantur.* Trajecti ad Rhenum, 1698.

———. *A Treatise on Regeneration.* Edited by Brandon G. Withrow. Translated by Anonymous. Morgan, PA: Soli Deo Gloria, 2002.

Watson, Thomas. *The Select Works of the Rev. Thomas Watson, Comprising His Celebrated Body of Divinity, in a Series of Lectures on the Shorter Catechism and Various Sermons and Treatises.* Edinburgh: A. Fullerton and Co., 1852.

Whichcote, Benjamin. "Moral and Religious Aphorisms." In *The Cambridge Platonists*, edited by Gerald Cragg. New York: Oxford University Press, 1968.

———. *The Works of the Learned Benjamin Whichcote, D.D.* Vol. 4. Aberdeen: J. Chalmers for Alexander Thompson, 1751.

Whitby, Daniel. *Six Discourses Concerning 1. Election and Reprobation. II. Extent of Christ's Redemption. III. The Grace of God. IV. Liberty of the Will. V. Defectibility of the Saints. VI. Answer to the Three Objections.* Worcester, MA: Isaiah Thomas, 1801.

White, John. *New England's Lamentations.* Boston: T. Fleet, 1734.

Wilkins, John. *Ecclesiastes, or A Discourse Concerning the Gift of Preaching As It Falls under the Rules of Art, Shewing The Most Proper Rules and Directions, for Method, Invention, Books, Expression, Whereby a Minister May Be Furnished with Such Abilities as May Make Him a Workman That Needs Not to Be Ashamed.* London: M. F., 1646.

———. *Of the Principles and Duties of Natural Religion.* London: A. Maxwell, 1676.

———. *Sermons Preached upon Several Occasions: By the Right Reverend Father in God, John Wilkins.* London: Thos. Basset, 1682.

Williams, William. *The Death of a Prophet Lamented and Improved in a Sermon Preach'd at Northampton, Feb. 13, 1729. On the Day of the Interment of the Reverend, Pious, & Learned, Mr. Solomon Stoddard their Pastor.* Boston: B. Green and D. Henchman, 1729.

Winthrop, John. *Winthrop's Journal: "History of New England," 1630–1649.* Vol. 1. Edited by James Kendall Hosmer. New York: Scribner's, 1908.

Secondary Sources

Alexander, Philip S. *The Targum of Lamentations.* Collegeville, MN: Michael Glazier, 2007.

Anderson, Wallace E. "Immaterialism in Jonathan Edwards' Early Philosophical Notes." *JHI* 25 (1964) 181–200.

Asiedu, F. B. A. "The Song of Songs and the Ascent of the Soul: Ambrose, Augustine, and the Language of Mysticism." *VC* 55:3 (2001) 299–317.

Ayres, Lewis. *Nicaea and Its Legacy: An Approach to Fourth-Century Trinitarian Theology.* New York: Oxford University Press, 2004.

Balthasar, Hans Urs von. *Origen: Spirit and Fire.* Translated by Robert J. Daly. Washington, DC: Catholic University of America Press, 1984.

Bebbington, D. W. *Evangelicalism in Modern Britain: A History from the 1730s to the 1980s.* London: Allen & Unwin, 1989.

Biddle, John C. "Locke's Critique of Innate Principles and Tolands' Deism." *JHI* 37 (1976) 411–22.

Billings, J. Todd. "John Calvin: United to God through Christ." In *Partakers of the Divine Nature: The History and Development of Deification in the Christian Traditions.* Edited by Michael J. Christensen and Jeffrey A. Wittung, 200–18. Grand Rapids: Baker, 2007.

Bizer, Ernst. "Reformed Orthodoxy and Cartesianism." In *Translating Theology into the Modern Age.* Edited by Robert W. Funk, 21–82. Tübingen: J. C. B. Mohr, 1965.

Bombaro, John. "Dispositional Peculiarity, History, and Edwards's Evangelistic Appeal to Self-Love." *WTJ* 66 (2004) 121–57.

———. "Jonathan Edwards' Vision of Salvation." *WTJ* 65 (2003) 45–67.

Bonner, Gerald. "Augustine's Conception of Deification." *JTS* 37:8 (1986) 369–86.

Bradley, James E., and Richard A. Muller. *Church History: An Introduction to Research, Reference Works, and Methods.* Grand Rapids: Eerdmans, 1995.

Brailsford, H. N. *The Levellers and the English Revolution.* Edited by Christopher Hill. Stanford: Stanford University Press, 1961.

Breslauer, S. Daniel. "Philosophy in Judaism: Two Stances." In *The Blackwell Companion to Judaism.* Edited by Jacob Neusner and Alan J. Avery-Peck, 162–80. Malden, MA: Blackwell, 2003.

Brown, Colin. *From the Ancient World to the Age of Enlightenment*. Vol. 1 of *Christianity and Western Thought: A History of Philosophers, Ideas and Movements*. Downers Grove, IL: InterVarsity, 1990.

Brown, Robert E. "Edwards, Locke and the Bible." *JR* 79 (1999) 361–84.

———. *Jonathan Edwards and the Bible*. Bloomington: Indiana University Press, 2002.

Bryant, Louise May, and Mary Patterson. "A List of Books Sent by Jeremiah Dummer." In *Papers in Honor of Andrew Keogh, Library of Yale University by the Staff of the Library, 30 June 1938*, 7–44. New Haven: Printed Privately, 1938.

Caldwell, III, Robert W. "The Holy Spirit as the Bond of Union in the Theology of Jonathan Edwards." PhD diss., Trinity Evangelical Divinity School, Deerfield, IL, 2003.

Chadwick, Henry. "Philo." In *The Cambridge History of Later Greek and Early Medieval Philosophy*. Edited by Arthur Hilary Armstrong, 137–57. New York: Cambridge University Press, 1967.

Chai, Leon. *Jonathan Edwards and the Limits of Enlightenment Philosophy*. New York: Oxford University Press, 1998.

Chamberlain, Ava. "The Theology of Cruelty: A New Look at the Rise of Arminianism in Eighteenth-Century New England." *HTR* 85:3 (1992) 335–56.

Champion, J. A. I. *The Pillars of the Priestcraft Shaken: The Church of England and its Enemies, 1660–1730*. Cambridge: Cambridge University Press, 1992.

Cherry, Conrad. "Symbols of Spiritual Truth: Jonathan Edwards as Biblical Interpreter." *Int* 39 (1985) 263–71.

———. *The Theology of Jonathan Edwards: A Reappraisal*. Gloucester, MA: Peter Smith, 1974.

Christensen, Michael J., and Jeffrey A. Wittung. *Partakers of the Divine Nature: The History and Development of Deification in the Christian Traditions*. Grand Rapids: Baker, 2007.

Coffman, Ralph J. *Solomon Stoddard*. Boston: Twayne, 1978.

Colie, Rosalie L. *Light and Enlightenment: A Study of the Cambridge Platonists and the Dutch Arminians*. London: Cambridge University Press, 1957.

———. "Spinoza and the Early English Deists." *JHI* 20:1 (1959) 23–46.

Copleston, Frederick. *Hobbes to Hume*. Vol. 5 of *A History of Philosophy*. Westminster, MD: Newman, 1964.

Cragg, Gerald. *The Cambridge Platonists*. New York: Oxford University Press, 1968.

———. *The Church and the Age of Reason, 1648–1789*. Baltimore: Penguin, 1970.

Cragie, P. C. "The Influence of Spinoza in the Higher Criticism of the Old Testament." *EvQ* 50 (1978) 23–32.

Craig, William Lane. *Time and Eternity: Exploring God's Relationship to Time*. Wheaton, IL: Crossway, 2001.

Crisp, Oliver D. *Jonathan Edwards and the Metaphysics of Sin*. Burlington, VT: Ashgate, 2005.

Coughenour, Robert A. "The Shape and Vehicle of Puritan Hermeneutics." *RefR* 30 (1976) 23–34.

Cudworth, Ralph, and Thomas Wise. *Abridgement of Dr. Cudworth's True Intellectual System of the Universe*. London: Oswald, 1732.

Daggy, Robert E. "Education, Church, and State: Timothy Cutler and the Yale Apostasy of 1722." *JCS* 13:1 (1971) 43–67.

Daniel, Stephen H. *The Philosophy of Jonathan Edwards: A Study in Divine Semiotics*. Bloomington: Indiana University Press, 1994.

Delattre, Roland André. *Beauty and Sensibility in the Thought of Jonathan Edwards: An Essay in Aesthetics and Theological Ethics*. New Haven: Yale University Press, 1968.
Dexter, Franklin Bowditch. *Documentary History of Yale University, 1701–1745*. Reprint, New York: Arno, 1969.
———. *Sketch of the History of Yale University*. New York: Henry Holt, 1887.
Dumont, Stephen. "John Duns Scotus." In *Routledge Encyclopedia of Philosophy*. Vol. 3. Edited by Edward Craig. New York: Routledge, 1998.
Ellison, Julie. "The Sociology of 'Holy Indifference': Sarah Edwards' Narrative." *AmLit* 56:4 (1984) 479–95.
Enns, Peter. *Inspiration and Incarnation: Evangelicals and the Problem of the Old Testament*. Grand Rapids: Baker, 2005.
Erdt, Terence. *Jonathan Edwards: Art and Sense of the Heart*. Amherst: University of Massachusetts Press, 1980.
Ferguson, Sinclair B. "John Owen and the Doctrine of the Person of Christ." In *John Owen: The Man and His Theology: Papers Read at the Conference of The John Owen Centre for Theological Study, September 2000*. Edited by Robert W. Oliver, 69–99. Philipsburg, NJ: P. & R., 2000.
Fiering, Norman. *Jonathan Edwards's Moral Thought and Its British Context*. Chapel Hill: University of North Carolina Press, 1981.
———. "The Rationalist Foundations of Jonathan Edwards's Metaphysics." In *Jonathan Edwards and the American Experience*. Edited by Nathan O. Hatch and Harry S. Stout, 73–101. New York: Oxford University Press, 1988.
Fishbane, Michael. *The Garments of Torah: Essays in Biblical Hermeneutics*. Bloomington: Indiana University Press, 1992.
Fisher, George P. "Richard Baxter's 'End of Controversy.'" *BS* (1855) 348–62.
———. "The Theology of Richard Baxter." *BS* (1852) 135–69.
Fonrobert, Charlotte Elisheva, and Martin S. Jaffee. *The Cambridge Companion to the Talmud and Rabbinic Literature*. New York: Cambridge, 2007.
Ford, Paul Leicester. *The New England Primer*. New York: Dodd, Mead, 1897.
Forstman, H. Jackson. *Word and Spirit: Calvin's Doctrine of Biblical Authority*. Stanford, CA: Stanford University Press, 1962.
Frank, Joseph. *The Levellers: A History of the Writings of Three Seventeenth-Century Social Democrats*. Cambridge: Harvard University Press, 1955.
Gamble, Richard C. "*Brevitas et Facilitas*: Toward an Understanding of Calvin's Hermeneutic." *WTJ* 47 (1985) 1–17.
———. "Exposition and Method in Calvin." *WTJ* 49 (1987) 153–65.
Gardiner, H. N. "The Early Idealism of Jonathan Edwards." *PhRev* 9 (1900) 573–96.
Gay, Peter. *A Loss of Mastery: Puritan Historians in Colonial America*. Berkeley: University of California Press, 1966.
Gilbert, Greg D. "The Nations Will Worship: Jonathan Edwards and the Salvation of the Heathen." *TJ* 23 (2002) 53–76.
Gerstner, John H. *The Rational Biblical Theology of Jonathan Edwards: In Three Volumes*. Vol. 2. Powhatan, VA: Berea, 1992.
———. *Steps to Salvation: The Evangelistic Message of Jonathan Edwards*. Philadelphia: Westminster, 1950.
Gerstner, John H., and Jonathan Neil Gerstner. "Edwardsian Preparation for Salvation." *WTJ* 42 (Fall 1979) 5–71.
Goodwin, Gerald J. "The Myth of 'Arminian-Calvinism' in Eighteenth-Century New England." *NEQ* 41 (June 1968) 213–37.

Grant, Robert with David Tracy. *A Short History of the Interpretation of the Bible.* Philadelphia: Fortress, 1973.
Griffin, Martin I. J., Jr. *Latitudinarianism in the Seventeenth-Century Church of England.* Leiden: Brill, 1992.
Grimm, Harold J. *Career of the Reformer.* Vol. 31 of *Luther's Works.* Philadelphia: Muhlenberg, 1957.
Guelzo, Allen C. *Edwards on the Will: A Century of American Theological Debate.* Middletown, CT: Wesleyan University Press, 1989.
Habets, Myk. "Reforming Theōsis." In *Theōsis: Deification in Christian Theology,* edited by Stephen Finlan and Vladimir Kharlamov, 146–67. Eugene, OR: Pickwick, 2006.
Hagen, Kenneth. "What Did the Term *Commentarius* Mean to Sixteenth-Century Theologians?" In *Théorie et Pratique de l'Exégèse: Actes du Troisième Colloque International sur l'Historie de l'Exégèse Biblioque au XVI Siècle [Genève, 31 août 2 Septembre 1988],* edited by Irena Backus and Francis Higman, 13–38. Geneva: Droz, 1990.
Hall, David D. *The Antinomian Controversy, 1636–1638: A Documentary History.* Middletown: Wesleyan University Press, 1968.
Hall, Richard A. S. "Did Berkeley Influence Edwards? Their Common Critique of the Moral Sense Theory." In *Jonathan Edwards's Writings: Text Context, Interpretation,* edited by Stephen J. Stein, 100–21. Bloomington: Indiana University Press, 1996.
Haller, William, and David Godfrey. *The Leveller Tracts, 1647–1653.* New York: Columbia University Press, 1944.
Halvini, David Weiss. *Peshat and Derash: Plain and Applied Meaning in Rabbinic Exegesis.* New York: Oxford University Press, 1991.
Hanson, R. P. C. *Allegory and Event: A Study of the Sources and Significance of Origen's Interpretation of Scripture.* Richmond, VA: John Knox, 2002.
Hardy, Edward R. *Library of Christian Classics: Christology of the Later Fathers.* Louisville: Westminster John Knox, 1954.
Harlow, Daniel C. *The Greek Apocalypse of Baruch* (3 Baruch). In *Hellenistic Judaism and Early Christianity.* Leiden: Brill, 1996.
Harrison, Verna E. F. "Allegory and Asceticism in Gregory of Nyssa." *Semeia* 57 (1992) 113–20.
Harrisville, Roy A., and Walter Sundeberg. *The Bible in Modern Culture: Baruch Spinoza to Brevard Childs.* Grand Rapids: Eerdmans, 2002.
Hastings, W. Ross. "'Honouring the Spirit': Analysis and Evaluation of Jonathan Edwards' Pneumatalogical Doctrine of the Incarnation." *IJST* 7:3 (2005) 279–99.
Hatch, Nathan O., and Harry S. Stout, editors. *Jonathan Edwards and the American Experience.* New York: Oxford University Press, 1988.
Hauck, Robert J. "'Like a Gleaming Flash': Matthew 6:22–23, Luke 11:34–36 and the Divine Sense in Origen." *AThR* 88:4 (2006) 557–73.
Heine, Ronald E. "Gregory of Nyssa's Apology for Allegory." *VC* 38 (1984) 360–70.
Helm, Paul. *Faith and Understanding.* Grand Rapids: Eerdmans, 1997.
Helm, Paul, and Oliver D. Crisp. *Jonathan Edwards: Philosophical Theologian.* Burlington, VT: Ashgate, 2003.
Holifield, E. Brooks. *The Covenant Sealed: The Development of Puritan Sacramental Theory in Old and New England, 1570–1720.* New Haven: Yale University Press, 1974.

Holmes, Stephen R. "Does Jonathan Edwards Use a Dispositional Ontology? A Response to Sang Hyun Lee." In *Jonathan Edwards: Philosophical Theologian*, edited by Paul Helm and Oliver D. Crisp, 99–114. Burlington, VT: Ashgate, 2003.

———. *God of Grace and God of Glory: An Account of the Theology of Jonathan Edwards*. Grand Rapids: Eerdmans, 2000.

Hopkins, Samuel. *The Life and Character of the Late Reverend Mr. Jonathan Edwards*. Boston: n.p., 1765.

Howe, Daniel Walker. "The Cambridge Platonists of Old England and the Cambridge Platonists of New England." In *American Unitarianism, 1805–1865*, edited by Conrad Edick Wright, 87–119. Boston: Massachusetts Historical Society and Northeastern University Press, 1989.

Hunsinger, George. "Dispositional Soteriology: Jonathan Edwards on Justification by Faith Alone." *WTJ* 66 (2004) 107–20.

Hylen, Susan. *Allusion and Meaning in John 6*. Berlin: de Gruyter, 2005.

Johnson, Thomas H. "Jonathan Edwards's Background of Reading." In *Publications of the Colonial Society of Massachusetts* 28, 193–222. Massachusetts: The Colonial Society of Massachusetts, 1931.

Johnson, William Stacy, editor. *H. Richard Niebuhr: Theology, History, and Culture: Major Unpublished Writings*. New Haven: Yale University Press, 1996.

Jones, Charles Edwin. "The Impolitic Mr. Edwards: The Personal Dimension of the Robert Breck Affair." *NEQ* 51 (1978) 64–79.

Jue, Jeffrey K. "'HEAVEN UPON EARTH': The Apocalyptic Thought of Joseph Mede (1586–1638)." PhD diss., University of Aberdeen, Scotland, 2003.

Kaiser, Christopher. *Creational Theology and the History of Physical Science*. Leiden: Brill, 1997.

Kang, Kevin Woongsan. "Justified by Faith in Christ: Jonathan Edwards' Doctrine of Justification in Light of Union with Christ." PhD diss., Westminster Theological Seminary, Glenside, PA, 2003.

Kapic, Kelly M. "The Son's Assumption of a Human Nature: A Call for Clarity." *IJST* 3:2 (2001) 154–66.

Kelley, Brooks Mather. *Yale: A History*. New Haven: Yale University Press, 1974.

Kelly, J. N. D. *Early Christian Doctrines*. New York: HarperSanFrancisco, 1978.

Kenny, Anthony. *The Oxford History of Western Philosophy*. New York: Oxford University Press, 1994.

Kittel, Gerhard, Gerhard Friedrich, and Geoffrey W. Bromiley. *Theological Dictionary of the New Testament: Abridged in One Volume*. Grand Rapids: Eerdmans, 2003.

Klauber, Martin I. "The Helvetic Formula Consensus (1675): An Introduction and Translation." *TJ* 11 (Spring 1990) 103–23.

Kraus, Hans Joachim. "Calvin's Exegetical Principles." *Int* 31 (1977) 8–18.

Kugel, James. L. *The Bible as It Was*. Cambridge: Belknap, 1997.

———. *How to Read the Bible: A Guide to Scripture, Then and Now*. New York: Free Press, 2007.

Kuklick, Bruce. "A Review Essay: An Edwards for the Millennium." *Relig Am Cult* 11 (Winter 2001) 109–17.

Laird, Martin. *Gregory of Nyssa and the Grasp of Faith: Union, Knowledge, and Divine Presence*. New York: Oxford University Press, 2007.

Laurence, David. "Jonathan Edwards, Solomon Stoddard, and the Preparationist Model of Conversion." *HTR* 72 (1979) 267–83.

Lee, Sang Hyun. *The Philosophical Theology of Jonathan Edwards*. Princeton: Princeton University Press, 1988.

———. *The Princeton Companion to Jonathan Edwards*. Princeton: Princeton University Press, 2005.

Lee, Sang Hyun, and Allen C. Guelzo. *Edwards in Our Time: Jonathan Edwards and the Shaping of American Religion*. Grand Rapids: Eerdmans, 1999.

Levine, Joseph M. "Latitudinarians, Neoplatonists, and the Ancient Wisdom." In *Philosophy, Science, and Religion in England, 1640–1700*. Edited by Richard Kroll et al, 85–108. New York: Cambridge University Press, 1992.

Lewalski, Barbara Kiefer. "Typological Symbolism and the 'Progress of the Soul' in Seventeenth-Century Literature." In *Literary Uses of Typology: From the Late Middle Ages to the Present*, edited by Earl Miner, 79–114. Princeton: Princeton University Press, 1977.

Logan, Samuel T. "The Doctrine of Justification in the Theology of Jonathan Edwards." *WTJ* 46 (1984) 26–52.

———. "The Hermeneutics of Jonathan Edwards." *WTJ* 43 (1981) 79–96.

Lohse, Bernhard. *Martin Luther's Theology: Its Historical and Systematic Development*. Translated by Roy A. Harrisville. Minneapolis: Fortress, 1999.

Lovejoy, Arthur O. *Essays in the History of Ideas*. Baltimore: Johns Hopkins University Press, 1948.

Louth, Andrew. "The Fouth-Century Alexandrians: Athanasius and Didymus." In *The Cambridge History of Early Christian Literature*, edited by Frances Young and Lewis Ayres, 275–82. New York: Cambridge, 2006.

———. *The Origins of the Christian Mystical Tradition: From Plato to Denys*. New York: Oxford University Press, 2007.

Lowance, Mason I. "Jonathan Edwards and the Platonists: Edwardsian Epistemology and the Influence of Malebranche and Norris." In *Studies in American Puritan Spirituality* 2. N.p., 1991.

———. *The Language of Canaan: Metaphor and Symbol in New England from the Puritans to the Transcendentalists*. Cambridge: Harvard University Press, 1980.

Lubac, Henri de. *Medieval Exegesis*. 4 Vols. Translated by Mark Sebanc. Grand Rapids: Eerdmans, 1998.

Ludlow, Morwenna. "Theology and Allegory: Origen and Gregory of Nyssa on the Unity and Diversity of Scripture." *IJST* 4:1 (2002) 45–66.

Lukin, Henry. *An Introduction to the Holy Scriptures, Containing the Several Tropes, Figures, Proprieties of Speech used Therein: with Other Observations Necessary for the Right Understanding Thereof*. London, 1669.

Lyon, Georges Henri Joseph. *L'idéalisme en Angleterre au XVIIIe siècle*. Paris: F. Alcan, 1888.

Macleod, C. W. "Allegory and Mysticism in Origen and Gregory of Nyssa." *JTS* 22 (October 1971) 362–79.

Marsden, George M. *Jonathan Edwards: A Life*. New Haven: Yale University Press, 2003.

———. "Perry Miller's Rehabilitation of the Puritans: A Critique." *CH* 39 (March 1970) 91–105.

Marshall, John. *John Locke: Resistance, Religion, and Responsibility*. New York: Cambridge University Press, 1994.

McClymond, Michael J. "Salvation as Divinization: Jonathan Edwards, Gregory Palamas and the Theological Uses of Neoplatonism." In *Jonathan Edwards:*

Philosophical Theologian, edited by Paul Helm and Oliver D. Crisp, 139–60. Burlington, VT: Ashgate, 2003.

McDermott, Gerald. *Jonathan Edwards Confronts the Gods*. Oxford: Oxford University Press, 2000.

———. "Jonathan Edwards on Justification: Closer to Luther or Aquinas?" *RefRJ* 14:1 (2005) 119–138.

———. "The Possibility of Reconciliation: Jonathan Edwards and the Salvation of Non-Christians." In *Edwards in Our Time: Jonathan Edwards and the Shaping of American Religion*, edited by Sang Hyun Lee and Allen C. Guelzo, 173–202. Grand Rapids: Eerdmans, 1999.

———. "Response to Gilbert: 'The Nations Will Worship: Jonathan Edwards and the Salvation of the Heathen.'" *TJ* 23 (2002) 77–80.

McGinn, Bernard. *The Foundations of Mysticism: Origins to the Fifth Century*. New York: Crossroad, 1991.

McGuckin, J. A. "The Strategic Adaptation of Deification." In *Partakers of the Divine Nature: The History and Development of Deification in the Christian Traditions*, edited by Michael J. Christensen and Jeffrey A. Wittung, 95–114. Grand Rapids: Baker, 2007.

McKim, Donald K. *Historical Handbook of Major Biblical Interpreters*. Downers Grove, IL: InterVarsity, 1998.

Miller, Perry. "Jonathan Edwards: A Theological Life." In *The Princeton Companion to Jonathan Edwards*. Edited by Sang Hyun Lee, 1–15. Princeton: Princeton University Press, 2005.

———. *The New England Mind: From Colony to Province*. Boston: Beacon, 1953.

———. *The New England Mind: The Seventeenth Century*. Boston: Beacon, 1939.

———. "'Preparation for Salvation' in Seventeenth-Century New England." *JHI* 4 (June 1943) 253–86.

———. *The Puritans*. New York: American, 1938.

———. "Solomon Stoddard, 1643–1729." *HTR* 34 (October 1941) 277–320.

Miller, Perry, and Thomas H. Johnson. *Jonathan Edwards*. Amherst: University of Massachusetts Press, 1981.

Minkema, Kenneth Pieter. "The Edwardses: A Ministerial Family in Eighteenth-Century New England." PhD diss., University of Connecticut, 1988.

Minnis, A. J. "*Quadruplex Sensus, Multiplex Modus*: Scriptural Sense and Mode in Medieval Scholastic Exegesis." In *Interpretation and Allegory: Antiquity to the Modern Period*, edited by John Whitman, 231–58. Leiden: Brill, 2000.

Mitchell, W. Fraser. *English Pulpit Oratory from Andrewes to Tillotson*. New York: Russell and Russell, 1962.

Morgan, John. *Godly Learning: Puritan Attitudes towards Reason, Learning, and Education, 1560–1640*. London: Cambridge University Press, 1986.

Morimoto, Anri. *Jonathan Edwards and the Catholic Vision of Salvation*. University Park: Pennsylvania State University Press, 1995.

Morris, William Sparkes. *The Young Jonathan Edwards: A Reconstruction*. Brooklyn: Carlson, 1991.

Muller, Richard. *God, Creation, and Providence in the Thought of Jacob Arminius: Sources and Directions of Scholastic Protestantism in the Era of Early Orthodoxy*. Grand Rapids: Baker, 1991.

———. "The Hermeneutic of Promise and Fulfillment in Calvin's Exegesis of the Old Testament Prophecies of the Kingdom." In *The Bible in the Sixteenth Century*, edited by David Steinmetz, 68–82. Durham: Duke University Press, 1990.

---. *Holy Scripture: The Cognitive Foundations of Theology.* Vol. 2 of *Post-Reformation Reformed Dogmatics: The Rise and Development of Reformed Orthodoxy, ca. 1520 to ca. 1725*. Grand Rapids: Baker, 2003.

---. *Prolegomena to Theology*. Vol. 1 of *Post-Reformation Reformed Dogmatics: The Rise and Development of Reformed Orthodoxy, ca. 1520 to ca. 1725*. Grand Rapids: Baker, 2003.

---. *The Unaccomodated Calvin: Studies in the Foundation of a Theological Tradition*. New York: Oxford University Press, 2000.

Murray, Iain H. *Jonathan Edwards: A New Biography*. Carlisle, PA: Banner of Truth, 1996.

Murray, John. *The Imputation of Adam's Sin*. Grand Rapids: Eerdmans, 1959.

Nadler, Steven. *Spinoza: A Life*. New York: Cambridge University Press, 1999.

Neele, Adriaan Cornelis. "A Study of Divine Spirituality, Simplicity, and Immutability in Petrus van Mastricht's Doctrine of God." ThM thesis, Calvin Theological Seminary, 2002.

Neuser, Wilhelm H. *Calvinus Sacrae Scripturae Professor: Calvin as Confessor of Holy Scripture*. Grand Rapids: Eerdmans, 1994.

Oberman, Heiko A. *The Dawn of the Reformation: Essays in Late Medieval and Early Reformation Thought*. Grand Rapids: Eerdmans, 1992.

---. *The Impact of the Reformation*. Grand Rapids: Eerdmans, 1994.

---. *Luther: Man Between God and the Devil*. Translated by Eileen Walliser-Schwarzbart. New Haven: Yale University Press, 1989.

Oliphint, K. Scott. "Jonathan Edwards: Reformed Apologist." *WTJ* 57 (1995) 165–86.

Ong, Walter J., SJ. *Ramus, Method, and the Decay of Dialogue: From the Art of Discourse to the Art of Reason*. Cambridge: Harvard University Press, 1958.

Osler, Margaret J. "John Locke and the Changing Ideal of Scientific Knowledge." *JHI* 31:1 (1970) 3–16.

Otto, Randall E. "The Solidarity of Mankind in Jonathan Edwards's Doctrine of Original Sin." *EQ* 62 (1990) 205–21.

Oviatt, Edwin. *The Beginnings of Yale, 1701–1726*. New York: Arno, 1969.

Ozment, Steven E. *The Reformation in Medieval Perspective*. Chicago: Quadrangle, 1971.

Packer, J. I. "The Puritans as Interpreters of Scripture." In *Puritan Papers*. Vol. 1, *1956–1959*, edited by Martyn Lloyd-Jones, 191–201. Phillipsburg, NJ: P. & R., 2000.

Parrington, Vernon Louis. *Main Currents in American Thought: An Interpretation of American Literature from the Beginnings to 1920*. New York: Harcourt Brace, 1930.

Passmore, J. A. *Ralph Cudworth: An Interpretation*. London: Cambridge University Press, 1951.

Pauw, Amy Plantinga. *"The Supreme Harmony of All": The Trinitarian Theology of Jonathan Edwards*. Grand Rapids: Eerdmans, 2002.

Pearse, Meic. *The Great Restoration: The Religious Radicals of the 16th and 17th Centuries*. Carlisle, PA: Paternoster, 1998.

Pease, Theodore Calvin. *The Leveller Movement: A Study in the History and Political Theory of the English Great Civil War*. Gloucester, MA: P. Smith, 1965.

Pelikan, Jaroslav. *The Emergence of the Catholic Tradition (100–600)*. Vol. 1 of *The Christian Tradition: A History of the Development of Doctrine*. Chicago, University of Chicago Press, 1971.

Peter, Francis E. *The Monotheists: Jews, Christians, and Muslims in Conflict and Competition*. Princeton: Princeton University Press, 2003.

Philo. *Who Is the Heir of Divine Things?* Vol. 4 of *Loeb Classical Library*. Edited by F. H. Colson and G. H. Whitaker. Cambridge: Harvard University Press, 1958.

Plantinga, Alvin. *Warranted Christian Belief.* New York: Oxford University Press, 2000.

Plato. *The Republic of Plato*. Translated by Alexander Kerr. Chicago: Kerr, 1911.

Pokorný, Petr, and Jan Roskovec. *Philosophical Hermeneutics and Biblical Exegesis*. Tübingen: Mohr/Siebeck, 2002.

Pope, Robert G. *The Half-Way Covenant: Church Membership in Puritan New England*. Princeton: Princeton University Press, 1969.

Powicke, Frederick J. *The Cambridge Platonists: A Study*. Westport, CT: Greenwood, 1970.

Pratt, Anne Stokely. "The Books Sent from England by Jeremiah Dummer to Yale College." In *Papers in Honor of Andrew Keogh, Library of Yale University by the Staff of the Library, 30 June 1938*. New Haven: privately printed, 1938.

Preus, J. Samuel. *Spinoza and the Irrelevance of Biblical Authority*. Cambridge: Cambridge University Press, 2001.

Puchniak, Robert "Augustine's Conception of Deification, Revisited." In *Theōsis: Deification in Christian Theology,* edited by Stephen Finlan and Vladimir Kharlamov, 122–33. Eugene, OR: Pickwick, 2006.

Pünjer, Bernhard. *History of the Christian Philosophy of Religion: From the Reformation to Kant*. Translated by W. Hastie. Edinburgh: T. & T. Clark, 1887.

Rahner, Karl. "'The Spiritual Senses' according to Origen." In Vol. 16 of *Theological Investigations*, 81–103. New York: Seabury, 1979.

Reedy, Gerard. "Interpreting Tillotson." *HTR* 86 (January 1993) 84.

Reventlow, Henning Graf. *The Authority of the Bible and the Rise of the Modern World*. Philadelphia: Fortress, 1985.

Roberts, James Deotis, Sr. *From Puritanism to Platonism in Seventeenth Century England*. The Hauge: Martinus Nijhoff, 1968.

Robertson, D. B. *The Religious Foundations of the Leveller Democracy*. New York: King's Crown, 1951.

Rogers, G. A. J. "Boyle, Locke, and Reason." *JHI* 27:2 (1966) 205–16.

———. "The Other-Worldly Philosophers and the Real World: The Cambridge Platonists, Theology and Politics." In *The Cambridge Platonists in Philosophical Context: Politics, Metaphysics and Religion,* edited by G.A.J. Rogers et al, 3–16. Boston: Kluwer Academic, 1997.

Rudy, Gordon. *Mystical Language of Sensation in the Later Middle Ages*. New York: Routledge, 2002.

Rupp, George. "The 'Idealism' of Jonathan Edwards." *HTR* 62 (1969) 209–26.

Ryken, Leland. *Worldly Saints: The Puritans as they Really Were*. Grand Rapids: Zondervan, 1986.

Sandys-Wunsch, John. "Spinoza—The First Biblical Theologian." *ZAW* 93 (1981) 327–41.

Saybrook Confession. *A Confession of Faith, owned and consented to, by the Elders and Messengers of the churches in the colony of Connecticut, in New-England, Assembled by Delegation at Saybrook, September 9th, 1708*. New London, CT: Bridgeport, 1710.

Schafer, Thomas A. "Jonathan Edwards and Justification by Faith." *CH* 20:4 (1951) 55–67.

———. "Solomon Stoddard and the Theology of the Revival." In *A Miscellany of American Christianity: Essays in Honor of H. Shelton Smith,* edited by Stuart C. Henry, 328–62. Durham, NC: Duke University Press, 1963.

Schaff, Philip, and Henry Wace. *The Evangelical Protestant Creeds*. Vol. 3 of *The Creeds of Christendom with a History and Critical Notes*. New York: Harper, 1919.

———. *Gregory of Nyssa: Dogmatic Treatises*. Vol 5 of *A Select Library of the Nicene and Post-Nicene Fathers of the Christian Church*, 2nd Series. New York: Scribner's, 1917.

Schenck, Kenneth. *A Brief Guide to Philo*. Louisville: Westminster John Knox, 2005.

Schoneveld, Cornelius W. *Intertraffic of the Mind: Studies in Seventeenth-Century Anglo Dutch Translation with a Checklist of Books Translated from English into Dutch, 1600–1700*. Leiden: Brill, 1983.

Schultz, Walter. "Jonathan Edwards's *End of Creation*: An Exposition and Defense." *JETS* 49 (June 2006) 245–73.

Segal, Alan F. "The Incarnation: The Jewish Milieu." In *The Incarnation: An Interdisciplinary Symposium on the Incarnation of the Son of God*, edited by Stephen T. Davis et al. 116–39. New York: Oxford University Press, 2002.

Shapiro, Barbara J. *Probability and Certainty in Seventeenth-Century England: A Study of the Relationships Between Natural Science, Religion, History, Law, and Literature*. Princeton: Princeton University Press, 1983.

Sharp, Andrew. *The English Levellers*. Cambridge: Cambridge University Press, 1998.

Sheldon-Williams, I. P. "The Cappadocians." In *The Cambridge History of Later Greek and Early Medieval Philosophy*. Edited by Arthur Hilary Armstrong, 432–56. New York: Cambridge University Press, 1967.

Skinner, Quentin. *Visions of Politics*, Vol. 1., *Regarding Method*. New York: Cambridge University Press, 2002.

Smalley, Beryl. *The Study of the Bible in the Middle Ages*. Notre Dame: University of Notre Dame Press, 1964.

Snyder, David C. "Faith and Reason in Locke's *Essay*." *JHI* 47:2 (1986) 197–213.

Sparks, Kent. "The Sun Also Rises: Accommodation in Inscripturation and Interpretation." In *Evangelicals & Scripture: Tradition, Authority and Hermeneutics*, edited by Vincent Bacote et al. 112–32. Downers Grove: InterVarsity, 2004.

Spellman, W. M. *The Latitudinarians and the Church of England, 1660–1700*. Athens: The University of Georgia Press, 1993.

Spicq, Çelsus. *L'épitre aux Hébreux*. 2 Vols. Paris: Gabalda, 1952.

Spivey Jr., "The Hermeneutics of the Medieval and Reformation Era." In *Biblical Hermeneutics: A Comprehensive Introduction to Interpreting Scripture*, edited by Bruce Corely et al. 101–15. Nashville: Broadman & Holman, 2002.

Sprunger, Keith L. "Ames, Ramus, and the Method of Puritan Theology." *HTR* 59 (1966) 133–51.

———. *Dutch Puritanism: A History of English and Scottish Churches of the Netherlands in the Sixteenth and Seventeenth Centuries*. Leiden: E. J. Brill, 1982.

———. *The Learned Doctor William Ames: Dutch Backgrounds of English and American Puritanism*. Chicago: University of Illinois Press, 1972.

———. *Trumpets from the Tower: English Puritan Printing in the Netherlands, 1600–1640*. Leiden: E. J. Brill, 1994.

Spurr, John. *The Restoration Church of England, 1646–1689*. New Haven: Yale University Press, 1991.

Stein, Stephen. *Jonathan Edwards's Writings: Text, Context, Interpretation*. Bloomington: Indiana University Press, 1994.

———. "'Like Apples of God in Pictures of Silver': The Portrait of Wisdom in Jonathan Edwards's Commentary on the Book of Proverbs." *CH* 54 (1985) 324–37.

———. "The Quest for the Spiritual Sense: The Biblical Hermeneutics of Jonathan Edwards." *HTR* 70 (1977) 99–113.
———. "Symbols of Spiritual Truth: Jonathan Edwards as Biblical Interpreter." *Int* 39 (1985) 263–71.
Steinmetz, David C. *The Bible in the Sixteenth Century*. Durham: Duke University Press, 1990.
———. *Calvin in Context*. New York: Oxford University Press, 1995.
Stoever, William K. B. *"A Faire and Easie Way to Heaven": Covenant Theology and Antinomianism in Early Massachusetts*. Middletown, CT: Wesleyan University Press, 1978.
———. "Nature, Grace and John Cotton: The Theological Dimension in the New England Antinomian Controversy." *CH* 44 (1975) 22–33.
Storms, C. Samuel. "Jonathan Edwards on the Freedom of the Will." *TJ* 3 (1982) 131–69.
Stoughton, John A. *"Windsor Farmes," A Glimpse of an Old Parish together with the Deciphered Inscriptions from a few Foundation Stones of a much Abused Theology*. Hartford, CT: Clark and Smith, 1883.
Stout, Harry S. *The New England Soul: Preaching and Religious Culture in Colonial New England*. New York: Oxford University Press, 1986.
———. "The Puritans and Edwards." In *Jonathan Edwards and the American Experience*. Edited by Nathan O. Hatch and Harry S. Stout, 142–59. Oxford: Oxford University Press, 1988.
Stout, Harry S. et al. *Jonathan Edwards at 300: Essays on the Tercentenary of His Birth*. Lanham, MD: University Press of America, 2005.
Strauss, Leo. *Spinoza's Critique of Religion*. Translated by E. M. Sinclair. Chicago: University of Chicago Press, 1997.
Studebaker, Steve. "Jonathan Edwards's Social Augustinian Trinitarianism: An Alternative to a Recent Trend." *SJT* 56:3 (2003) 268–85.
———. "Jonathan Edwards' Social Augustinian Trinitarianism: A Criticism of and an Alternative to Recent Interpretations." PhD diss., Marquette University, 2003.
Studer, Basil. *Trinity and Incarnation: The Faith of the Early Church*. Collegeville, MN: Liturgical, 1993.
Sugenis, Robert A. *Not By Faith Alone: The Biblical Evidence for the Catholic Doctrine of Justification*. Santa Barbara: Queenship, 1997.
Sweeney, Douglas A. *Jonathan Edwards and the Ministry of the Word: A Model of Faith and Thought*. Downers Grove, IL: InterVarsity, 2009.
———. "Jonathan Edwards and the World Religions: A Response to Gerald McDermott." Unpublished paper, presented at the Annual Meeting of the Evangelical Theological Society, Toronto, Ontario, on November 20–22, 2002.
———. "Longing for More and More of It: The Strange Career of Jonathan Edwards's Exegetical Exertions." In *Jonathan Edwards at 300: Essays on the Tercentenary of His Birth*. Edited by Harry S. Stout et al., 25–37. Lanham, MD: University Press of America, 2005.
———. *Nathaniel William Taylor, New Haven Theology, and the Legacy of Jonathan Edwards*. New York: Oxford University Press, 2003.
Sweeney, Douglas A., and Brandon G. Withrow. "Jonathan Edwards: Continuator or Pioneer of Evangelical History?" In *The Emergence of Evangelicalism: Continuities in Evangelical History*, edited by Michael A. G. Haykin and Kenneth Stewart, 278–301. Nottingham: Apollos, 2008.

Swete, Henry Barclay. *The Holy Spirit in the Ancient Church: A Study of Christian Teaching in the Age of the Fathers*. London: Macmillan, 1912.
Tamburello, Dennis E. *Union with Christ: John Calvin and the Mysticism of St. Bernard*. Louisville: Westminster John Knox, 1994.
Thomas de Aquinatis. *Summa Theologica*. Edited by Nicolai et al. Paris: Bloud and Barral, 1880.
Thompson, John L. "Calvin as a Biblical Interpreter." In *The Cambridge Companion to John Calvin*, edited by Donald K. McKim, 58–73. New York: Cambridge University Press, 2004.
Thuesen, Peter J. "Edwards' Intellectual Background." In *The Princeton Companion to Jonathan Edwards*, edited by Sang Hyun Lee, 16–33. Princeton: Princeton University Press, 2005.
Todd, Margo, editor. *Reformation to Revolution: Politics and Religion in Early Modern England*. New York: Routledge, 1995.
Tracy, Patricia J. *Jonathan Edwards, Pastor: Religion and Society in Eighteenth-Century Northampton*. New York: Hill & Wang, 1980.
Trueman, Carl R. *The Claims of Truth: John Owen's Trinitarian Theology*. Carlisle, Cumbria, UK: Paternoster, 1998.
———. *John Owen: Reformed Catholic, Renaissance Man*. Aldershot: Ashgate, 2007.
———. *Luther's Legacy: Salvation and English Reformers, 1525–1556*. Oxford: Clarendon, 1994.
———. "Puritan Theology as Historical Event: A Linguistic Approach to the Ecumenical Context." In *Reformation and Scholasticism: An Ecumenical Enterprise*, edited by Willem J. Van Asselt and Eef Dekker, 253–75. Grand Rapids: Baker, 2001.
———. "Why I am Not A Christian Historian of Ideas." Unpublished paper presented at The Conference on Faith and History Biennial Meeting, Huntington, IN, October 2002.
Trumper, Timothy J. R. "An Historical Study of the Doctrine of Adoption in the Calvinist Tradition." PhD diss., University of Edinburgh, 2001.
Tufts, James H. "Edwards and Newton." *PhRev* 49 (November 1940) 609–622.
Twain, Mark. *A Connecticut Yankee in King Arthur's Court*. New York: Harper, 1917.
Van Asselt, Willem J., and Eef Dekker. *Reformation and Scholasticism: An Ecumenical Enterprise*. Grand Rapids: Baker, 2001.
Van Leeuwen, Henry G. *The Problem of Certainty in English Thought, 1630–1690*. The Hague: Martinus Nijhoff, 1970.
Waddington, Jeffrey C. "Jonathan Edwards's 'Ambiguous and Somewhat Precarious' Doctrine of Justification?" *WTJ* 66 (2004) 357–72.
Walker, Williston. *The Creeds and Platforms of Congregationalism*. Boston: Pilgrim, 1960.
Wallace, Ronald S. *Calvin's Doctrine of the Christian Life*. Edinburgh: Oliver and Boyd, 1959.
Warch, Richard. *School of the Prophets: Yale College, 1701–1740*. New Haven: Yale University Press, 1973.
Ward, Graham. "Allegoria: Readings as a Spiritual Exercise." *MT* 15:3 (1999) 272–95.
Watson, I. B. "Yale, Elihu." In *Oxford Dictionary of National Biography: From the Earliest Times to the Year 2000*, edited by H. C. G. Matthew and Brian Harrision. New York: Oxford University Press, 2004.

Watts, Emily Stipes. "Jonathan Edwards and the Cambridge Platonists." PhD diss., University of Illinois, Urbana, 1963.
Weddle, David. "Jonathan Edwards on Men and Trees, and the Problem of Solidarity." *HTR* 67 (1974)155–75.
Weinsheimer, Joel C. *Eighteenth-Century Hermeneutics: Philosophy of Interpretation in England from Locke to Burke*. New Haven: Yale University Press, 1993.
Weir, David A. *The Origins of the Federal Theology in Sixteenth-Century Reformation Thought*. Oxford: Clarendon, 1990.
Williams, Garry J. "Was Evangelicalism Created by the Enlightenment?" *TynBul* 2 (2002) 283–312
Williamson, R. *Philo and the Epistle to the Hebrews*. Leiden: Brill, 1970.
Willis, E. David. *Calvin's Catholic Christology: The Function of the So-Called Extra Calvinisticum in Calvin's Theology*. Leiden: Brill, 1966.
Winslow, Ola Elizabeth. *Jonathan Edwards, 1703–1758: A Biography*. New York: Octagon, 1979.
Withrow, Brandon G. "An Empty Threat: Jonathan Edwards on Y2K and the Power of Preaching." *RefRJ* 9:1 (2000) 69–92.
———. "'Full of Wondrous and Glorious Things': The Exegetical Mind of Jonathan Edwards in His Anglo-American Cultural Context." PhD diss., Westminster Theological Seminary, Glenside, PA, 2007.
———. "A Future of Hope: Jonathan Edwards and Millennial Expectations." *TJ* 22:1 (2001) 75–98.
———. "Introduction." In Peter van Mastricht, *Treatise on Regeneration*, vii–xxxii. Morgan, PA: Soli Deo Gloria, 2002.
———. "Jonathan Edwards and Justification: Help for Current Evangelical Discussion? Part One." *RefRJ* 11:2 (2002) 93–109.
———. "Jonathan Edwards and Justification: Help for Current Evangelical Discussion? Part Two." *RefRJ* 11:3 (2002) 98–111.
———. "Jonathan Edwards as a Resource for Current Evangelical Discussion over the Language of Justification." MA Thesis, Trinity Evangelical Divinity School, 1999.
Wodrow, Robert. *The History of the Sufferings of the Church of Scotland, From the Restoration to the Revolution: Collected from the Public Records, Original Papers, and Manuscripts of that Time, and Other Well Attested Narratives*. 2 Vols. Edinburgh, 1721–22.
Wolfe, Don Marion. *Leveller Manifestoes of the Puritan Revolution*. New York: Nelson, 1944.
Wolterstorff, Nicholas. *John Locke and the Ethics of Belief*. Cambridge: Cambridge University Press, 1996.
Woolsey, Theodore D. *An Historical Discourse Pronounced Before the Graduates of Yale College, August 14, 1850; One Hundred and Fifty Years after the Founding of that Institution with an Appendix*. New Haven: Yale College, 1850.
Wright, Conrad. *American Unitarianism, 1805–1865*. Boston: Massachusetts Historical Society and Northeastern University Press, 1989.
———. *The Beginnings of Unitarianism in America*. Boston: Beacon, 1966.
Wright, J. Edwards. *The Early History of Heaven*. New York: Oxford, 2000.
Yarchin, William. *History of Biblical Interpretation: A Reader*. Peabody, MA: Hendrickson, 2004.
Zakai, Avihu. "The Conversion of Jonathan Edwards." *JPH* 76:2 (1998) 127–38.
———. *Jonathan Edwards' Philosophy of History: The Enchantment of the World in the Enlightenment*. Princeton: Princeton University Press, 2003.

Index

activism, 4
Adam (and Eve), 17, 61, 95–96, 133, 138, 159–64, 167–68
Ames, William, 48–49
Anglicanism, 46n3, 59, 64, 66, 72, 75, 79–80, 139, 139nn6–7, 174, 175
Apocrypha, 15
Arminianism, 1, 59n45, 66, 75–76, 81, 90, 95, 136–42, 144, 145, 156, 159
antichrist, 48, 92–93
antinomianism, 138, 142–45, 156
Antiochene School, 33
Athanasius of Alexandria, 5, 26, 35, 41, 129, 201
Augustine of Hippo, 5, 26, 34–35, 41, 122–23, 181–83, 192

Bach, J. S., 119
Bates, William, 181n36
Baxter, Richard, 48, 50n17, 112
Bebbington, David, 4–8, 13, 72, 116, 198
Berkeley, George, 106, 112n13, 139n9
Bible. *See* Scripture
biblicism, 3, 4–5, 198, 199–201
Blount, Charles, 70n98
Bombaro, John, 149n45, 154n67, 158–59n84
Book of Common Prayer, 75
Breck, Robert, 138–41, 143
Brown, Robert E., 54, 117, 141, 200

Caldwell, III, Robert W., 158
Calvin, John, 1, 8, 37–43, 49–53, 107, 129, 143, 158, 202, 204
Calvinism, 1–3, 40, 41, 48, 66, 68, 76, 77, 88, 90, 96, 98n74, 105, 139, 139n7, 199, 201, 205
Cambridge Platonism, 2, 44, 46, 58–63, 64, 71, 101, 105–7, 180, 194
Chalcedon, 130, 133, 166, 192
Chamberlain, Ava, 137, 144
Chauncy, Charles, 144–45
Chillingworth, William, 64–65, 67
Christ. *See* Jesus Christ
Chrysostom, John, 33–34, 166, 181
Chubb, Thomas, 140
College of New Jersey (Princeton), 2, 173, 178–79
commentary, biblical (as a literary form), 8, 15, 27, 32, 35, 38–40, 51, 52n23, 71–72, 92, 174, 176–78, 181
Congregationalism, 84
conversionism, 4–6, 87, 88–94, 198
Craig, William Lane, 102
Crellius, John, 129
Crisp, Oliver, 162n97
crucicentrism, 4
Cudworth, Ralph, 58–63, 71, 180, 187
Culverwel, Nathanael, 58–59
Cutler, Timothy, 75–77, 79–81, 90, 96, 111, 136–39

227

Davenport, John, 80
Descartes, René, 46, 55–58
deification, 3, 5–7, 14, 20, 26–30, 32–35, 37, 41, 77, 96–97, 104, 137–38, 146, 166–68, 173, 200–205. *See also* union with the divine
Deism, 54, 69–70, 70n98, 80, 140, 141
Delattre, Roland Andre, 118
Didymus the Blind (of Alexandria), 107, 123, 127n66, 129, 181, 192
Diodore of Tarsus, 33
divine knowledge, 13, 20, 27–30, 31, 50, 61–63, 68–69, 108, 115–16, 122, 130, 133–34, 144, 155, 157, 171, 182–84, 188–92, 203
divine light, 5, 14, 23, 30, 31–33, 35, 75, 104, 106n106, 107, 110–17, 144, 153, 166–67, 173, 182–84, 204
divine participation. *See* deification
Doddridge, Philip, 177, 181
Dummer, Jeremiah, 78–79, 102, 112, 180
Durham, James, 50, 52

Edward, Lord Herbert of Cherbury, 70n98
Edwards
on beauty, 118–21, 126, 132, 179, 185
on excellency, excellencies, 6, 91, 104, 106n106, 114–18, 120–26, 132–134, 136–37, 146, 156, 157, 165, 168, 184, 203
on faith, 3, 95–98, 105, 120–21, 125, 134, 137, 139–40, 142, 145–56, 159, 164, 167
on fitness (moral and natural), 146–47, 150, 175

on grace, 88–89, 91, 96–98, 104, 114, 124, 127, 130, 148, 150, 152–57, 164, 167. *See also* grace
on happiness, 95, 100, 121, 124, 126, 136, 197, 203
on incarnational analogy, 2, 109, 131–34, 138, 145, 157–67, 179, 188–95. *See also* incarnation
on joy, 3, 6, 9, 91, 99, 100, 104, 105–7, 110, 124, 136, 165, 183–84, 196, 197, 201
and melancholy, 9, 110, 112, 113
and New York, 18, 91, 98, 108, 110, 175
on redemption, 2, 89–90, 105, 111
and science, 9, 92, 100–3, 175, 194–95, 198
Sermons of,
"A Divine and Supernatural Light," 115
"Application on Love to Christ," 105
"Christ, the Light of the World," 98
"Christ's Sacrifice," 105
"Glorious Grace," 96
"God's All-Sufficiency for the Supply of Our Wants," 194
"Heeding the Word," 13
"Life Through Christ Alone," 98
"Living Peaceably One with Another," 110
"Living to Christ," 98
"None Are Saved by Their Own Righteousness," 156, 167
"Nothing on Earth Can Represent the Glories of Heaven," 121

Edwards
- Sermons of (*cont.*)
  - "Perpetuity and change of the Sabbath," 193
  - "Profitable Hearers of the Word," 108
  - "The Pure in Heart Blessed," 75
  - "Spiritual Understanding of Divine Things Denied to the Unregenerate," 115, 120
  - "Striving after Perfection," 197
  - "The Terms of Prayer," 136
  - "The Threefold Work of the Holy Ghost," 133
  - "True Love to God," 175
  - "True Repentance Required," 96
  - "Way of Holiness," 94, 100
- on the Holy Spirit, 5, 43, 50, 71, 86, 97–98, 106, 110, 113–17, 119, 122–34, 144–45, 149, 151–54, 157–58, 165–67, 171, 173, 177–79, 181–83, 188–91, 193, 196–97, 201, 204
- on the spiritual sense, 9, 26, 37, 71–72, 81, 99–100, 106–7, 114–21, 182, 151, 173–74, 179–88
- on the Trinity, 3, 5–6, 77, 114, 121–27, 132, 134, 158, 167, 187, 202
- Works of,
  - "The Blank Bible," 13, 45, 146, 176–79, 181, 185, 197
  - *A Faithful Narrative of the Surprising Work of God*, 141
  - *The Great Christian Doctrine of Original Sin Defended*, 159–63
  - "Catalog of Reading," 19, 46n3, 96, 112, 127, 165, 174, 182, 200
  - *Charity and Its Fruits*, 104, 148, 204
  - *Concerning the End for which God Created the World*, 202–3
  - "Diary," 90, 93, 112–13
  - *Distinguishing Marks of a Work of the Spirit of God*, 7
  - *Freedom of the Will*, 1
  - "God Glorified in Man's Dependence," 104, 136, 144
  - "Images of Divine Things," 1, 45, 108
  - *Justification by Faith Alone*, 125, 135, 237, 139, 140–42, 145–49, 157, 161, 163, 165, 204
  - "Natural Philosophy," 101, 110
  - "Notes on the Apocalypse," 92, 94, 176
  - "Notes on Scripture," 176, 200
  - *Personal Narrative*, 81, 91, 94, 100, 112, 114
  - *Quaestio*, 76, 90–92, 94, 95–97, 99, 110, 134, 139
  - "A Rational Account of the Main Doctrines of the Christian Religion," 134
  - "Resolutions," 6, 90, 91
  - "Shadows of Divine Things," 185
  - *A Treatise Concerning Religious Affections*, 71, 116–17, 181–82
  - *Treatise on Grace*, 153
  - "Types of the Messiah," 184–85

Edwards, John, 66, 96, 105, 106n108, 124n51, 174–75, 181
Edwards, Sarah Pierpont, 106n107, 109, 113, 171–73
Edwards, Timothy (father of Jonathan Edwards), 77, 79, 82, 85–87, 90
Edwards, Timothy (son of Jonathan Edwards), 197–98
emanation, 60, 71, 202–4
Evangelicalism, 2, 4–7, 13, 40, 93, 174–75, 195, 198
extra calvinisticum, 128

First Enoch, 15

Gale, Theophilus, 180
Gay, Peter, 198
Gerstner, John, 98n74, 161
grace, 26, 29, 35, 43, 82, 87–88, 89, 91, 96–97, 104, 114, 124, 127, 130–31, 134, 143, 148, 150–56, 164, 167, 172, 190. *See also* Edwards, on grace
Great Awakening, The, 92–93, 137, 171
Gregory (the Great), 35–36
Gregory (Nazianzus), 30–31, 189, 192
Gregory of Nyssa, 31–33, 34

half-way covenant, 83–85
Harrison, Verna E. F., 32
Harvard College, 78, 136, 139
heaven, 5, 7, 13, 26, 30, 33, 36, 62, 71, 98–100, 109–10, 117, 121, 126, 127, 132, 143, 144, 166, 172, 173, 179, 185–88, 192, 201, 203
Henry, Matthew, 52, 105, 112, 177
Heraclitus, 19–20
Holy Spirit, 5, 14, 22, 29, 30, 36, 40–43, 46, 49–53, 55, 71, 86, 97–98, 104, 106, 110, 113–19, 122–34, 142–44, 149, 151–54, 157–58, 164–67, 171, 173, 177–79, 181–83, 188–91, 193, 196–97, 201, 204
Hopkins, Samuel, 2
Hurrion, John, 166n116, 181
Hutchinson, Anne, 142–45

incarnation, 3, 5, 7, 14, 24, 26–29, 31–33, 36, 41–42, 67, 97, 107, 109–10, 126–34, 144, 149, 157–67, 179, 185–187, 188–95, 200–202, 204. *See also* Edwards, on incarnational analogy
inerrancy. *See* infallibility
infallibility, 7, 56, 69

Jesus Christ, 1, 3, 5–6, 7, 9, 14, 24, 26–27, 27–37, 40–43, 45, 49, 50, 52, 67, 72, 76–77, 82, 88, 89, 91, 93–100, 105, 107–10, 114, 117, 121, 123, 125–34, 136–139, 143–49, 152, 154–55, 157–68, 172, 173, 177–79, 181, 185–94, 196–98, 201, 203, 204
Jewish interpretation. *See* Scripture, and PaRDeS
Jue, Jeffrey K., 48
Justin (Martyr), 180, 187

Kabbalah, 18
Kang, Kevin, 158, 158n84
Kelley, Brooks Mather, 78
Kugel, James L., 23–24
Latitudinarianism, 44, 46, 63–71, 75, 76, 79, 80, 136, 139, 175
Laud, William, 147–48
laws of nature, 101, 109, 151, 162
Lee, Sang Hyun, 150–52
Levellers, The, 61

light. *See* divine light; light of reason
light of reason, 55–64, 106n106
Locke, John, 2, 64, 67–72, 107, 116–17, 177, 198
Logos, 19–30, 36, 127–32, 157–58, 179, 187, 188–91, 194
Lohse, Bernhard, 38
Lowman, Moses, 92
Luther, Martin, 37–38, 49

Malebranche, Nicolas, 106
marriage, 45, 52
Marsden, George M., 8, 82, 87–88, 110, 113, 140, 199
Mather, Cotton, 100, 102, 195
Mather, Increase, 85
Mather, Richard, 83–85
McDermott, Gerald, 149n45
Mede, Joseph, 48
Miller, Perry, 83, 198–99
Milton, John, 120
"Miscellanies" (general discussion), 71, 91, 92, 94, 96, 100, 106, 115, 154, 156, 157, 163, 176, 180, 194
"Miscellanies" No. a, 94, 94n59, 114n17
"Miscellanies" No. b, 94n59, 97n72
"Miscellanies" No. l, 97n73, 154n68
"Miscellanies" No. m, 105n102
"Miscellanies" No. p, 97n73, 154n68
"Miscellanies" No. r, 98n74
"Miscellanies" No. s, 94n59, 95n63
"Miscellanies" No. aa, 115n18
"Miscellanies" No. ff, 6n, 99n80, 201n18
"Miscellanies" No. gg, 99n81, 103n95, 115n19
"Miscellanies" No. nn, 94n59, 96n68, 96n69
"Miscellanies" No. oo, 94n59, 96n69
"Miscellanies" No. pp, 103, 103n94
"Miscellanies" No. 2, 94n59, 97n71
"Miscellanies" No. 3, 115n20
"Miscellanies" No. 27b, 94n59, 97, 97n73, 154, 155n70
"Miscellanies" No. 30, 94n59, 96n66
"Miscellanies" No. 32, 94n59
"Miscellanies" No. 33, 94n59, 97n71
"Miscellanies" No. 34, 115n20
"Miscellanies" No. 35, 94n59, 96n66
"Miscellanies" No. 36, 97n71
"Miscellanies" No. 38, 94n59
"Miscellanies" No. 41, 94n59
"Miscellanies" No. 42, 115n19
"Miscellanies" No. 45, 94n59
"Miscellanies" No. 77, 97, 97n73, 154
"Miscellanies" No. 78, 96n64, 118n31
"Miscellanies" No. 81, 187, 187n54,
"Miscellanies" No. 87, 124n53, 125n55
"Miscellanies" No. 89, 125n56
"Miscellanies" No. 94, 123, 123n49, 126n64
"Miscellanies" No. 96, 123n49
"Miscellanies" No. 105, 126n61
"Miscellanies" No. 108, 126n59, 126n61
"Miscellanies" No. 112, 126n61
"Miscellanies" No. 114, 126n61
"Miscellanies" No. 117, 123n49, 125n54
"Miscellanies" No. 119, 105n104
"Miscellanies" No. 138, 75
"Miscellanies" No. 143, 123n49
"Miscellanies" No. 144, 123n49
"Miscellanies" No. 151, 123n49
"Miscellanies" No. 155, 133n93
"Miscellanies" No. 157, 123n49
"Miscellanies" No. 160, 193, 193n76
"Miscellanies" No. 184, 127n65, 131n87, 132n88
"Miscellanies" No. 186, 96n66
"Miscellanies" No. 205, 191
"Miscellanies" No. 229, 194n77

"Miscellanies" No. 241, 151n55, 154
"Miscellanies" No. 281, 133n92
"Miscellanies" No. 293, 126n63
"Miscellanies" No. 376, 132, 132n91, 155n71
"Miscellanies" No. 393, 154
"Miscellanies" No. 471, 153, 153n63,
"Miscellanies" No. 487, 127, 131, 131n86, 132n89, 132n91, 134n95, 144, 157n76, 157n78, 188–89, 190n63
"Miscellanies" No. 513, 157n76
"Miscellanies" No. 614, 153, 154n64, 154n66
"Miscellanies" No. 624, 157n76,
"Miscellanies" No. 709, 157n76, 157n77, 190n63
"Miscellanies" No. 716, 72n105
"Miscellanies" No. 736, 166
"Miscellanies" No. 738, 157n76,
"Miscellanies" No. 763, 194n79
"Miscellanies" No. 766, 157n76, 158, 158n79, 171, 187n70
"Miscellanies" No. 767, 157n76, 190n63
"Miscellanies" No. 722, 157n76
"Miscellanies" No. 781, 157n76
"Miscellanies" No. 851, 171, 171n1
"Miscellanies" No. 874, 72n107
"Miscellanies" No. 972, 72n105
"Miscellanies" No. 1011, 72n105
"Miscellanies" No. 1047, 127n66
"Miscellanies" No. 1060, 72n107
"Miscellanies" No. 1162, 184
"Miscellanies" No. 1217, 72n105
"Miscellanies" No. 1256, 187n55
"Miscellanies" No. 1343, 71n104
"Miscellanies" No. 1355, 187, 187n57
"Miscellanies" No. 1358, 190, 71n104
"Miscellanies" No. 1359, 71n104, 187n56

moral certainty, 64–67, 68
More, Henry, 58, 63n67, 101–2, 112
Morimoto, Anri, 152–56, 166
Muller, Richard, 36, 39–40
mysticism, 4, 6, 8, 9, 14, 16, 18, 24, 34, 42, 165, 172, 199, 200, 201–2, 204

National Covenant, 81, 82–89
New England Primer, 82
Newton, Isaac, 2, 9, 101–2, 107, 151, 194
Northampton, Massachusetts, 2, 108–9, 113–14, 136–37, 140, 141, 142, 144, 172, 195

Oberman, Heiko, 37–38
Origen of Alexandria, 5, 8, 27–30, 31, 33, 34, 43, 168, 180, 182–83, 187, 194
original sin, 159–63, 165
Owen, John, 48, 49, 107, 112, 127–31, 157–59, 165, 181, 189–92

Palamas, Gregory, 103–4, 198
Patrick, Simon, 63–64
Pauw, Amy Plantinga, 72, 122–23, 128, 158, 190
Philo of Alexandria, 21–26, 28, 34, 173, 180, 181, 187
Plato, 7, 20–21, 28, 58, 60, 120, 180
Platonism (Middle Platonism, Neoplatonism), 21, 24, 26–27, 44, 58, 100, 105, 185, 204
Plotinus, 21, 26–27, 31, 58, 60
Poole, Matthew, 50–53, 105, 177
Porphyry, 31
preaching manuals, 66, 173–75
preparationism, 87–88, 89, 98n74, 154
Presbyterianism, 18, 47, 64n69, 84, 91

Proclus, 31
Protestant Reformation. *See* Reformation
Pseudepigrapha, 15
Puritans, 43, 46, 47–53, 57, 59, 60, 83, 87–88, 143, 184, 199
Putney Debates, 61

Reformation, 8, 9, 14, 15, 36, 37–44, 46, 49, 57, 71, 86, 92–93, 95, 148, 176
Ramsay, Andrew Michael, 187
Rogers, G. A. J., 59

Saybrook Confession, 77–78, 81, 95–97, 111
Schafer, Thomas, 84–85, 87, 94n58, 115, 149–50
Scripture,
 allegorical interpretation of, 14–19, 25–36, 40, 52, 55, 180, 184
 and PaRDeS (*peshat, remez, derash, sod*), 15–19
 and Quadriga (four-fold method), 25–36
 typological interpretation of, 9, 14, 24–25, 29–30, 33, 35, 37–38, 40, 43, 49–53, 105n102, 105–6, 121, 174–76, 178–79, 183–87, 196
Second Temple Period, 15
sensus divinus, 29, 183
Sewall, Samuel, 195
sex, 18, 50, 113
sin, 28, 49, 83, 87–88, 95–98, 109, 115, 128, 130, 133, 151, 159–65
Skinner, Quentin, 2
Smith, John, 58, 62–63, 71, 194
Socinianism, 112, 128, 129, 189, 192
sola scriptura, 38, 55

Spinoza, Benedict (Baruch), 44, 45–46, 53–60, 67–69, 70n98, 71
Spirit-Christology, 41–43, 126–34, 157, 165, 181, 188–91
Sprunger, Keith L., 48
Stapfer, Johann, 163n101
Stein, Stephen, 37, 40, 179n30, 200
Stillingfleet, Edward, 64–65, 112
Stoddard, Solomon, 83–90, 108, 110, 113
Stout, Harry S., 83, 86, 89
Strauss, Leo, 54
Studebaker, Steve, 123
Sweeney, Douglas A., 7, 71n104, 180, 200

Tanak, 15–17
Targum of Lamentations, 16–17
Taylor, John, 159–62
Tertullian, 18
theosis. *See* deification
Tillotson, John, 63, 65–67, 71, 72n105, 112, 139, 175
Toland, John, 67, 69, 70n98
Trinity, 36, 67, 121–27, 140. *See also* Edwards, on the Trinity
Trueman, Carl R., 127n66
Twain, Mark, 1–2

union with the divine, 3, 5–6, 8, 9, 14, 20, 26, 29, 30–34, 36, 37, 41–43, 45, 72, 76–77, 90, 96–100, 104, 107–9, 114–16, 117, 119, 121, 126–34, 137–39, 142, 143, 145–49, 152–54, 157–59, 163–68, 173, 179, 188–90, 197, 201–4. *See also* deification

Van Mastricht, Peter, 57–58, 98
vestigia Trinitatis, 122
Voetius, Gisbertus, 57
Waddington, Jeffrey C., 154, 158n84

Whichcote, Benjamin, 58–60, 63–64
Wilkins, John, 63, 65, 175–76
Williams, William, 108, 111, 140
Winslow, Ola Elizabeth, 198
Winthrop, John, 142–43

Yale, Elihu, 78
Yale College, 47, 75–81, 95, 102, 105, 109, 111–13, 136–38, 139, 144, 174, 178, 179n30, 180, 199
Yarchin, William, 19, 23

Zeno of Citium, 21